KHRUSHCHEV and the
SOVIET LEADERSHIP
1957–1964

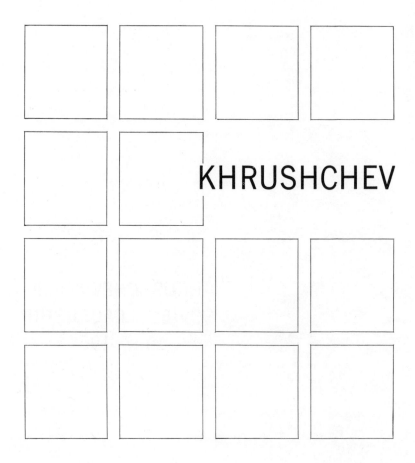

KHRUSHCHEV

Published in co-operation with the Institute for
Sino-Soviet Studies, George Washington University

and the SOVIET LEADERSHIP
1957–1964

CARL A. LINDEN

THE JOHNS HOPKINS PRESS
Baltimore, Maryland

FOREWORD
BY ROBERT C. TUCKER

POLITICAL LEADERS OFTEN have to fight their way to power, by whatever methods their diverse political systems prescribe. And the struggle does not always end with the attainment of this goal. In some instances, circumstances compel the victorious politician to go on fighting after he has reached high office, both to preserve and increase the power that he has won and to set the course of policy according to his desires. This can happen in an authoritarian political system like that of Soviet Russia as well as in a democracy. A notable case in recent Soviet political history is the career in power of former First Secretary of the Soviet Communist Party, Nikita S. Khrushchev.

Even when his career reached its peak at the time of the Twentieth Party Congress in 1956, and again after his triumph in 1957 over the anti-Khrushchev coalition in the Presidium, Khrushchev remained a challengeable leader. He never became an absolute dictator over the Soviet ruling group. It is true that he attempted to be a strong personal leader in the tradition of Lenin and Stalin before him. He lacked, however, both the immense authority that enabled Lenin to dominate the ruling group even when it disagreed with him, and the police-based personal power that enabled Stalin to terrorize it into agreement. So he continually had to contend with forces in the Soviet oligarchy which opposed his policies and which compelled

v

him, on occasion, to backtrack and maneuver. His fall in October, 1964, was not his first lost political battle after coming to power; it was only the one that he lost catastrophically.

Using published Soviet materials as its prime source of evidence, Carl Linden's work sheds much new light upon the complex course and issues of Khrushchev's political struggle from the victory in 1957 to the final defeat in 1964. It is a measure of Dr. Linden's mastery of these materials and grasp of the Soviet internal political situation that he produced and published a short statement of the main theses in 1963, when Khrushchev was still in power and appeared to many in the West to be unchallengeably strong. Subsequent Soviet events have indicated the soundness of Dr. Linden's assessment, which has been fully elaborated in these pages. The volume will stand as a distinguished contribution to scholarship in Soviet studies and a model of the sophisticated analysis of Soviet internal political processes which contemporary Western students of this subject are able to produce.

ACKNOWLEDGMENTS

My THANKS ARE DUE to a number of persons for their aid, advice, and criticism. I owe special debts to Professor Wolfgang H. Kraus, Chairman of the Department of Political Science at George Washington University, for his wise guidance during the writing of the study and to Dr. Matthew Gallagher, whose thinking in many discussions over a period of time was invaluable in the formulation of my views. I also wish to express particular appreciation to Professor Robert Tucker and to Professors Raymond Garthoff, Sidney Ploss, and Ronald Thompson as well for many thoughtful and useful comments and suggestions. Mr. Set Mardirosian, Mr. Earl Scott, and Mr. Ronald Stivers also gave generously of their knowledge and aid at various points and Mrs. Tybel Litwin offered some valuable editorial suggestions.

I am also grateful for the warm interest and support of Professor Kurt London, Director of the Institute of Sino-Soviet Studies, and Mr. J. Thomas Weiss, who helped make this study possible. My thanks also go to the editors of *Problems of Communism* for permission to adapt some materials from my articles in that journal.

CONTENTS

KHRUSHCHEV and the
SOVIET LEADERSHIP
1957–1964

INTRODUCTION: The CASE for the "CONFLICT MODEL" of SOVIET POLITICS

THIS STUDY EXAMINES a question that has occupied Western students of Soviet politics over the past decade: What was the nature of Khrushchev's political leadership and high-level Soviet politics during his incumbency? This question must inevitably hold a central place in any scholarly assessment of Soviet Russia's post-Stalin political transition. Valid answers to it are necessary if we are to develop a sound perspective on what has and what has not changed in the Soviet political system and on the factors and forces that shape contemporary Soviet politics. While events are still too close at hand for anything like a comprehensive or definitive political history of the Khrushchev period, there are ample materials from which it is possible to isolate the major elements which must figure in any systematic reconstruction of the politics of that era.

The scope of this study is the last seven years of Khrushchev's incumbency—the period after he overcame the attempt of the Molotov-Malenkov faction to overthrow him in 1957 until his downfall at the hands of another Presidium faction in 1964. Evidence is offered to show that, despite his primacy, Khrushchev in the years after 1957 continually engaged in an intensive and complex battle behind the scenes to sustain and extend his power within the leading group. From this perspective his fall was neither

1

fortuitous nor preordained, but was an outgrowth of an on-going conflict.

While various issues implicated in the conflict are discussed, major attention is given throughout to the Stalin question in Soviet politics, the issue of Khrushchev's defeated enemies, the so-called anti-party group, issues of party economic policy, and the "dogmatism-revisionism" issue as among the most persistent tell-tales of conflict. Each of these issues was closely linked to the party's political strategy at home and abroad.

The existence of a real and serious battle over Khrushchev's power and policy was rather widely doubted among Soviet specialists during Khrushchev's incumbency. After he overcame his challengers in June, 1957, the prevailing view was that he had become the new dictator of the party, something of a functional equivalent of a Stalin minus terror. However, a dissenting minority saw in accumulating signs of high-level conflict after 1957 evidence that Khrushchev's leadership was not as stable or unchallengeable as was widely assumed. This observation raised broader questions regarding political dynamics in the post-Stalin regime and prompted me to seek a more adequate picture of the character of Khrushchev's leadership.

The differences among students of Soviet politics on the question of Khrushchev's power mirrored a broader divergence of outlook regarding the general nature of Soviet leadership politics since Stalin's death. Two schools of thought emerged. One stressed the element of conflict in Soviet leadership politics. The other and more conventional school emphasized the stability of the Soviet leadership process once a political figure becomes the recognized leader of the regime.[1] While not denying that conflict over power and

---

[1] A sample of the argument between the two schools was provided in a series of articles and commentaries appearing in *Problems of Communism* in late 1963 and early 1964 under the title "Conflict and Authority: A Discussion." An article of mine, taking the standpoint of the conflict school, provided the starting point. See the following articles and commentaries: Carl Linden, "Khrushchev and the Party Battle," *Problems of Communism*, XII (Sept.–Oct., 1963), 27–35; Thomas H. Rigby, "The Extents and Limits of Authority (A rejoinder to Mr. Linden)," 36–41; Robert Conquest, "After Khrushchev: A Conservative Restoration?," 41–46; Carl Linden, "Facts in Search of a Theory" (a reply), XII (Nov.–Dec., 1963), 56–58.   Robert C. Tucker, "The 'Conflict Model,' "

policy occurs, this latter approach has not treated conflict as a *continuous* and *crucial* fact of Soviet political life. It has posited two phases in the cycle of leadership, the first being the period when the leading figure has left the scene and a struggle develops between contenders for the "succession." During this phase, power struggle occupies a prime place in leadership politics; however, once a leader emerges victorious in the struggle a phase of dictatorial rule begins and stability is restored to the leadership. Conflict in this phase no longer involves the top man but shifts to his subordinates, who vie for the boss's ear and support. This, essentially, is how Khrushchev's leadership was viewed by this school from 1957 to his fall in 1964.[2]

The conflict school sees this two-cycle scheme of leadership politics as inadequate for understanding the Khrushchev period, though it more fairly describes what happened in the period from Lenin's death to the establishment of Stalin's dictatorship. According to the conflict school the above approach has made too much of the distinction between phases of oligarchy and one-man rule in the post-Stalin period. It asserts that, especially in the absence of a terror-imposed discipline in the leadership, the opposing tendencies toward oligarchy and dictatorship remained in constant interplay throughout the Khrushchev era. This view sees Soviet leadership politics under Khrushchev as inherently dynamic and unstable.[3]

59–61; Wolfgang Leonhard, "An Anti-Khrushchev Opposition?," 61–64; Michel Gordey, " 'Vanka-Vstanka,' " 64–65.

A sequel to the above discussion was provided after Khrushchev's fall in the same journal in its January–February, May–June, and July–August issues for 1965 under the title "The Coup and After." Articles and commentaries were contributed by Merle Fainsod, Richard Lowenthal, Robert Conquest, Uri Ra'anan, Adam Ulam, Leon Smolinski, Seweryn Bialer, T. H. Rigby, J. W. Cleary, and myself.

[2] For example, Thomas Rigby focuses on the distinction between "monocratic" and "oligarchic" phases of Soviet leadership. See Thomas H. Rigby, "Crypto-Politics," *Survey*, No. 50 (Jan., 1964), pp. 183–94. Myron Rush also sees a "qualitative" difference between periods of "personal rule" and "succession" in Soviet leadership politics in the introduction to his *Political Succession in the USSR*, (New York: Columbia University Press, 1965), p. xi.

[3] Among those who have adopted this broad outlook have been such scholars as Robert Conquest, Robert Tucker, Sidney Ploss, David Burg, Peter Wiles, Boris Meissner, Wolfgang Leonhard, Victor Zorza.

The specialists who have seen this period as something of a repetition of the *succession crisis–personal dictatorship* cycle of the Stalin period also might justly be called the totalitarian school of Soviet leadership politics. They have relied heavily on the modern concept of totalitarianism developed by such political scientists as Karl Friedrich, which views modern Fascist and Communist regimes as historically unique political formations. In the Soviet field the concept has been most effectively and consistently applied by Merle Fainsod in his classic study of the Soviet system, *How Russia is Ruled*. The concept as applied to Soviet politics has drawn on mature Stalinism for its main content and has profoundly influenced contemporary students of Soviet politics. From it we receive the image of the Leviathan cemented by terror and ideology into a political monolith. From the standpoint of political anatomy the Soviet regime is viewed as a system of internal pressures and tensions manipulated by a totalitarian supreme ruler. Thus the tendency of this approach is to seek explanations of the regime's actions in the "dictator" himself. Since he remains basically above challenge from his associates, concrete policy is seen more as the product of the ruler's decrees "from above" rather than as a complex resulting from the leader's on-going struggle in the leading group to sustain and promote this power and policy. Professor Fainsod in the concluding chapter of his revised edition of *How Russia Is Ruled* (Cambridge, Mass.: Harvard University Press, 1963) clearly expresses this view in such statements as: "Khrushchev, like Stalin before him, tolerates no derogation of his own authority, permits no opposition to raise its head within the Party, and insists that the Party function as a unit in executing his will" (p. 583). Elsewhere, "Like Stalin before him, Khrushchev monopolizes control of the media of mass communications, saturating the channels of public opinion with party propaganda and permitting no outlet for political programs which challenge his own" (p. 581).

Most adherents of the conflict school probably would accept such statements as descriptive of Khrushchev's motives, but not of what he in fact accomplished. In short, the conflict school questions the adequacy of the totalitarian concept as a tool for plumbing the Soviet regime's inner political realities. While the usefulness of the totalitarian concept in understanding the psychology and mental outlook of the party leadership is not in question, its tendency to discount the importance of a dualistic or multiplistic politics within the regime itself is challenged.

Those who have stayed more or less within the framework of the totalitarian concept also have placed heavy emphasis on the formal structure of power in the regime. From this standpoint, Khrushchev's formal positions, virtually by definition, provided him with all the levers of power necessary to insure his dominance in the leadership and put him beyond the reach of effective challenge. This theory was the basis of the argument by Professor Lowenthal in *Problems of Communism* in 1960 taking issue with another article by Robert Conquest that had emphasized Khrushchev's vulnerabilities.

Those who stressed the stability of Khrushchev's leadership also turned to concepts in contemporary political science borrowed from modern sociological and behavioral studies which focus on the stabilizing elements in any political leadership. General considerations taken from contemporary "group theory" about the solidarity of "decision-making groups" under a leader have at times been offered in argument. However, a crucial point about Soviet politics has been the absence of well-defined or regularized methods of resolving problems of authority and decision-making within the leadership.[4] The conflict school sees in this condition a major source of disorder and conflict in the regime throughout its history.

The pioneer of the conflict school after World War II was Boris I. Nicolaevsky. He saw the Soviet leadership as a scene of perpetual conflict behind a monolithic façade. Those specialists who followed his lead and searched the Soviet press and publications for clues of conflict in the leadership earned for themselves the not always complimentary title of "Kremlinologists."

Kremlinology, at least initially, shared with the totalitarian concept a predominating focus on the power rather than the policy side of the Soviet political equation. In contrast, however, Kremlinology emphasized the *struggle* for power rather than the *structure* of power within the regime. Thus early Kremlinology tended to see conflict

---

[4] See Linden, "Facts in Search of a Theory."

among politicians as scarcely more than a pure power struggle where policy issues are mere pawns in the fight for supremacy. It sought to lay bare factional alignments within the regime mainly by identifying the personal followings of various leaders as well as the career and associational groupings within the regime on which a leader builds power.

The Kremlinologist sought to correct what he regarded as the tendency of the totalitarian school to obscure the role of factionalism in regime politics. He thereby contributed a key element in the outlook of the conflict school, which sees the emphasis on factional politics in the Soviet leadership as more in tune with the broader testimony of Soviet and Communist history. At the same time the conflict school has moved beyond the initial Kremlinological tendency to play down the policy dimension of Soviet politics, that is, the question of power for what?

Attention to policy issues has in turn led to an effort to define the spectrum of forces in the regime within which such issues are decided. Thus the adherents of the conflict school have turned to the general conceptual device of conventional political science, where attempts are made to define cleavages in terms analogous to left-right or conservative-reforming tendencies in other political systems. They have seen the post-Stalin period as one in which the normal dualisms of politics have increasingly influenced contemporary Soviet leadership politics.[5] It is worth stressing, however, that neither of the two approaches to Soviet leadership politics outlined above has been made of whole cloth. Soviet specialists have variously employed general concepts of politics, both traditional and contemporary, and their work is mainly distinguished by their greater or lesser reliance on one or another unifying concept. In general, it can be said the adherents of the conflict model have drawn more heavily on insights from traditional studies of politics and history than on the sociological, behavioral, and structural-functional orientations of contemporary American political science. Robert Conquest, for example, has drawn extensively

[5] For a recent example of current work being done from this perspective, see: Sidney Ploss, *Conflict and Decision-Making in Soviet Russia, A Case Study of Agricultural-Policy, 1953-1963* (Princeton, N.J.: Princeton University Press, 1965).

and fruitfully on political history past and present in his major contribution to the development and defense of the conflict approach to Soviet leadership politics.[6]

This study takes the general perspective of the conflict school in its view of Soviet leadership politics under Khrushchev, though it differs from other work of its kind in various particulars, points of emphasis, and interpretations of certain events. For example, the stress on the importance of the policy dimension in its own right, the portrayal of Khrushchev as a reformer with an underlying consistency of outlook informing his policies, the interpretation of the role of conservative-reformist cleavages in leadership politics are all areas where differences are likely to arise.

The study attempts to strike a balance between the power and policy sides of leadership politics under Khrushchev. It questions the view that conflict between Soviet politicians is nothing more than conflict about power for power's sake. Policy is seen as the twin, not the pawn, of power; thus the focus is on the *nexus* of power and policy, and on the combustion produced by their interaction. In the Soviet context personalities and policies count as much as the formal apparatus of power. Moreover, a political figure's formal position and authority must not be confused with his actual or effective powers. Over time it has been the political struggle that has shaped Soviet political institutions rather than the other way around.

Khrushchev's political power is viewed as being at no time a definite quantum but rather an unstable mixture of his native political skills, his accumulated prestige, his control over and influence in the political organization he headed, the assets and liabilities his leadership acquired through policy successes and failures, and finally the balance of forces in the political environment with which he had to deal. Those around Khrushchev are seen not as nonentities or mere toadies, but men òf power who represented real political and organizational interests. At no point do they appear

[6] See Robert Conquest, *Power and Policy in the USSR* (New York: St. Martin's Press, 1961). Also Conquest's article "After the Fall: Some Lessons," *Problems of Communism*, XIV (Jan.–Feb., 1965), 17–22, and his *Russia After Khrushchev* (New York: Praeger, 1965).

as wholly malleable to the leader's purposes and, while oppor-
tunistic and skilled tacticians, they also are seen as men who more
often than not possessed political identities which placed them to
one side or the other in the political spectrum of the party. It was
through such territory and with such company that Khrushchev
made his way and finally stumbled.

As will be apparent, the major, but not exclusive, focus here is
the narrow circle of a few dozen figures at the level of the party
Presidium and Secretariat. While this does not enclose the whole
arena of Soviet politics, it is where ultimately all major political
decisions in the U.S.S.R are made. Despite the many changes of the
post-Stalin era, the comment made by the American sociologist
Daniel Bell some years back remains basically true. In his article
on the various approaches to the study of the Soviet world, he
cautioned some of his own colleagues in sociology that the U.S.S.R.'s
"social system" could not be meaningfully defined outside of the
context of Soviet politics, a politics which is a "command system"
where "the decisions of a few men—and in the case of Stalin of one—
become decisive in changing the nature of the system."[7]

It is also true, however, that with the passing of Stalin's system
of terror this small group of men has become less and less insulated
from the pressures issuing from the various strata of the Soviet new
class. The various bureaucratic, professional, and intellectual
groupings within the system have become increasingly articulate.
While none of these groupings speaks with a single voice, they each
represent communities of interest and outlook. Soviet leaders can
less and less afford to ignore their weight and influence.

A final word about "methodology." The popular conception
of a "black art" of Kremlinology based on a set of prescribed
techniques for breaking the communications code of the inner
sanctum has yet, unfortunately, to be exorcised. The evidence
available to the student of Soviet politics remains, it is true, discrete
and usually tangential. But evidence relating to conflicts in the
party has become increasingly abundant in the post-Stalin period.
We need not grope in the dark nearly as much as we did during

[7] Daniel Bell, "Ten Theories in Search of Reality: The Prediction of Soviet
Behavior in the Social Sciences," *World Politics*, X (April, 1958), 327–65.

Stalin's day, and there is less justification than ever before for saying there is not enough to go on in the public utterances of the leadership. Close and continuing scrutiny of the Soviet political and historical experience through the medium of these utterances, against the broader background of politics and history, remains the best tool at the disposal of the student of the Soviet political scene.

1

SOVIET LEADERSHIP POLITICS —
The TERRAIN of BATTLE

CONFLICT OVER POWER and policy animates the political process everywhere and Soviet politics is no exception. Politics within the Soviet one-party state has been no less prone to the divisions that occur among political men generally. Political conflict within the ruling group, however, has traditionally been concealed from public view and the image of a unified and indivisible leadership projected to the outside world. The battles between rival figures and factions in the party press are conducted by indirection, ambiguous allusion, and subtle manipulation of ideological and policy formulas. Only when conflict reaches culmination does it break into the open in the form of a political shake-up or the purge and denunciation of the losers by the victors. The facade of unified leadership is usually quickly restored and until a new falling-out occurs the ruling group strives to camouflage its internal struggles.

This pattern lies deeply imbedded in the conventions and conditions of Soviet politics and reaches back to the origins of the regime. The impulses for concealment, unity, and discipline grew out of the conspiratorial and ideological character of the early Bolshevik movement, were reinforced during the struggle for survival of the Bolshevik dictatorship during its first years of rule, and became over-riding compulsions in the Stalin era. Under Stalin the mythology of the monolithism, continuity, and infallibility of the leadership was carried to its extreme. Despite these things, perhaps because of them, the Soviet leadership from its inception has been peculiarly vulnerable to intense factionalism within its ranks.

The party itself was born a creature of factional struggle. Lenin's Bolsheviks were the product of schism in the early Russian Marxist movement. Up to 1917 the Bolshevik faction not only engaged in sharp struggles with other Marxist groups but was often divided within itself. After seizing power in 1917 the Bolshevik regime during its first years was ridden by conflict over its basic policy direction. Lenin was haunted by the fear of a link up of oppositional currents inside the party with the discontents in society at large. Following the shock of the Kronstadt revolt against Bolshevik rule in 1921 factionalism was formally outlawed within the party at Lenin's insistence. Despite the proscription Lenin's death was followed by years of bitter conflict in the leadership until Stalin secured his place as Lenin's successor.

Stalin eventually resorted to terror to settle the issue of his own power, but the terror itself was a manifestation of the naked confrontation of wills that has characterized higher party politics. After Stalin's death his heirs locked themselves in bitter struggle for primacy. In 1957 Khrushchev gained supremacy only to lose it seven years later at the hands of a formidable coalition of oligarchs who joined to oust him. Whether at the end of 1964 the old play had simply reopened or whether the plot itself is changing is not yet clear, but factional in-fighting is likely to remain a basic feature of the Soviet leadership.

Part of the reason for the intensity of factional struggle within the leadership throughout its history must be sought in the official ideology as it was shaped by Lenin and Stalin. Politics in general is seen as a life and death struggle between irreconcilable forces—an outlook aptly summed up in Lenin's favorite maxim, the not precisely translatable Russian expression "Kto Kogo?" (Who whom? or, Who wins?). While Lenin observed limits in his vendettas against those who opposed him within the party, Stalin carried the doctrine into literal practice not only against outside enemies but against opponents, both real and imagined, inside the party. Under Khrushchev limitations on struggle once again came to be observed; with the exception of the execution of Beria, unsuccessful leaders suffered not death but political disgrace or demotion. Also, however tentatively, party literature in recent years has acknowledged that differences of opinion among leaders are a normal part of the process of policy formulation. Nonetheless, only the slimmest formal grounds are allowed for disagreement and the new party statutes adopted in 1961 reaffirm in emphatic terms the traditional injunctions against factional activity in the party.

The party leadership thus remains formally committed to the proposition that there can only be one correct policy flowing from one correct interpretation of doctrine at any particular historical juncture. As a result disagreements among leaders even on seemingly practical and concrete issues easily grow into head-on collisions. The room for pragmatic compromise between disputants is cramped and when compromises are struck they tend to be highly fragile. Flying in the face of the natural tendency of political men to divide over issues of power and policy, the insistence on political monolithism reinforces rather than reduces the potentials for conflict.

The absence of defined and regularized methods for resolving problems of authority and decision-making within the leading group is another major factor adding to the potential for conflict. Despite the trappings of party statutes and a state constitution, the relationships within the leading group, both among individuals and the ruling bodies of the regime, are ill defined. The division of functions between the top organs of the party and state—the party Central Committee, its Politburo and Secretariat, the Council of Ministers, and the Presidium of the Supreme Soviet—are not clearly spelled out. Furthermore, while the executive bodies of the state apparatus have a hierarchy of ranks, the highest council of the party, the Politburo (called the Presidium under Khrushchev) has no formally designated chairman, in accord with the concept that it is a "collective" of equals. The relation and authority of the highest executive official of the party, the general Secretary (formerly First Secretary), to the Politburo remains equivocal. Under Khrushchev party literature was inconsistent on this point and mirrored contention over the issue. Khrushchev's closest supporters promoted the idea that their leader was "head" of the Presidium and the initiator of policy, but discussions in the party journals often stressed that the main business of the First Secretary was carrying out the letter of the collective decisions of the Presidium.

At the same time, there is no specific regulation for choosing particular individuals to fill vacancies in the leadership, nor for the selection of a successor to the top leader, although the party statute adopted at the Twenty-second Congress for the first time contained a general formula for the rotation of leading party personnel. A loophole was left, however, which exempts figures of "recognized authority" from the limitations on terms of office. In these conditions, the informal political relations among individual leaders rather than their formal authority or functions becomes a prime determinant of the configuration of power and influence in the ruling group.

Most Soviet leaders have risen to the top through one or more of the centralized bureaucratic apparatuses that make up the political, administrative, and economic institutions of the Soviet regime. They have gathered personal followings around themselves during their rise by rewarding the faithful and punishing the disloyal. They confront each other in the no man's land at the apex of the bureaucratic pyramid of party and state, and their conflicts often bear a family resemblance to the bitter struggles among machine politicians elsewhere. The lack of any political arrangements of a genuinely constitutional character makes the enterprise of leadership especially difficult for those who venture to undertake it.

Although Lenin dominated the Soviet regime through his combative skill, a polemic-sharpened intellect, and his immense prestige as the maker of the revolution, he was constantly embroiled in conflicts with party factions and oppositional currents. And while Stalin came to rule over and not through the party as Lenin did, the factional tendency of the regime conditioned his method of rule. He exploited and often encouraged the endemic factionalism of the leading elements in the regime. It might be said that Stalin's regime was paradoxically a faction-ridden "monolith." He ruled through factions to implement his policies and used his apparatus of terror to master the factions. This was a risky undertaking even for that master of intrigue.

Khrushchev inherited the factional regime but had to control it through more normal methods of politics. Like Lenin, he did not rule over the party but through it. Further, he had neither won a revolution nor consolidated one. He had neither the prestige of a Lenin nor of a Mao Tse-Tung, nor the despotic power of a Stalin. He had to rely heavily on his own political dynamism and skill. Despite his defeat in October, 1964, his occupancy of the post of party First Secretary for eleven years was no mean achievement.

The factional tendency then has been persistent throughout Soviet history and has permeated the politics at the apex of the one-party regime. It is not simply a phenomenon which appears in a period of succession crisis and disappears when a dominant leader emerges. Furthermore a leader cannot easily insulate himself from the underlying instability of the leadership arrangements at the pinnacle of the party structure. Unless he acquires massive coercive powers over his associates a leader cannot disregard without peril the political weight of the leading group. Stalin succeeded in extricating himself from the restraining influence of the leading group only after he had instituted a reign of terror. Even then the specter of the repressed oligarchy lived on in Stalin's pathological suspiciousness of those around him.

Thus the logic of Soviet politics inclines the leader to seek absolute power over the leading group, but the same logic also impels them to strive to inhibit or prevent the prime leader from acquiring it. In 1934, for example, long after Stalin had routed his opponents and had piled up massive powers, Kirov and others apparently joined in an effort to restrain him. Stalin's resort to terror after 1934 to secure his dictatorship was probably in part a reaction to Kirov's effort to curb his power.[1] Under Khrushchev the conflicting tendencies between one-man rule and oligarchy remained in interplay.

---

[1] See Leonard Schapiro, *The Communist Party of the Soviet Union* (New York: Random House, 1960), pp. 394–98, for a careful piecing together of some of the evidence suggesting that Kirov was involved in a move against Stalin. In 1964 the Soviet press published articles indicating that such an episode did take place. See, for example, the article signed by L. Shaumyan, *Pravda*, Feb. 7, 1964.

Perhaps profoundly significant for the Soviet political future, the oligarchy prevailed over Khrushchev's personal power at the end of 1964.

The Soviet leader must therefore engage in continual maneuvering to prevent aggregations of power around him from raising threats to his own. No "office" or formal position he holds automatically assures him against such threats. He neither rules on a solid foundation of constitutional authority or through powers inherent in his office but rather as the fruit of continuing struggle. Nor is he an elected official who can bank on a set term of office. Thus policy conflicts, personal rivalries, and personnel shifts at the top levels bear on his continuing effort to sustain or expand his dominance. He cannot be the disinterested judge of factional conflicts going on around him since he must lead and have a program. He inevitably offends some political forces and pleases others in pressing his policies, thereby generating conflict within the regime. He must register success and is not free from the corrosive effects of failure. Too many failures can erode not only his prestige and influence, but ultimately his power position. Khrushchev's power and prestige were, to a far greater extent than Stalin's, dependent on the success of his policies. Events like the U-2 incident, the Cuban crisis, the 1963 agricultural debacle, and the weakening of Soviet authority in the Communist world under the impact of the Sino-Soviet conflict must be included in any reckoning of Khrushchev's ultimate downfall.

Our picture of Soviet leadership politics remains incomplete as long as we restrict our account to the mechanics of power struggle and disregard the battle over policy. How an issue is defined is intimately intertwined with the question of power. A leader seeking power tries to define the issue in a way that brings him the strategic advantage in the political battle. Once in power he seeks to sustain his definition of the issue and prevent conflicts around him from encroaching on that definition, for such conflicts contain the seeds of challenge to his leadership. In fact, it is the way the issue is defined by the leader or faction in power that gives shape and tone to all the tensions and contentions within the political regime. In these respects Soviet politics is like other politics.

Soviet politicians must also seek winning issues and develop policy lines within the specific context of the political spectrum in the party. That spectrum both conditions and limits the alternatives open to them; the Soviet leader who aims to win and hold power must have a healthy respect for this element of the political terrain in which he operates. Over its history the Soviet party, like other Communist parties, has been divided into opposing wings contending over alternative political strategies. These divisions can usefully be seen as bearing a kinship to cleavages between conservative and reforming tendencies in other political systems.

The Soviet party regime before the onset of the blood purges of the thirties, it will be recalled, was torn by left-right cleavages. Stalin used terror to impose a strait jacket on this phenomenon of politics, but he did not succeed in liquidating it. After World War II powerful pressures for reform began to build up under the tight wraps of Stalinist orthodoxy. The aging leader had apparently hoped to repress them with a new reign of terror but death prevented him from executing his plans. In the Khrushchev era the split between reforming and orthodox tendencies—given freer play in the absence of the terror—pervaded the Soviet political atmosphere.

The root of this cleavage can be located in the tension between the imperatives of a revolutionary ideology and the requirements of ruling and managing an increasingly complex industrial society. As early as 1924 Stalin sensed that out of this tension a challenge to orthodoxy would emerge. In his lectures to party cadres at Sverdlov University he saw the Bolshevik politician torn by ambivalent tendencies which he aptly characterized as "Russian revolutionary sweep" and "American efficiency." The first, Stalin said, carried the Bolshevik away from reality, the second from the revolutionary cause. While cautioning against excessive revolutionary zeal, he made it clear that the champion of efficiency provided the greater danger to the party. Stalin's portrayal of the latter type incidentally serves admirably as a thumbnail sketch of Khrushchev's style of leadership from an orthodox viewpoint. Stalin said:

American efficiency has every chance of degenerating into narrow and unprincipled practicalism if it is not combined with Russian revolutionary sweep. Who has not heard of that disease of narrow empiricism and unprincipled practicalism which has not infrequently caused certain "Bolsheviks" to degenerate and to abandon the cause of the revolution? We find a reflection of this peculiar disease in a story by B. Pilnyak, entitled *The Barren Year*, which depicts types of Russian "Bolsheviks" of strong will and practical determination who "function" very "energetically," but without vision, without knowing "what it is all about," and who, therefore, stray from the path of revolutionary work.[2]

Yet Stalin could not prevent the rise of a class of party functionaries of the type he most feared. Khrushchev was to be a representative par excellence of this class. Stalin's policy of forced draft industrialization and modernization of Russia only intensified the division in the party. However, he sought to prevent it from shaping the orientation of the regime. Stalin's holding total power over the regime and pronouncing ex cathedra on doctrine and policy protected ideological orthodoxy from the corrosive pressures for rationality and efficiency; the new class of managers and pragmatic party executives were prevented from becoming autonomous forces within the regime.

After World War II, as noted, pressures for reform of doctrine and practice to meet the changing world nonetheless began to build up. Views favoring reforms disturbed the surface calm of the regime in the dictator's last years and marked the beginning of the contemporary conflict between reformist and orthodox tendencies. Stalin himself wrote the prologue to the struggle in his political testament.

His *Economic Problems of Socialism*—the keynote of the Nineteenth Party Congress in 1952—condemned various "un-Marxist" and "erroneous" views abroad in the party. The ideas Stalin sought to suppress were destined to turn up again as key elements in Khrushchev's own program for reform after the dictator's death. For instance Stalin attacked the proposals for abolishing the Machine Tractor Stations in the countryside, which were later imple-

[2] J. V. Stalin, *Foundations of Leninism*, in *Works* (Moscow: Foreign Languages Publishing House, 1953), pp. 195–96.

mented by Khrushchev in 1958. He attacked "some comrades" who argued that war in the post-war world was no longer inevitable, a doctrine Khrushchev would announce at the Twentieth Congress. He condemned "comrades" whose views on economic policy foreshadowed both Malenkov's and Khrushchev's pro-consumer policies. These views, according to Stalin, meant "giving up the primacy of output of the means of production in favor of consumer goods production." Stalin labeled the theory of another economist as an un-Marxist substitution of "rational" economics for Marxist "political economy"—a theme bearing kinship with Khrushchev's own reversal of the traditional dictum that "politics" not "economics" must guide party policy.

Stalin saw the maintenance of a militant and rigid ideological regime as vital to the survival of the party dictatorship in Russian society. The conception of the party as a disciplined missionary elite whose purposes transcend the day-to-day affairs of the society it dominates was essential in the Stalinist view. By contrast, the guiding motive of the party's pro-reform wing has been to seek to adapt the regime's theory and practice to the realities of a modernized Russia and a changing outside world. In this view, the party's survival becomes dependent on its assumption of a vital functional role in an industrialized Russia. Khrushchev succeeded in effecting a shift of the party's political ground toward the reformist orientation despite his ultimate downfall. Yet no real solution to the problem of the role of the party in the Soviet future has been found and an important element of the Khrushchevian solution—his party reform designed to give the lead to the "economic organizers" over the "political agitators"—was eliminated with his fall.[3]

The antagonism in the post-Stalin period between those leaning toward orthodoxy and conservatism, on the one hand, and those disposed to reform and innovation, on the other, can be roughly defined in terms of an internal versus an external orientation in policy. The more orthodox emphasize the necessities of the world

[3] The "rediscovered" chapters of a Lenin work in 1918, released at the time Khrushchev's reform was being prepared, called for replacing political agitators with economic organizers in the new Soviet regime. The chapters were published in *Pravda*, Sept. 28, 1962.

struggle and the dangers from the outside enemy. Those inclined toward reform stress internal problems, the prospects for a relatively stable international environment, and the possibilities of developing less dangerous forms of struggle with the adversary abroad. In domestic policy the orthodox stress the ideological function of the party, doctrinal continuity, the need for limits on de-Stalinization, maintenance of centralized control of the economy, close supervision of the intelligentsia, and a heavy industry-defense weighted resource allocations policy. The reformers, by comparison, lean toward innovation in theory and practice, pragmatic solutions to economic problems, greater reliance on material rewards than on ideological stimuli, more local initiative and less centralization, and concessions to the consumer.[4]

These, broadly speaking, are the poles around which the political struggle in the party has turned. Between them, of course, the struggle over power and policy has produced a complex pattern of changing political combinations and shifting alignments. At the same time, these poles have kept relatively steady because both wings of the party so far remain dedicated to the preservation of the domination by the party over society at large. Thus the reformers are not conscious champions of some kind of broad process of democratization leading to the dismantling of the party dictatorship over society, though party conservatives may accuse them of this. Neither are the more orthodox or conservative elements in the contemporary Soviet party dyed-in-the-wool Stalinists, though the reforming elements may label them as such. Both wings merely offer diverging approaches to a common goal, namely, the preservation of the vitality of the party dictatorship. In other words

---

[4] This study uses the terms "orthodoxy" and "conservatism," and "reform" rather than "right" and "left" to describe divisions in the regime, since right and left have acquired their own somewhat inverted meanings in the Communist lexicon and can be a source of confusion for the reader. "Orthodox" and "conservative" however are useful in describing those wedded to inherited doctrine and defending continuity rather than promoting change in theory and practice. "Reform" rather than "liberal" or "left" is used as the correlative of the latter terms for obvious reasons. "Liberal" in the West has carried the connotation of special concern for the individual's civic and political liberties. So far at least there has been no sign of any significant element within the Soviet party making such a concern a part of its platform.

they operate in the context of the official "Marxist-Leninist" ideology. The ultimate justification for the existence of the party institution lies in its claim that it is the agency appointed by history for transforming Marxist ideology into political reality. However we conceive the thorny question of the precise political role of the ideology, it provides the language of that politics and serves as a vehicle both of consensus and conflict within the party regime.

Cleavages analogous to right-left or conservative-reformist alignments in the party are thus not intelligible outside of their ideological context. Moreover, the various political, institutional, and other forces in the regime have vested interests in particular aspects of doctrine. The leader or faction that seeks to alter the balance among such forces in the pursuit of certain aims must usually seek to revise or modify existing doctrine. Such efforts generate resistance. Thus, for example, Khrushchev's efforts to revise the Stalinist dogma on heavy industry involved him in battle with a powerful constellation of political and bureaucratic forces. Even his revisions of formulations on such an abstruse question of Marxist doctrine as the withering away of the state under communism encountered resistance and raised issues bearing on practical and fundamental matters of policy. Indeed, there is usually an intimate intertwining of political conflicts with debates over doctrinal issues.

At the same time, such conflicts occur in the institutional as well as ideological context of the one-party state. Inevitably, conflicts among the leaders also reflect the rivalries among the various apparatuses and bureaucracies in both the party and state structure. A leader must win and hold the support of a combination of such organizational groupings adequate to secure his position. His actual or potential rivals can look for aid from those bureaucratic elements discontented with a leader's policy. With the loss of an absolute political will such as Stalin's and the waning of the system of terror, conflict and controversy both within and among the bureaucratic, professional, and intellectual groupings staffing the modern Soviet state increasingly resonate in the politics of leadership. Though short of being formal pressure groups, they have come to play influential roles in regime councils. Few of them however express wholly uniform outlooks on all issues and each contains its own special mix of conservative and reforming tendencies.

It is important to recognize that within the narrow confines of Soviet leadership politics there is a genuine political spectrum that helps shape the character of that politics. The Khrushchev era cannot be properly understood unless it is seen that Khrushchev was on the reforming end of that spectrum and that the issues raised by his policy as well as his power gave shape to the leadership struggle.

2

KHRUSHCHEV'S POWER
and POLICY—
The FOCUS of CONFLICT

STALIN'S HEIRS, for four years after his death, engaged in an inter-twined struggle over power and policy, a struggle veiled at the time by the façade of unified leadership that the regime turns toward the outsider. During this period, Beria's execution, Malenkov's removal as Premier, and Molotov's *mea culpa* on an obscure point of doctrine marred the surface of collective harmony and the careful eye caught both symptoms of the fight for Stalin's mantle and the clash between the forces of reform and orthodoxy in the regime. Only after the conflict reached its climax and Khrushchev emerged victor in the leadership crisis of June, 1957, were its full dimensions exposed to public view.

Khrushchev's rise in the interval between Stalin's death and his victory in 1957 involved a complicated interplay between the struggle for power among the individual leaders and the broader conflict between conservative and reforming trends in the regime as a whole. Khrushchev had to overcome two formidable rivals in the leading group: Malenkov, the head of the state apparatus and a figure whom Stalin had given the lead in his last years, and the prestigious Molotov, who had known Lenin and had held the highest posts throughout the Stalin era. In his drive to unseat Malenkov, Khrushchev briefly assumed the pose of a defender of orthodox policy against Malenkov's New Course. He then turned on Molotov, attacking him as a die-hard conservative opposing long overdue changes in policy. In 1957 Khrushchev finally disposed of both these men who had joined in an effort to unseat him, and he thereby established his personal supremacy in the leadership.

With this capsule view of the post-Stalin leadership struggle in mind, it is easy enough to conclude that Khrushchev was a mere political opportunist engaged in a pure power struggle. Further, an historical parallel automatically suggests itself. Khrushchev had simply followed Stalin's footsteps, first destroying a rival and then proceeding to take over his policies. From this standpoint we might decide that it was only late in the game that he struck the pose of a reformer, namely when he resorted to anti-Stalinism as a weapon against his enemies at the Twentieth Congress in 1956. Such a line of reasoning is one-dimensional, however, and can cause us to misread Krushchev's political personality as well as the character of the struggles in the leadership in the post-Stalin period.

Even in Soviet politics, generally characterized by opportunism in political struggle, leading personalities more often than not possess political outlooks that influence their political orientation. Political necessity occasionally led Khrushchev to assume the colors of an orthodox militant; expediency frequently put him in a centrist position, but personal conviction moved him more and more toward radical reform within the context of the party regime. He took up the latter cause whenever possible and undertook grave risks for its sake. It is this, not his twists and turns in political in-fighting, that gives rhyme and reason to the course of his leadership, a point that can be missed because he, like other Soviet leaders, had to work in the midst of formidable political forces and had to wage complicated battles both to maintain mastery over them and to bend them to his purposes.

When we examine Khrushchev's rise we discover that he was

clearly distinguishable from his associates in his general political approach even before Stalin's death. His penchant for innovation, radical projects, and reform was not something that came as an afterthought late in his rise. As far back as the end of World War II he displayed some of the essential traits of the future reformer. The testimony of Milovan Djilas is revealing in this regard. His impressions of Khrushchev during a visit to the Soviet Union in 1945 correspond basically with the Khrushchev the world came to know as the leader of the Soviet Union. Djilas was struck by two characteristics that marked him out from the rest of Stalin's entourage—an eminently practical, down-to-earth approach and an absorption in the Soviet agricultural problem. In the context of Stalinism such tendencies in a top leader betrayed the latent reformer.

In his *Conversations with Stalin* Djilas notes that "all the Soviet leaders have distinguished themselves by their practicality and, in Communist circles, by their directness . . . N. S. Khrushchev stood out from the rest in both respects."[1] At another point Djilas notes that he was the only one among the leaders who delved into the daily problems of the party rank and file and the populace and "did look into matters and remedy them."[2] During an automobile ride into Kiev from an outlying collective farm they had visited, Djilas recalls how Khrushchev "kept coming back to the question of the collective farms and openly brought out shortcomings."[3] He also noted that Khrushchev's own entourage were of the same mold as their chief, practical and attentive to actual problems.[4]

It is noteworthy that within the year after Djilas' visit Khrushchev came under fire from Moscow for his neglect of ideology. Thus in August, 1946, he found it necessary to engage in tacit self-criticism for inadequate ideological work in the Ukrainian party under his direction.[5] In a report to a Ukrainian party plenum he referred

---

[1] Milovan Djilas, *Conversations with Stalin* (New York: Harcourt, Brace, and World, Inc., 1962), p. 120.

[2] *Ibid.*, p. 122.

[3] *Ibid.*

[4] *Ibid.*

[5] See Lazar Pistrak, *The Grand Tactician, Khrushchev's Rise to Power* (New York: Praeger, 1961), pp. 227–28, for a description of this episode.

to a decision from the Central Committee in Moscow criticizing the Ukrainian Central Committee for underestimating the "significance of ideological work" and for "not paying enough attention to the selection and the political and ideological education of the cadres in science, literature and art," as well as failure to organize a campaign against "hostile bourgeois ideology."[6] These were charges to which a practical-minded party leader is naturally vulnerable and they would appear again in the course of his rise and fall.

At the same time, while Khrushchev was practical-minded, it would be an error to view him as a mere pragmatist. The other side of his political character was vividly exposed in his proposal in 1950–51 for the creation of *agrogorods* (agri-cities) in the countryside. Here Khrushchev first displayed his own brand of "revolutionary sweep." The ambitious *agrogorod* scheme was the precursor of the economic reform projects which characterized his rule and which were aimed at overcoming the grave dislocations in the economy left behind by Stalinism. Khrushchev's reformism, while showing contempt for the rigid and restrictive doctrines of Stalinism, also revealed an attachment to the ultimate social and economic goals projected in Communist ideology.

Indeed Khrushchev's reformism also exposed him to attack for promoting impracticable schemes and in this respect too the *agrogorod* episode was a portent of things to come. In fact it was on such grounds that Malenkov discredited the plan at the Nineteenth Party Congress in 1952, an action taken apparently with Stalin's approval. The radical character of the *agrogorods*, in fact, even seemed to identify Khrushchev more as an ideologically oriented "leftist" than as a pragmatic "rightist" in the Communist sense of those terms. The curious point, nonetheless, was that Malenkov did not charge Khrushchev with a deviation in this direction; rather, the *agrogorods*, Malenkov asserted, mirrored a "consumer approach" to agriculture—a charge of rightism, not leftism.[7]

---

[6] *Ibid.*, p. 228. This well-aimed attack on Khrushchev and his practical-minded entourage may well have been inspired by Malenkov.

[7] As quoted in Conquest, *Power and Policy in the USSR*, p. 123.

While the circumstances and exact motives of the principals in the *agrogorod* episode remain obscure, some points suggest themselves. Khrushchev evidently thought that the sweeping character of his project would appeal to Stalin's post-war penchant for the grandiose "construction projects of communism." Further, the scheme was lent a seal of orthodoxy by its obvious tie-in with the ultimate Marxist goal of erasing the differences between town and country. Yet Malenkov did put his finger on a real implication of the project that was at odds with a basic tenet of Stalinist orthodoxy. The plan would have entailed major diversions of regime resources into the long-neglected countryside. It would have given agriculture priority that Stalinist doctrine had consistently denied to it in favor of heavy industrialization. Also its apparent long-term aim was to give the Russian collectivized peasantry an incentive to produce, which Khrushchev from first-hand knowledge knew was virtually non-existent in Stalin's order of things. On a closer look then Khrushchev's proposal was not so far out of character. It reflected, it would appear, his desire to make a real dent in the problem of a prostrate agriculture, which had become the scandal of Stalinist orthodoxy. While allowing for political exaggerations, there does seem to have been justification for the complaint raised against Stalin at the Twenty-second Party Congress in 1961 for rejecting the *agrogorod* scheme. In his speech to the Congress Ilichev, one of the ideologists in the Khrushchev regime, asserted that the Stalinist leadership regarded the very idea of improving the working and living conditions of the collective farms as "dangerous."

Unfortunately there is little evidence of exactly where Khrushchev stood in 1952 regarding the series of proposals for major economic reforms Stalin condemned in his last work, *The Economic Problems of Socialism*. It was apparent, however, that he was already a part of the trend those proposals mirrored. But his sponsorship or approval of one of them was at least probable—the plan to abolish the Machine Tractor Stations and to turn their machinery over to the collective farmers.

The genuine frustration Khrushchev experienced in his failure to move Stalin in favor of his ideas for lifting agriculture out of its morass was expressed in his complaints after the Twentieth Congress that Stalin insisted on viewing the collective farms through rose-colored glasses. In his "secret speech" Khrushchev, for example, asserted that "we" repeatedly told Stalin of the critical situation in agriculture but that he gave no heed and was content to accept the Potemkin-style picture of the collective farm drawn in propaganda films.[8] At agricultural plenums in subsequent years Khrushchev recited instances of how Stalin rejected "our" proposals for agricultural improvement. His story that Stalin once accused him of being a *narodnik*—a reference to the nineteenth-century Russian revolutionaries who made the peasant problem the key to a reformed Russia—and the report that Khrushchev's opponents in 1957 had accused him of being a "rightist peasant deviationist" are both believable.[9]

KHRUSHCHEV'S RISE TO LEADERSHIP

Even in the earliest stages of his rise to power after Stalin's death, Khrushchev began staking out a claim as a leader of reform. This was already apparent in what served as his inaugural address, his speech to the Central Committee plenum of September, 1953, where he acquired the formal title of the First Secretary of the party and thus established himself as the co-equal of Malenkov both in power and policy. His report to the plenum in fact served to take the torch away from Malenkov. Just the month before at the Supreme Soviet Malenkov had announced measures designed to stimulate greater agricultural production. Khrushchev now pitted himself against Malenkov with his own program of agri-

[8] N. S. Khrushchev, *"Secret Speech" to the 20th CPSU Congress*, in a selection of documents edited by the Russian Institute, Columbia University, *The Anti-Stalin Campaign and International Communism* (New York: Columbia University Press, 1956), p. 77.

[9] The *narodnik* reference appeared in Khrushchev's 1957 speeches on literature and art published in *Kommunist*, No. 12, 1957, p.13. The charge of "rightist peasant deviation" was mentioned in an account of the June, 1957, leadership crisis in the organ of the Polish party, *Trybuna Ludu*, July 9, 1957. See Appendix I of Roger Pethybridge, *A Key to Soviet Politics, The Crisis of the Anti-Party Group* (New York: Praeger, 1962), p. 191.

cultural reform and concessions to the peasantry. In his speech he set forth positions that became premises of his domestic program throughout his rule.

While careful to avoid Malenkov's controversial formulations on consumer policy, his opening words nonetheless stressed that the regime was now in a position to turn its attention to "the task of creating an abundance of consumer goods in our country."[10] In support of this point he advanced a formulation that he would return to again and again in future years. He said that the U.S.S.R. now had developed "an integrated heavy industry," which set the stage for "marked advances" in the development of consumer industries. True, he was careful not to assert the idea of equal rates of growth for the consumer and heavy industries as Malenkov did, but his position opened the way for adopting such a line sometime in the future. He stressed here that "the basic goal and chief task of socialist production" was the "maximum satisfaction" of the needs of society but contended that the first order of business in domestic policy was the recovery of Soviet agriculture. He asserted that the regime must in a few years greatly increase food supplies for the entire population and raise the living standards of the peasantry. According to Khrushchev, only a rapid increase in food output could close the gap between growing demand and lagging output and lead the way to an abundance of consumer goods.

His argument tended to shift the traditional policy emphasis from industry toward agriculture. In support of the goals he set forth, he offered a program of increased farm prices, tax relief for the peasantry, and increased capital investment in agriculture. He declared that the material interests of the peasantry had been grossly violated, tacitly referring to the deprivations the peasantry had suffered under Stalin's policy. And he invoked statements from Lenin that a Communist economy could not be built on enthusiasm alone but must rely on personal interest and incentive.

Khrushchev proceeded in characteristic style to expose in the frankest terms the deplorable condition in which agriculture had

[10] *Pravda*, Sept. 15, 1953.

been left by the Stalin regime. Among other things, he made public figures showing that the U.S.S.R. in 1953 had fewer cattle and cows than prerevolutionary Russia in 1916. His presentation as a whole was an implicit refutation of Malenkov's assertions at the Nineteenth Party Congress eleven months earlier that the Soviet grain problem had been basically solved. At the same time, Khrushchev projected the local party apparatus, not the state administration under Malenkov, as the agency that would play the guiding role in carrying out the agricultural program. Underlying these statements was the argument that the country needed food for the population more than it did the washing machines and other appliances the officialdom was destined to receive under Malenkov's conversion of various industrial plants to consumer goods production.

Just a few months later Khrushchev unveiled his radical project for converting vast areas of semi-arid virgin lands in Siberia and Central Asia to grain cultivation, designed to show that he was the Soviet leader who could solve the grain problem "in a few years." This sweeping attack on the grain problem contrasted with Malenkov's more cautious approach favoring intensified use of existing agricultural land. The project—entailing a massive gamble since there was no assurance that the marginal virgin lands could sustain large grain crops for any extended period—was designed both to focus the party's energies on the critical agricultural problem at home and assert its primacy in the economic sphere as against the state apparatus headed by Malenkov.

Khrushchev's recurrent theme during this initial phase of his rise was the necessity of "on-the-spot" guidance of the economy by local party executives. He offered himself as the exemplar of the party executive who understood and did something about problems at the grass roots. He was constantly on the go in the countryside, looking into local conditions, offering local officials, farmers, and workers practical advice, and displaying his own considerable practical knowledge of everything from plumbing to corn-growing.

Behind this furious activity was Khrushchev's goal of reshaping the party into an effective agency of internal economic leadership. His strategy was producing an inevitable clash with the economic administrators of the state under Malenkov's leadership. Both figures were offering rival programs for rationalizing the political-economic order left by Stalin: Malenkov through streamlining the economic-administrative apparatus of the state and Khrushchev through a redirection of the energies of the party toward long-neglected internal problems. From the outset Khrushchev sought to give the lead to the "managerial" rather than the "ideological" element within the party—to its cadre of working executives rather than its political-ideological overseers, to the territorial party machines and not the central apparatus. On the other hand, Malenkov had spent most of his career as a representative of the party center in Moscow and, as Premier, placed his reliance on the centralized ministerial and planning organs of the state. He even sought to perfect the cumbersome economic machinery of the state through further centralization of the ministerial apparatus. He amalgamated the profusion of ministries left by Stalin into a small number of super-ministries, a project which soon aborted. Both Khrushchev and Malenkov were seeking to reform the system but from different perspectives and by different means.

In an important sense Khrushchev's approach involved a more significant departure from past practice than Malenkov's. Under Stalin the state apparatus was the agency entrusted with the direction and management of the economy. Khrushchev was seeking to shift the party's attention from its political-ideological functions to an economic mission, upsetting the roles of the party and state as established under the Stalin regime.

When Khrushchev moved to topple Malenkov from his position, toward the end of 1954, a rivalry over the reform issue already underlay the power struggle between the two. Malenkov as Premier was pre-empting the reform theme with his pro-consumer line and policy of relaxation of international tensions under the rubric of his war-would-end-civilization theme. Within a few months after Malenkov's ouster Khrushchev would quickly develop his own version of such a policy; at this moment, however, he needed a powerful lever to achieve his purpose. He tipped the balance against Malenkov by making a temporary alliance with hard-line forces in the leadership. He took up the theme that Malenkov's policy was undercutting the basic party doctrine on heavy industrial priority and was weakening the U.S.S.R.'s position in relation to Western military power. By this strategem he mustered the support of such figures as Molotov and Kaganovich, as well as the military. At the Supreme Soviet session in February, 1955, which removed Malenkov from the Premiership, Molotov vigorously asserted his orthodox outlook on policy. He appropriately drummed up the theme of the military danger from the "imperialist" enemy abroad and generally indicated that there were no grounds for departing from traditional policy either in foreign affairs or domestic policy. While Khrushchev was not ready to challenge Molotov on policy at this juncture, he had obviously inspired certain passages in Malenkov's written resignation. Malenkov said he was responsible for past failures in agricultural policy and indicated that not he but the Central Committee was the author of the 1953 agricultural reforms. He also confessed inexperience in "local work," the area in which Khrushchev claimed special competence.

Khrushchev evidently wanted to make it clear that he had not given up his identification with reform. It is notable in this connection that at the Twenty-second Congress various Khrushchev supporters took special pains to show that Molotov and Khrushchev were at loggerheads on the reform issue throughout the 1953–55 period before Malenkov's fall. For example, Furtseva, in seeking to show that this was the case, mentioned that Molotov had "ferociously" objected to Khrushchev's proposal for reorganizing housing and industrial construction in late 1954. Khrushchev had unveiled his plan in December, 1954, at the time he was indicating his opposition to Malenkov's line on heavy industry. Furtseva in her congress speech sought to depict Khrushchev's proposal as a question of "big reforms."[11] She also stressed that Molotov had opposed the "new course of the party," citing as illustration the 1953 agricultural reforms and the virgin lands policy.

However the most striking thing about Khrushchev's marriage of convenience with Molotov was how quickly he proceeded to dissolve it. He immediately began undercutting the Molotov hard line and stole Malenkov's fire with his own coexistence line

[11] *Ibid.*, Oct. 22, 1961.

abroad and welfare line at home. In the face of Molotov's bitter opposition he went to Belgrade and patched up relations with Tito, promoted the signature of the Austrian State Treaty, and capped these moves by joining Bulganin at the summit meeting with President Eisenhower in July, 1955. Armed with the Spirit of Geneva Khrushchev had prepared the way for unveiling his program for reform of party doctrine and policy at the Twentieth Party Congress the coming February.

By the fall of 1955 Khrushchev's foreign policy initiatives were already breaking the bonds with the Stalinist past. This was highlighted by the publication of a letter from Molotov in *Kommunist* in September admitting that he had committed an ideological error in his speech to the Supreme Soviet the previous February. This humiliation for Molotov was the upshot of his defeat at the July, 1955, plenum where he had clashed with Khrushchev over the latter's foreign policy initiatives. Molotov noted that this Supreme Soviet speech had employed an obsolete doctrinal formulation which implied that the U.S.S.R. was still at an early stage in the development of "socialism." The lapse had harmonized with the general orthodoxy of the speech. He had indicated that the U.S.S.R. was facing a long struggle with the capitalist enemy and that the time was not ripe for any relaxation in foreign or domestic policy.

At the Twenty-second Party Congress in February, 1956, Khrushchev introduced the doctrinal underpinnings for his long-range policy of limited détente abroad and a popular welfare line at home. He revised the pessimistic Leninist doctrine on war, now declaring that the balance of forces in the world was tipping in favor of the Communist bloc and thus war was no longer "fatalistically inevitable." He also stated that Communist parties no longer were necessarily committed to achieve their aims in the outside world by violence but that "peaceful transitions to socialism" were now possible through parliamentary means.

Along with his portrayal of long-term coexistence on the international plane, he also introduced what became his basic line on the domestic role of the party. He declared that Lenin had taught that in certain periods the "solving of problems of practical economics" takes the fore in questions of Marxist-Leninist theory and indicated that time had now arrived. At the same time he vented his spleen against the old-line ideologues of the party, obviously including Molotov, depicting them as doctrinaire pedants divorced from the real problems facing the regime.

Khrushchev's decentralization of economic management in early 1957 was an action consistent with his concept of the party. He reduced the central apparatus of the state and the role of high-level functionaries of the state in economic policy and correspondingly enhanced the role of territorial party organizations in overseeing the economy. The action also cleared the way for his later attempt in 1962 to convert the party itself into a hierarchy of industrial and agricultural committees charged with guiding the national economy.

The coalition that formed in mid-1957 in the attempt to overthrow Khrushchev was in part a reaction to his strategy. That coalition included both orthodox party figures like Molotov and Kaganovich, who objected to Khrushchev's tendency to de-politicize and de-ideologize the party, and the high-level managers of the state apparatus like Pervukhin, Saburov, and Malenkov, who objected to his effort to strip the state of its economic prerogatives. His strategy, however, proved itself in the 1957 crisis. His repeated grass-roots campaigns into the provinces seeking the support of the middle-level functionaries of the territorial party organizations bore fruit. The bulk of this group threw their weight behind Khrushchev at the June, 1957, Central Committee plenum, which sealed the defeat of his challengers. Nonetheless his effort to reshape the party remained a generator of conflict after 1957 and once again emerged as an underlying issue in his downfall in 1964.

THE ATTACK ON STALIN

However late Khrushchev decided on his plan to launch an all-out attack on Stalin at the Twentieth Congress, the action flowed logically from the policy line he had developed after the defeat of Malenkov. In fact such action was becoming virtually the prerequisite for any further development of a reform policy. Strong medicine was required if he hoped to shake loose the political and bureaucratic forces with vested interests in the status quo and to shift the political ground in the party. The doctrinal and political legacy of Stalinism provided a powerful bulwark against change.

The available evidence suggests that Khrushchev planned the action in advance of the Congress but knew that if he were to succeed he would have to put his more cautious colleagues off balance by tabling his plan with minimal forewarning. At the Twenty-second Congress Khrushchev in his concluding speech on October 27 said that a sharp conflict had been generated in the leading group in reaction to the proposal to tell the Congress of Stalin's misdeeds. According to Khrushchev, Molotov, Kaganovich, Malenkov, Voroshilov, "and others" yielded on the issue only when Khrushchev threatened to raise the matter before the Congress delegates themselves. There is corroborative evidence that the Stalin issue had been raised in the Presidium in the weeks before the Congress.[12]

In any case, Khrushchev's frontal attack on Stalin at the Twentieth Party Congress in 1956 was the decisive event in his struggle for primacy among Stalin's heirs. With his attack on Stalin he set the mold of his leadership and irrevocably labeled himself as a leader of reform. Like political struggles elsewhere, the figure who strikes for power must define the issue at stake in a manner that will give him the strategic advantage in political battle and carry him to the commanding heights. The question of Stalin provided Khrushchev with such an issue. The whole party had suffered under Stalin's lash and the political potency of the Stalin issue had not yet been tapped despite some of the cautious and halting de-Stalinizing moves that had been made by the leadership after Stalin's death. By taking the issue head-on Khrushchev could draw forces outside the immediate ruling circle into the struggle and undercut his rivals. The anti-Stalin platform was especially

---

[12] The leadership's birthday greeting to Voroshilov on his seventy-fifth anniversary, for example, omitted the customary reference to the elder figure as a "comrade-in-arms" of Stalin. See *ibid.*, Feb. 4, 1956. Also, an attack on Stalinism in historical science had already developed prior to the Congress at an historians' conference at the end of January, 1956.

attractive to the rising generation of party secretaries in the territorial apparatus whom he was bringing into the center. Khrushchev was forging this group, relatively less compromised by direct involvement in the purges and terror of the Stalin era, into a phalanx that could be turned against the Old Guard in Moscow.

In one sense, of course, all of Stalin's heirs were committed to internal relaxation of the Stalin regime. The issue facing them at the time of the great dictator's death was not whether Stalinism should be preserved in undiluted form. The rivals for the succession were agreed at the outset that terror and the secret police must no longer be final arbiters of politics within the ruling group. This consensus was duly registered in the rapid demise of Secret Police Chief Beria soon after Stalin's death. Even Beria in the few months he remained in the post-Stalin Presidium had sought to win credit for a policy of relaxation. Such a course had been a virtual necessity for Stalin's successors. Their grip on the reigns of power was yet untested.

The real issue was whether measured change within a framework of continuity or a break with the past was to be the keynote of the successor regime. This issue marked the divide between the orthodox and reforming wings in the party leadership. After his defeat of Malenkov, Khrushchev quickly became the champion of reform in the party's doctrine and practice while Molotov led the defense of political continuity and reliance on tried and tested methods of rule. As long as no direct attack on the Stalinist heritage was made, the defenders of orthodoxy held the advantage in regime politics. Any real effort at reform necessitated a breaking of the Stalinist mold both in doctrine and practice. Khrushchev grasped the nettle suddenly and firmly in his "secret speech" to the Twentieth Congress in 1956.

However, he chose a paradoxical means to power when he made anti-Stalinism his platform. It was both his steppingstone to personal primacy and a potent weapon in his efforts to adapt the old regime to the changing realities of the post-Stalin era. But at the same time his attack on Stalin represented a pledge to his party associates and to the Soviet population as well that he would not resort to Stalin-style coercion as his method of rule. As a result he helped bring about a situation that fettered his ability to impose his will on his party colleagues—the general foreclosure of terror as a means of enforcing discipline at the top levels of the party. Khrushchev faced the iconoclast's problem of finding a substitute for what he had destroyed. Having shaken the foundations on which Stalin built dictatorial power, he attempted to find a new basis for his own.

He sought to sustain the momentum of his leadership through a dynamic policy of reform. His strategy had its successes and it worked for eleven years. It proved less effective, however, than Stalin's system of ideological terror politics in preventing entrenched political and bureaucratic forces from obstructing the leader's purposes. Ultimately, he was overthrown by a formidable combination of such forces.

The dilemma of Khrushchev's leadership was increasingly revealed in the years after 1957 in his effort to convert what had begun as a guarantee against a return to Stalinism into a means of enforcing his dominance over the leading group and the party. He strove to forge the Stalin issue and an attack on his fallen rivals into a weapon for subduing and ultimately suppressing opposition within the regime to his purposes, and for aggrandizing his personal position in the leading group. Ironically, the technique was drawn from Stalin's own maxims of political struggle; the attack on his defeated foes became so virulent at the Twenty-second Congress that it was reminiscent of the denunciations of politically disgraced leaders in Stalin's times. In fact, anti-Stalinism as a factional weapon was something of a boomerang. When it missed its mark it became a threat to its wielder and an aid to the intended victims. Whenever opportune, the victims were able to accuse Khrushchev of dangerously corroding the prestige and authority of the party institution through his anti-Stalinist excesses.

The dilemma of power Khrushchev faced reflected the collision of two tendencies in post-Stalin politics: the impulsion of the leader to expand his power over his associates in the leading group encountered the pressure within the regime as a whole for a regularization and normalization of the political process. For Khrushchev anti-Stalinism became the means of meeting the dilemma.

The first tendency is rooted in the ill-defined leadership arrangement within the ruling group and was the offspring of Lenin's concept of a centralized revolutionary dictatorship directed by a band of professional revolutionaries. A leader must build his power in the absence of either constitutional or traditional arrangements that would help secure his authority. As a result, he is, like Hobbes' political man, likely to be gripped by a "perpetual and restless desire for power after power." This tendency, reinforced by the ideology's demand for an authoritative guide to doctrine and policy, creates the potential for personal dictatorship in the U.S.S.R.

The second tendency, at work even in Stalin's crisis state, acquired massive impetus in the near universal reaction against institutionalized terror after the great dictator's death. The pressure for normalization favors the natural interplay that develops in most established political orders between forces of change and of status quo, between reformers and conservatives, between a "left" and a "right." In the Soviet context, as Stalin well understood, it favors the entrenchment of political and bureaucratic forces capable of limiting a leader's freedom of action. Furthermore, in regard to the question of power within the leading group, it assists the basically conservative countertendency toward oligarchy within the regime. The same logic that inclines a leader to seek absolute power also inclines the top group to impose limits on the powers of the prime leader. Under Khrushchev the dictatorial and oligarchic tendencies remained in constant interplay even after 1957 and in October, 1964, met in head-on collision. In 1964 the oligarchs of the party prevailed. This unstable power condition within the leadership accounts in part for the stormy and dynamic quality of Soviet politics in the Khrushchevian era. It contradicted any idea that after Khrushchev disposed of his 1957 challengers the regime settled into a stable dictatorship whose calm would only be disrupted with the onset of a new succession crisis after the leader's passing.

After June, 1957, however, the regime once again turned its more-or-less monolithic face outward. The temptation was strong to assume that the image now roughly corresponded with the reality—the cycle of "collective leadership" then personal dictatorship had completed its round with Khrushchev in the role of the new Stalin, without the latter's paranoia and blood thirst. However, indications of conflict in the leadership told a different story. Khrushchev emerged from the 1957 crisis as the regime's recognized leader, but he had neither destroyed the will of significant elements in the leadership to resist his effort to make his power over them absolute nor routed all the forces capable of raising roadblocks in the way of his political program. The resulting conflicts overlapped and impinged on one another and eventually culminated in Khrushchev's downfall in October, 1964.

The submerged conflict over the leader's power and policy after 1957 was revealed in the tortuous history of a number of key political issues. The questions of Stalin and of Khrushchev's fallen foes, the so-called anti-party group, became deeply implicated in the issue of Khrushchev's powers within the leading group. The ruling group displayed its instinct for self-preservation and intention to prevent the leader from acquiring automatic purge powers over it. Here something of a common interest developed within the leading group that cut across political outlooks and made some strange bedfellows. However, more conservative party elements had additional motives for opposing Khrushchev on the Stalin and anti-party group issues because he exploited these issues not only to expand his power but also to attack traditional policy positions. The conflict over policy, while it reverberated in various spheres of Soviet political life, was most steadily apparent in running disputes over resource allocations and the party's role in the Soviet economy, disputes mirroring the conflict produced by Khrushchev's long-term effort to reorient party policy in favor of a neglected agriculture and the long-deprived Soviet consumer. The question of resource allocations, in particular, was a storm center of regime politics where the forces favoring change and those defending the status quo collided. This issue entailed more than narrow questions of economic policy but was intimately related to the premises of the general political strategy of the party leadership both at home and abroad. Contention over the general direction of party strategy was also echoed, especially at critical points, in the question of the relative danger that "revisionism," on the one hand, and "dogmatism," on the other, posed to correct party strategy.

The prosperity of Khrushchev's leadership was deeply implicated in each of the above issues. The revisionism-dogmatism issue, especially, became intertwined with the conflict with the Chinese Communists and at times echoed differences between Khrushchev and his colleagues on handling the Chinese challenge. The increasing pressure on Khrushchev from Peking also spurred him to double and redouble his effort to secure his power and implement his political program at home.

3

KHRUSHCHEV'S
INCOMPLETE VICTORY—
The 1957 LEADERSHIP CRISIS

THE SEEDS OF CONFLICT over Khrushchev's power and policy were immediately visible in the aftermath of the June, 1957, leadership crisis. The picture of a sweeping, even easy, Khrushchev victory portrayed in the Soviet press after the event was deceptive. A close look revealed the symptoms of a strenuous struggle won by hard bargaining and intricate maneuver.

Like the anti-Khrushchev faction itself, the forces Khrushchev marshaled to overcome his challengers were diverse. Among those casting their lot with him were figures who were less than ardent supporters either of his more far-reaching power ambitions or of his penchant for reform, and they sought to place limits on his victory. It is this factor that goes far in accounting for Khrushchev's less-than-complete rout of his foes at the June plenum. They were retained in the party and half of them remained unexposed in high posts. His victory had been won at the cost of compromise both tacit and explicit.

With the ink of the plenum resolution hardly dry, it became evident that the matter of the anti-party group was not settled and that there were splits over the mandate Khrushchev had won in the field of policy. In contrast to his portrayal of the purge as a victory for his reform policies, some saw in it a vindication of basic orthodoxy in policy.

SIGNS OF HARD STRUGGLE

The struggle for power between Khrushchev and his challengers in June, 1957, raged for three days within the Presidium and it took another eight days of closed sessions of the Central Committee to put an end to the crisis. Even the inevitably one-sided accounts of the struggle that came from Khrushchev and his supporters belied the notion of either an easy or automatic victory. These accounts, especially those given at the Twenty-second Party Congress in 1961, conveyed a picture of intrigue and maneuver in the classic manner of a palace struggle. They suggest that Khrushchev upon his return from a visit to Finland found himself confronted by a large majority in the Presidium not simply critical of his policies but seeking his overthrow.

The detail revealed at the Twenty-second Congress that Bulganin had posted his own guards in the Kremlin during the critical Presidium session indicated that Khrushchev's enemies had laid a trap for him rather than the other way around.[1] While they may have been careful to conceal their plan to oust him, they apparently had not hesitated to contend with him over policy issues in the previous months. In an interview with a Western correspondent in May Khrushchev himself had referred openly to "heated" arguments in the Presidium which had required a vote to settle.[2] Premier

[1] See Shelepin's speech to the Twenty-second Congress in *Pravda*, Oct. 28, 1961. Shelepin alleged: "Abusing his office, Bulganin, during June, 1957, when the factionalists turned to an open attack against the Central Committee, placed his bodyguards around the Kremlin and stationed guards at supplementary posts who let no one pass without his instructions into the government building where the meeting of the Presidium of the Central Committee was being held."

[2] Khrushchev's interview with Turner Catledge of *The New York Times* on May 10, 1957 (*The New York Times*, May 11, 1957.)

Bulganin, who joined the attack on Khrushchev, evidently did not even consider it necessary to conceal his contempt for him in the weeks before the encounter in the Presidium. He apparently staged a walk-out designed to embarrass Khrushchev during his visit to an agricultural exhibit in Moscow at the beginning of June.[3] These were scarcely signs that Khrushchev's opponents regarded him as so powerful that he could not be crossed.

N. G. Ignatov, who gained Presidium membership in June, 1957, gave a blow-by-blow account of the three-day struggle within the Presidium, which, however distorted by political motives, conveyed a clear impression that the scales had been delicately balanced. At the Twenty-second Congress he exclaimed how "fortunate" it was for the party that Khrushchev and Mikoyan had gained approval from the Presidium to accompany Bulganin and Voroshilov to a meeting with those Central Committee members who had gotten wind of the struggle in the Presidium and were petitioning for convocation of a plenum. The "mathematical" Presidium majority opposed to Khrushchev, according to Ignatov, had intended to send Bulganin and Voroshilov alone to meet with the Central Committee members who had "literally illegally" entered the Kremlin.[4] The clear implication was that the outcome might have been different if this tactic had succeeded.

Khrushchev's strategy, of course, was to transfer the struggle to the Central Committee where his supporters were in a majority. Apparently much depended on getting his scattered supporters to the Kremlin to build pressure for such action, but it was not even certain that the Central Committee would have automatically

[3] At the party plenum in December, 1958, Matskevich charged that at the opening of the All-Union Agricultural Exhibit on June 2, 1957, which he attended, "Bulganin created a disturbance for Comrade Khrushchev and quit the exhibit at the head of a factional group." See *Plenum tsentral'nogo komiteta kommunisticheskoy partii sovetskogo soyuza, 15–19 dekabrya 1958 goda, stenograficheskiy otchet* [*Plenum of the Central Committee of the Communist Party of the Soviet Union, December 15–19, 1958, Stenographic record*] (Moscow: 1958), pp. 421–23. While the accuracy of the official versions of the 1957 struggle must be suspect, such details had a ring of authenticity because they did not contribute to the propaganda image of a triumphant leader who had easily overcome a small factional minority in the party.

[4] See Ignatov's speech to the Twenty-second Congress in *Pravda*, Oct. 25, 1961.

supported Khrushchev if the Presidium had presented it with a *fait accompli* rather than with an issue to be resolved. This seems to be the purport of Ignatov's reference to the "good fortune" of the party that Khrushchev saw through the opposition's tactic of proposing that only Voroshilov and Bulganin meet with the Central Committee petitioners and insisted on going along with them.

Furthermore, Khrushchev's support in the Central Committee at the outset was less than total, despite the claim that it was "unanimous" in condemning the opposition faction. Shortly after the plenum *Kommunist* virtually admitted as much. The journal drew pointed attention to the "decisive" role the *expanded* Central Committee—a reference to Khrushchev's success in packing the body with about one-third more members at the Twentieth Congress —had played in preserving party unity.[5] It recalled that Lenin had used a similar tactic. The illogic of *Kommunist*'s point was apparent. If the Central Committee was "unanimous" in opposing the group, the fact that it had been expanded at the Twentieth Congress was irrelevant.

It also must be kept in mind that the outside assistance of Marshal Zhukov was important, if not decisive, in Khrushchev's success. Both Zhukov's elevation to full Presidium membership—the highest party post ever held by any Soviet professional military figure— and his sudden ouster a few months later strongly suggest this conclusion. In other words, it appears that Khrushchev regarded his political debt to Zhukov of sufficient magnitude to pose a genuine threat to his rule, making the preventative purge imperative. In this action he evidently had full support from his party colleagues, who probably also saw in Zhukov a menace to party rule as such. Whether Zhukov actively entertained the idea of challenging party rule or not, the party leaders' fear was echoed in the characterization of him as a "new Bonaparte" by his successor as defense minister.[6]

Khrushchev at the same time had to use all his skill at maneuver, cajolery, and pressure tactics to break up the two-to-one majority initially confronting him in the Presidium. He divided, then

[5] *Kommunist*, No. 10, 1957, p. 8.
[6] See Malinovskiy's speech to the Twenty-first Congress in *Pravda*, Feb. 4, 1959.

conquered. He first succeeded in weaning Voroshilov, Bulganin, Pervukhin, and Saburov away from Molotov, Malenkov, Kaganovich, and Shepilov. Here he may have already obtained Zhukov's backing and was using this as a wedge with which to split the opposition.[7] Also in the heat of the struggle Khrushchev evidently offered these figures assurances that they would not suffer reprisals in return for their defections from the opposition. Such assurances probably were a factor in their retention in high posts after the June purge.

Suslov's part in the leadership crisis remains ambiguous. Whether by accident or intention, when the confrontation in the Presidium was beginning he was away from Moscow touring in the provinces. Saburov in his statement to the Twenty-first Congress on his participation in the anti-Khrushchev faction did not mention Suslov's name in referring to the "healthy" section of the members of the Presidium who sided with Khrushchev.[8] Saburov mentioned only Mikoyan and Kirichenko in this connection, apparently the only two who stood by Khrushchev at the opening of the fateful session. According to Saburov, the two figures had persuaded him to break with the opposition. Here was a possible hint that Suslov was not among Khrushchev's firmest supporters in the crisis. Although he obviously had come out in support of Khrushchev by the time the Central Committee was convened, his selection to report to the plenum on the issues between the contenders raised the further suspicion that he may have initially attempted to act as an "honest broker" in the conflict.

If such was Suslov's tactic, it would accord with previous hints that he had occupied middle ground between the factions. It was he, for example, who gave the October Revolution anniversary speech in 1956 shortly after the Hungarian and Polish upheavals.

---

[7] Probably linked with Khrushchev's bid to Zhukov was a gratuitous reference to Zhukov's role in turning back Japanese incursions into Soviet territory during the Thirties in Khrushchev's interview with a Japanese correspondent on June 18. The Western press picked up various rumors at the time that Zhukov provided Khrushchev with the aircraft used to carry his Central Committee supporters from the provinces into Moscow.

[8] Conquest points out this seeming omission in *Power and Policy in the USSR*, pp. 317–18.

At this point Khrushchev's opponents had gained ground and Khrushchev was on the defensive under the impact of Hungary. The October speech normally reflects the consensus of the leadership on policy, and Suslov may have been chosen to deliver it as the representative of the new balance in the Presidium after Hungary. His conservative leanings were suggested by his role in the crackdown after the Twentieth Congress on the most zealous of the de-Stalinizing historians. Under his supervision they were condemned as "revisionists." And on the eve of the struggle in the Presidium, on June 15, the leader of these historians, Burdzhalov, was ousted as editor of the professional historical journal.[9]

The Incomplete Purge

In the aftermath of the June plenum various indications appeared that Khrushchev's victory rested on a coalition of diverse elements and depended on certain compromises between the hard-core Khrushchevites and other important figures outside his circle. The nature of these compromises soon became evident.

The retention of Khrushchev's foes in party ranks was a key part of the arrangement, and his unfinished business was to dispose of them. Khrushchev and his confederates almost immediately began registering dissatisfaction with the portrayal in the plenum resolution of Malenkov, Molotov, and Kaganovich as "comrades" guilty merely of political error. They began building the case for party expulsions and even eventual trial by raising charges of crimes against them. At the Twenty-second Congress a strong backer of further punishment of the group directly revealed the intentions of the Khrushchev faction.

They had failed in an earlier effort to gain the party ouster of his foes at the plenum. Ignatov's account of the purge recalled that

[9] Agit-prop chief Konstantinov mirrored the hard-line trend in the social sciences at this juncture in his speech at the social science conference held in Moscow June 14–22. He stressed the limits of de-Stalinization and warned that the attack on the Stalin cult could not be a pretext for disparaging Stalin's "immense theoretical work" and defense of Leninism against hostile attacks.

"many" participants at the plenum considered it "impossible" to retain the group leaders in the party.[10] Yet the impossible was done. Obviously a compromise on the point had been made. The plenum resolution papered over the failure of the expulsion effort. It pictured a "unanimous" Central Committee withdrawing its demand for party expulsions of the opposition to Khrushchev only after the group admitted its errors and pledged that it would abide by party decisions. But the explanation was lame. A few paragraphs further the resolution registered Molotov's refusal to comply.

The resolution also contained a passage justifying party expulsion as a penalty for factionalism, but in a way that amounted to a binder on Khrushchev to emulate Lenin's restraint toward opponents and to eschew the Stalinist tactic of resorting to the pretext of political crime in disposing of opponents. The resolution recalled the Tenth Party Congress decision drafted by Lenin outlawing factionalism but describing the penalty of expulsion as an "extreme" measure. It also noted the requirements that such action against a Central Committee member must be approved by a two-thirds majority of all Central Committee and party Control Commission members sitting in general session.[11] The June plenum resolution thus hinted that the Central Committee did not deem Khrushchev's foes as deserving of extreme penalties and that his forces did not have the two-thirds vote to carry through its attempt to expel the defeated faction.

Nonetheless Khrushchev immediately began the long, drawn-out process of exposing and weeding out that portion of the anti-party group that had escaped censure in the plenum resolution. This piecemeal process would take over four years to complete. The

[10] *Pravda,* Oct. 25, 1962.

[11] Conquest, *Power and Policy in the USSR*, p. 462 (text of June plenum resolution.) Undoubtedly some of those present at the June, 1957, plenum recalled that Lenin himself failed in his efforts to use the ban on factions against dissenters inside the party following the Tenth Congress. Lenin's attempt to have A. G. Shlyapnikov, a leader of the Workers' Opposition faction, expelled from the party fell three votes short of the necessary two-thirds majority at a joint session of the Central Committee and Central Control Commission in August, 1921. Later, in 1922 at the Eleventh Party Congress, proposals for the expulsion of Shlyapnikov and his associates, Madame Kollantai and Medvedev, also failed to be carried.

resort to a highly circuitous means of disposing of his hidden opponents was scarcely testimony of Khrushchev's political strength and something more than an elaborate way of avoiding political embarrassment. It was rather intimately related to the resistance to new vendettas against the defeated faction which Khrushchev had encountered from various top figures. The presence of such resistance was already echoed in the month after the purge in *Pravda's* complaint that the Soviet press was not giving enough attention to the purge.[12] Somebody in the agitation-propaganda department of the Central Committee apparatus was apparently dragging his feet.

Another arrangement between Khrushchev and his Presidium colleagues appears to have been made: anti-Stalinism would be more or less shelved as a weapon in factional politics. Such a consensus within the leadership was registered in the issuance of the official biography of Stalin in November, 1957, in Volume 40 of the *Great Soviet Encyclopedia*. The volume originally had been scheduled to appear in the spring of 1956 but had been held up by Khrushchev's attack on Stalin. The new biography, however, contained none of the vitriol against Stalin of Khrushchev's Twentieth Congress "secret speech." Rather, it continued to reflect the balanced assessment of Stalin's pros and cons that characterized the public stance of the party after the Twentieth Congress as well as the increased attention to his merits after the Hungarian revolt. Rolling with the blow that Hungary dealt his de-Stalinization policy, Khrushchev himself had defended Stalin against his detractors in early 1957.

His own renewal of that defense after the fall of his challengers in June served as reassurance to the ruling group that the Stalin issue had been laid to rest in internal politics. The abridged Khrushchev speeches released in August, 1957, conveyed the impression that the anti-Stalin campaign he had initiated at the Twentieth Congress had reached its limit and would go no further. He admonished those who mistook his attack as a "sweeping denial" of Stalin's positive role and went on to indicate that his merits

[12] *Pravda*, July 21, 1957.

outweighed his demerits.[13] He even shifted some of the blame for abuses from Stalin to Beria and Malenkov—whom he pictured as unscrupulously exploiting Stalin's personal weaknesses. He thus kept separate for the moment the issue of Stalin and the anti-party group, but not to a degree that would make the joining of the two issues in the future overly difficult. Even at this stage his treatment of Stalin betrayed his real intent. He began to imply a link between the "dogmatic" views of his anti-party foes and their violations of legality under Stalin. The portion of the abridgement of Khrushchev's speeches implying the link apparently was taken from his speech to the Moscow party organization on the day the purge was announced in the Soviet press.[14]

In line with this it is reasonable to infer that one of the factors contributing to Zhukov's sudden downfall at the end of October lay in the fact that he, wittingly or not, threatened to upset the consensus of the leadership on the Stalin and anti-party group issues. Speaking to enthusiastic crowds in Leningrad on July 5, Zhukov began none too subtly urging that the whole question of Stalin and the role in the repressions played by the leaders he purged be brought into the open. *Pravda* edited the speech and excised an obviously sensitive passage where Zhukov spoke of documents proving the guilt of the purged leaders.[15] Zhukov was playing with political dynamite. Although he may have been thinking principally in terms of righting the wrongs perpetrated against himself and the professional military under Stalin in the 1930's and World War II, the party leaders as a body must have regarded Zhukov's speech as a possible first step in a bid for power. Khrushchev himself must have viewed it as an effort to take the Stalin issue out of his hands; he was not about to be deprived of his prime political weapon.

[13] *Kommunist*, No. 12, 1957, p. 19.

[14] *Kommunist*'s editors appended a note to Khrushchev's statement on literature and art saying it was an abridged version of three speeches, two before the purge and the third "at a party *aktiv* in July." Only the last speech would have contained direct attacks on the anti-party group.

[15] *Pravda*, July 16, 1957. *Pravda* at one point in the text inserted the statement that Zhukov had cited "facts" on the "anti-party group's" "violations of legality" without further elaboration.

ORTHODOX WARNINGS

Omens of approaching conflict over Khrushchev's policy of economic reform also appeared in the aftermath of the purge. In contrast to his portrayal of the fall of his foes as a decisive victory for his economic reforms and pro-consumer line, some voices saw in it a reaffirmation of basic orthodoxy in economic policy. The treatment of the key issue of party policy on heavy industry and consumer goods signaled an incipient split between Khrushchev and the conservatives. This issue had taken a central place in the leadership crisis, yet the party resolution on the purge and Khrushchev ignored that fact while others concentrated on it.

The resolution conspicuously failed to note that Khrushchev's rivals had judged him vulnerable to the same charge he had used in bringing down Malenkov in 1955. Thus it overlooked the fact that at the June plenum they had specifically attacked Khrushchev for violating the party's line on heavy industrial primacy and had cited his program for matching American consumption of meat, milk, and butter within "a few years" as case in point.[16] The resolution only briefly referred to the sacrosanct heavy industry dogma, treating it as an accepted element of party policy rather than a contentious issue. It was soon evident, however, that some wanted to make it unmistakably clear that the regime was still pledged to keeping the dogma inviolate in future policy.

Thus the *Pravda* editorial on party unity on the eve of the purge announcement noted where the resolution had failed to say that the primacy of heavy industry was the party's *general line*. Without naming them, *Pravda* stressed that the Central Committee and the Twentieth Party Congress had censured *both* Malenkov's pro-consumer heresy on the heavy industry question and Molotov's

---

[16] The resolution cites the anti-Khrushchev faction's opposition to the meat, milk, and butter line but not their charge that this line was a violation of the heavy industry dogma. This linkage was, however, made explicit, for example, in an article by A. Rumyantsev in *Kommunist*, No. 11, 1957, p. 19. Mikoyan in a speech in Yerevan in March, 1958, gave the most revealing account of the faction's attack on Khrushchev for putting butter before steel. See the Armenian party newspaper *Kommunist*, March 12, 1958.

pessimistic view of the U.S.S.R.'s progress in building socialism.[17] The tacit message was that neither the extreme of Malenkov's reformism or Molotov's conservatism was acceptable to the party. The latter half of the editorial was irrelevant; there was little danger that the party would err in the direction of excessive conservatism under Khrushchev's lead.

After the purge certain party figures—notably Kosygin and Kozlov—pressed *Pravda's* point about heavy industry as if to compensate for the resolution's reticence on the matter. Kosygin, who won a place as a Presidium candidate at the June plenum, revealed that the group had directly charged Khrushchev with deviation on heavy industry. Reporting on the purge to the Moscow party organization, Kosygin said: "The group sought to contrast the rate of development of agriculture to the rate of development of heavy industry. But everyone is well aware that successes in agriculture do not at all mean that heavy industry should develop more slowly in this connection. The party always has been and always will be concerned for the preponderant development of heavy industry. It never has and never will deviate from this line."[18]

Kosygin seemed to protest too much. The passage not only conveyed the impression that the group had exposed a chink in Khrushchev's political armor but also advertised that the post-purge regime was committed to toeing the traditional line on resource allocations.

At the same time Frol Kozlov, who was elevated to full Presidium membership at the June plenum, added another point overlooked in the purge resolution in his report to the Leningrad party organization. He recalled Malenkov's consumer heresy in 1954–55 which the resolution, despite a lengthy recital of the group members' offenses, conspicuously failed to mention. Kozlov declared that "as Chairman of the Council of Ministers Comrade Malenkov . . . made crude political mistakes, distorting the Leninist line on the preferential development of heavy industry, and giving confused and harmful directives on questions of foreign policy and the international situation."[19]

[17] *Pravda*, July 3, 1957.
[18] *Ibid.*, July 4, 1957.
[19] *Leningradskaya Pravda*, July 5, 1957.

Here we get a clear indication of Kozlov's conservative orientation on domestic and foreign policy. In his first speech after the purge he had publicly intimated his orthodox leanings on domestic policy and, by implication, in foreign policy. His reference to Malenkov's "harmful" directives on foreign policy unmistakably alluded to the ex-Premier's soft line in foreign affairs, which was expressed in his formula that a new world war could destroy civilization.

Khrushchev's own first post-purge public speech a few days later was in marked contrast to both Kosygin's and Kozlov's.[20] He treated the heavy industry question with seeming unconcern. Without referring either to the charge he had personally pinned on Malenkov in 1955 or to the fact that his foes had turned that very charge against him, he repeated the resolution's brief passage on heavy industry. Notably it stressed that Soviet industry had assumed such "tremendous" proportions and was proceeding at such a "high rate" that conditions necessitated the 1957 decentralization of industrial management which the anti-Khrushchev faction had opposed. Khrushchev would return again and again to this same argument to justify a shift away from heavy industry to consumer goods. Moreover, in contrast to Kozlov's reference to Malenkov's foreign policy errors, Khrushchev asserted that his rivals, especially Molotov, opposed détente and coexistence and "found a policy of tightening all screws more convenient."[21]

Kozlov's pointed recollection of Malenkov's heresy obviously did not fit with Khrushchev's picture of the issues at stake in the purge. Not only was the reminder on Malenkov disruptive to Khrushchev's effort to show that Malenkov, Molotov, and Kaganovich were uniformly die-hard, but it also invited invidious comparison with his own expanding pro-consumer line.

In the months after the June plenum Khrushchev worked to revise the record to show that Malenkov had always been conservative. The party press carried articles indicating that Molotov and Malenkov were birds of a feather and that Malenkov's association with post-Stalin reform measures was pure demagogy and opportunism. Thus while Khrushchev sought to blot out

[20] *Pravda*, July 7, 1957.
[21] *Ibid.*

Malenkov's record as a reformer and gather all the credit himself, the defenders of traditional policy sought to preserve the memory of Malenkov's pro-consumer "right" deviation as an object lesson to other would-be reformers.

One other key regime element indicated its sympathy with the orthodox position on economic policy: the military press made no bones about the military's stake in continued preferential development of heavy industry. The emphasis on the point had no equivalent in the general editorial comment on the purge in the press at large. The day after the release of the June plenum resolution *Red Star* carried an article declaring:

> To whom is it not clear that enormous harm to our state would occur if, instead of being stepped up, the tempos of further development of industry—including heavy industry—and the material basis of the economic might and defense capability of the country were weakened? . . . Thanks to the fact that the possibilities of the socialist economy have grown and above all to heavy industry, and to the achievements of Soviet science and technology, our armies . . . are supplied with the latest military equipment and arms which are the material basis of the Soviet Union's armed forces.[22]

The article, like Kozlov, noted that primacy of heavy industry was the party's "Leninist line" and it further recalled that the Twentieth Congress had instructed the party to implement that line "unswervingly." Clearly *Red Star* was warning Khrushchev that tampering with the traditional line on heavy industry would incur the resistance of the military. Here was a harbinger of Khrushchev's future troubles with the generals over military policy, as well as the danger of an alliance between the military and more conservative elements in the leadership in opposition to his program of economic reform.

Khrushchev's challengers in June, 1957, obviously had hoped to bring all those favoring traditional economic policy to their side with the attack on him as a violator of the heavy industry line. Though the military was evidently uneasy about Khrushchev's economic policy, it appears that Zhukov at least was most concerned

[22] *Krasnaya Zvezda [Red Star]*, July 5, 1957.

with redress of the military's grievances over the depredations they suffered under Stalin. In this respect he apparently regarded Khrushchev as the most receptive among the leaders to his demand. In her speech to the Twenty-second Congress Furtseva in fact asserted that Khrushchev at a Presidium meeting shortly before the June crisis had called for the rehabilitation of the generals Stalin had shot in 1937.

If Zhukov had remained in the Presidium he might have become a stumbling bloc to Khrushchev's domestic program, a consideration which may have been among the reasons that impelled Khrushchev to act quickly to remove him. Zhukov had earlier aligned himself with those who opposed Malenkov's 1953–54 consumer program as endangering the policy of heavy industrial priority. Indeed, *Red Star's* veiled warning against any tampering with the priority for the heavy industrial defense sector of the economy probably also expressed Zhukov's views. While he approved Khrushchev's de-Stalinization policy he would not necessarily go along with his internal economic program. Apparently Khrushchev had already clashed with Zhukov over one aspect of his program—the industrial decentralization in early 1957. Under this reform Khrushchev originally intended to decentralize even the ministries dealing with defense production, but when it was formalized both the Ministry of Defense Production and the Ministry of Aviation Industry were not decentralized—an apparent concession to the Army. Soon after Zhukov's fall in December, 1957, however, both these ministries were included in the reform and were converted to state committees. Zhukov also on various occasions had denigrated the importance of nuclear weapons in contrast to Malenkov's assertion that such weapons could destroy "civilization." Zhukov most likely would have opposed Khrushchev's later forays aimed at cutting defense costs of the Army and his effort to develop a strategy placing heavy reliance on a rocket-nuclear deterrent.

While all the causes for the failure of the 1957 anti-Khrushchev faction may never be known, it is worth noting that the Leningrad party under Kozlov had a special score to settle with Malenkov for his role in the Leningrad purge under Stalin. Interestingly, Malenkov was placed at the head of the anti-party leaders in the

June plenum resolution, possibly as a gesture to the Leningraders, but at the Twenty-second Congress Khrushchev put Molotov at the head. In any case, Malenkov took the butt of the post-purge attacks on the opposition from a number of party leaders for his alleged participation in the Leningrad affair. The head of the Leningrad party organization, Spiridonov, also took the lead in the attack on Malenkov both at the Twenty-first and Twenty-second Congresses.

These post-plenum developments were further indications that Khrushchev's June victory was born of a coalition and that he depended in part on political understandings with conservative-leaning elements who had denied their support to the anti-Khrushchev faction. The reference in the party resolution to heavy industry as the basis of party policy may be read as an assurance to these elements that Khrushchev did not intend a major shift in industrial priorities despite his attack on his opponents' disregard of popular welfare. The arrangement was inherently unstable. Khrushchev would seek to undo it and other forces in the regime would seek to sustain it.

WHAT IS THE MAIN DANGER?

Khrushchev not only faced formidable powers defending orthodox policy within the Soviet party after his June victory but also had to contend with similar forces within the bloc as a whole, principally from the Chinese. Even at this stage before the Sino-Soviet conflict had fully developed the Chinese Communists already were beginning to put a crimp in Khrushchev's favored strategy. At the meeting of the bloc parties in Moscow in November, 1957, Mao Tse-tung began mounting resistance to the Khrushchev line. The cleavage was echoed in the question of whether revisionism or dogmatism was the greater danger to correct Communist strategy. Khrushchev had set the terms of the conflict as early as the Twentieth Congress when he revived the polemical epithet "dogmatist" to describe the orthodox elements in the party. In June, 1957, he applied the term to his fallen foes; the plenum resolution, for example, focused heavily on Molotov's "dogmatic" and "conservative" errors.

Shortly after that he declared the danger of dogmatism was not only an internal problem of Soviet politics but also of the Communist bloc as a whole. He went to Czechoslovakia in July and issued a statement with Czech party leader Novotny, asserting that the struggle against dogmatism was as "equally necessary" as the struggle against revisionism.[23] Here he was initiating an effort to curb the strong anti-revisionism line the Soviet leadership had adopted after the Hungarian revolt.

As was the case during the remainder of his rule, Khrushchev's call for struggle against dogmatism was tied to a policy of rapprochement with Tito, the leading revisionist of the Communist world in orthodox lights. Also in Czechoslovakia Khrushchev pressed another theme he had previously used to promote Soviet-Yugoslav rapprochement—the theme that ruling parties could pursue "different roads to socialism." He had advanced this line after the Twentieth Congress attack on Stalin and it had culminated in the Khrushchev-Tito statement in Moscow in June, 1956, which recognized Yugoslavia's right to a "different road to socialism" and spoke of Soviet-Yugoslav party ties. Molotov had vigorously opposed Khrushchev's effort to renew ideological and party ties with the Yugoslavs. At the end of 1956 Molotov had his day, however; Khrushchev's pro-Yugoslav policy collapsed under the impact of the Hungarian revolt.

The line Khrushchev took in Czechoslovakia in July, 1957, was thus the prelude to an effort to restore ties with the Yugoslavs; he met with Tito the next month. The warming trend in Soviet-Yugoslav relations was also duly registered in the October Revolution slogans released in mid-October by the CPSU Central Committee, fostering the impression that the links broken by the Hungarian revolt had been repaired.[24] Yugoslavia was pictured as an integral member of the bloc by the device of placing in alphabetical order with the other bloc states the Yugoslav slogan, which specifically noted that Yugoslavia was "building socialism"—

[23] *Pravda*, July 17, 1957.
[24] *Ibid.*, Oct. 13, 1957.

a point that had been dropped from the May Day slogans issued six months after Hungary.[25] This developing line, however, was cut short by the November meeting in Moscow of the bloc parties.

At the November summit meeting of bloc party leaders Mao threw his full weight behind a crackdown on revisionist deviation in the bloc. He called for urgent struggle against revisionism and succeeded in putting a damper on Khrushchev's anti-dogmatism line. Mao's point of view was duly reflected in the twelve-party statement. It made revisionism a greater sin than dogmatism and stressed that Communist unity was a consideration prior to the recognition of "national peculiarities."

That Khrushchev accepted this line at the time did not mean he personally favored it: this was the price of Chinese support or, more precisely, acquiescence to his leadership. Further, he was in need of tranquility in the bloc, especially in Eastern Europe, while he consolidated his June victory at home. Yet it did not follow that he regarded a vendetta against Yugoslav revisionism as the best means to this end and his portrayal of his June victory as a victory over dogmatism in policy was not compatible with Mao's line that revisionism was the greater danger to policy; indeed, within the month after the November meeting Khrushchev tried to minimize the effect of the Yugoslav refusal to sign the twelve-party Moscow statement which had attacked revisionism. While he noted that ideological and political differences with the Yugoslavs remained, he stressed that there were now fewer such differences than before.[26]

The Chinese position at the November meeting was undoubtedly welcomed by the more orthodox elements in the Soviet party as well as in Eastern Europe who were fearful of the unsettling effects, both internal and external, of political commerce with the Yugoslav revisionists. Notably there was already an intimation that Suslov was a more zealous anti-revisionist than Khrushchev. He played a major role in the talks at the meeting of the parties in Moscow in November, 1957, by presenting the position of the Soviet party.

[25] *Ibid.*, April 21, 1957. Compare Yugoslav slogans No. 22 in April and No. 29 in October.

[26] Speech to Supreme Soviet, *ibid.*, Dec. 22, 1957.

Little is known of the specific contents of his presentation but an East German Politburo member, reporting on the meeting at an SED plenum, singled out Suslov's stress on the dangers of revisionism and the need to combat it.[27]

The anti-revisionism line was reaffirmed in mid-1958 by the Soviet attack on the new Yugoslav party program—here following the Chinese lead—and again at the Twenty-first Congress, where an effort was made to paper over the rift produced in Sino-Soviet relations by Chinese claims that they had found a short cut to communism through the communes. At a time when Khrushchev was still suffering from the blow the U-2 incident dealt to his détente strategy, the thesis that revisionism was a greater danger than dogmatism was once more incorporated, under heavy pressure, in the 1960 Moscow statement of the world's Communist parties. It was imperative, however, for Khrushchev to break from the confines imposed by the anti-revisionism line if his political strategy were to be freed of the albatross the Chinese had tied to it, and he worked toward this end. But there were those who sought to hinder his efforts.

Khrushchev had, in the final analysis, won only a limited victory in June, 1957. By the rule of politics a limited victory involves a limited mandate. His unfinished business was to make the victory complete and the mandate unconditional. To the very eve of his fall in October, 1964, he struggled to accomplish this.

[27] *Neues Deutschland*, Nov. 30, 1957.

4

CONSOLIDATION and ADVANCE— The MTS REFORM and CHEMICALS

DURING THE SECOND HALF of 1957 and up to the fall of 1958 Khrushchev worked to consolidate his June victory and to break ground for a broad attack on the bases of traditional policy. He moved with relative caution, however, in the first six months after the purge of his challengers and more or less stayed within the confines of the political arrangement that gave him victory. He struck the pose of a moderate reformer still wedded to the essentials of orthodoxy, but his pose disguised preparations for major moves aimed both at expanding his power and pressing a program of reform. Shifts in leadership in December, 1957, strengthened his base in the Secretariat and his leverage in the Presidium.

Following these changes he further tightened his personal grip on power and policy by taking on the role of Premier as well as First Secretary. And he now introduced his MTS reform—abolition of Machine Tractor Stations, the most radical change in the Soviet countryside since collectivization. This measure was soon followed by the unveiling of a plan for basically reorienting industrial policy, entailing a shift in the focus of economic policy from steel and metal to chemicals production. The MTS reform and the chemicals program were part of his developing strategy aimed against the traditional economic structure.

THE CLOAK OF ORTHODOXY

Up to the end of 1957 Khrushchev did not initiate any major policy moves; his first pronouncement after the purge was in fact a model of moderation. The abridged speeches on literature and art released in August presented a Khrushchev not only opposing undue denigration of Stalin's memory but favoring strict, paternalistic party control over the intellectuals.[1] This posture was related to a more important issue than literary policy per se: it reduced his vulnerability to the charge that his attack on Stalin at the Twentieth Congress had produced the wave of unrest among Hungarian intellectuals which had ignited the Hungarian revolt, not to speak of near-rebellion in Poland and a rash of protest literature in the U.S.S.R. itself.

Khrushchev also made a show of militancy in foreign policy at this time. In an interview with James Reston he once more emphasized that capitalism, not socialism, would perish in a new war.[2] Thus he underscored the distinction between his coexistence line and Malenkov's heretical view that a new war could "end civilization." He linked the theme with a display of bluster that became his hallmark in the years prior to the Cuban crisis—that peculiar mixture of declarations of peaceful intent and rocket-rattling.

His bent toward reform, however, was evident even in his invocations of orthodox themes. In his speech on the fortieth anniversary of the Bolshevik revolution he duly reiterated the proposition that heavy industry was the "foundation of foundations" of party domestic policy, but at the same time he qualified his assertion in a manner reminiscent of Malenkov. He said that the basic industries of the U.S.S.R. "had reached such a level that, without detriment to the interests of consolidating the defense of

[1] *Kommunist*, No. 12, 1957, pp. 11–29.
[2] *TASS*, Oct. 11, 1957.

the country, without detriment to further development of heavy industry and machine-building, we can develop light industry at a considerably higher speed."[3] Though the statement was ambiguous on the relative rates of growth he had in mind, the emphasis on boosting consumer output was clearly the operative part. It foretold of his long-term effort to reduce the citadel of heavy industry in Soviet policy in favor of the consumer and agriculture.

Even Khrushchev's insistence on party vigilance toward deviation among the intellectuals was counterbalanced by a promise of a less repressive regime. He revived the long-defunct doctrine that the Soviet state was destined to wither away and that indeed the process had already begun, and he declared that class struggle was on the wane in the U.S.S.R., reducing the need for political arrests.

There also was a significant omission in his renewed emphasis on Stalin's merits and basic soundness as a "Marxist-Leninist and strong revolutionary" in the speeches released at the end of August, 1957.[4] He made no mention of Stalin's contributions to Communist theory. In contrast, the new Stalin biography in the *Great Soviet Encyclopedia* had restored the portrayal of Stalin as an "outstanding" theoretician who "creatively developed" theory—a standard characterization that had been dropped from the sketch of Stalin in the official *Political Dictionary* released in the summer of 1956 after the Twentieth Congress. Khrushchev had good cause not to advertise Stalin's theoretical prowess: he was on the verge of launching a major attack on Stalinist theory and practice in a key area of policy—Soviet agriculture. At the beginning of 1958 he introduced the MTS reform, the first major innovation since the fall of his challengers.

He prepared for this radical departure in agriculture by significantly augmenting his power base in the Central Committee Secretariat and his leverage in the top policy-making Presidium. At an organizational plenum in December he succeeded in creating a situation unique in party history—the members of the Secretariat now represented the majority of the voting Presidium membership. Khrushchev's protégé, Mukhitdinov, was given both full Presidium

[3] *Pravda*, Nov. 7, 1957.
[4] *Kommunist*, No. 12, 1957, p. 19.

status and a secretarial post, and Presidium members Kirichenko and Ignatov joined the Secretariat. Prior to the June purge only Khrushchev and Suslov had held dual membership in the Presidium and the Secretariat. The June, 1957, plenum had raised the dual membership to seven and the December plenum to nine, making a majority of secretaries in the fifteen-member Presidium of the time. The effect of the shifts was to enhance the influence of Khrushchev's closest confederates in the June crisis and accentuate the increased voice in policy of the party Secretariat, where his most reliable support was lodged. The Secretariat now was in a position to exercise a controlling voice in Presidium decisions if at least eight of the nine Presidium-member secretaries shared a common view on any particular policy issue. These changes obviously eased the way for Khrushchev's take-over of the Premiership from Bulganin within a few months—a move not only securing his grip on the executive posts of the regime but also effecting the removal of his still unexposed anti-party opponent from a position of power.

The MTS Reform—Orthodox Protests

Within the month after this redistribution of power Khrushchev introduced the MTS reform. Despite his enhanced organizational strength the introduction and implementation of the reform was accompanied by sharp controversy. He had routed the "dogmatists" and "conservatives" of the anti-party group, but there were still those who dared criticize the project on the grounds that it departed from orthodoxy in agricultural policy. The conflict demonstrated that his June victory had not immunized his policy initiatives from criticism in the party. Although neither Khrushchev nor the critics of the reform mentioned Stalin in the debate over the measure, the prime issue at stake was whether Stalinist doctrine in agriculture, symbolized in the MTS, could be nullified.

The reform struck at one of the foundation stones of the traditional economic structure of the regime. Quite literally, the Machine Tractor Station was the counterpart in agriculture to the dogma of heavy industrial priority for Soviet industry; it assured the regime control over the product of the collectivized peasantry in support of forced draft industrialization. Khrushchev's reform made use, without significant change, of the plan of the two regime economists Stalin had roundly condemned in his political testament. Stalin had seen in their proposal to abolish the MTS a major retreat from communism and an attempt to "turn back the wheel of history." To him the plan meant expanding the market economy of the collective farm system and the release of uncontrolled economic forces within the system. It meant handing over the "basic means of production" in agriculture to a less than fully socialist economic institution, the collective farm. These, according to Stalin, were a form of co-operative property inferior to full public or state owner-ship. The MTS represented the "higher" form of public property in the countryside, which would replace the "lower" collectivized property. Stalin thus made the elimination of the collective farms, not their preservation, a programmatic goal of party policy.[5] The objections attending Khrushchev's introduction of the reform faithfully echoed those Stalin had made.

Khrushchev had been unable to initiate the MTS reform while his rivals remained in the Presidium. In early 1957 there were numerous signs of an effort to build up pressure behind the plan. The press carried reports of experiments on local Ukrainian collective farms with joint MTS-collective farm tractor brigades and references to cases of individual transfers of tractor brigades to collective farm control. A Central Committee journal in March, 1957, revealed that outright proposals for sale of MTS equipment to the collective farms had been made at an agricultural conference in Moscow at the time but had been rejected out of hand.[6] Khrushchev betrayed his frustration over the failure of the effort

[5] J. V. Stalin, *Economic Problems of Socialism* in L. Gruliow (ed.), *Current Soviet Policies, Documentary Record of the 19th Communist Party Congress* (New York: Praeger, 1953), pp. 1–18.

[6] An article by S. Kolesnev in issue No. 3 (March), 1957, in the journal *In Aid of Political Self-Education* said:

"In the course of the discussion of the problem of the relations between the MTS and the farms some comrades have put forward the proposal for the sale to the collective farm of the equipment of the MTS. Is this proposal acceptable? No, it is not.

to get the MTS plan off the ground in this period in his abridged speeches published in August, 1957. In these speeches, which he had given just before and after the June crisis, he vented his ire at "theoreticians" and "pedants" who among other things "seek out a citation from the classics" in determing "how to act in case of an MTS in a certain rayon."[7] He was almost certainly alluding to the opposition against his plan.

In fact later at the December, 1958, CPSU plenum Molotov, Kaganovich, and Shepilov were directly charged with having led the effort to sabotage Khrushchev's MTS project. According to the then Agriculture Minister, V. V. Matskevich, when the question of the reform was raised in the leadership, "Molotov and Kaganovich attempted literally to terrorize the apparatus of the Ministry of Agriculture in order to get hold of, or rather to concoct, any kind of materials which would defame this measure."[8] Matskevich further charged that "Shepilov and his assistants, in the person of Academician Laptev, attempted 'theoretically' to substantiate the 'erroneousness' of the proposals which had been worked out."[9]

Soon after the June purge the proposal to abolish the MTS resurfaced in the press. Appropriately the November issue of *Oktyabr* raised the question in an article by I. Vinnichenko containing an account of a conversation with the two economists Sanin and Venzher, whom Stalin had attacked in 1952 for proposing sale of the MTS to the collectives.[10] The proposal did not go unchallenged this time either, and right up to the very eve of Khrushchev's own

"The whole experience of collective farm production shows that concentration of the basic tools of agricultural production in the hands of the MTS is the main method of insuring a rapid tempo of development of socialist agriculture and livestock breeding."

[7] *Kommunist*, No. 12, 1957, p. 17.

[8] *Stenograficheskii Otchet, Plenum Tsentralnogo Komiteta KPSS* [*Stenographic Record, Plenum of the Central Committee of the CPSU*] Dec. 15–19, 1958 (Moscow: Gospolitizdat [State Publishing House for Political Literature], 1958), p. 422.

[9] It is notable that despite Laptev's involvement with the anti-party group he continued to occupy a prominent position as a member of the Academy of Agricultural Sciences. Khrushchev did not settle accounts with him until 1962. Laptev lost his post following Khrushchev's complaint that he had made no contribution to agricultural science. Khrushchev also revealed he had been appointed rather than elected to the academy in violation of its rules.

[10] *Oktyabr*, No. 11, 1957, pp. 205–23.

presentation of the plan it was attended by controversy in the press. A series of articles countered the arguments of the reform's advocates. Soviet economist V. Dyachenko in *Problems of Economics* in mid-December voiced an orthodox Stalinist objection to the idea, saying it would be "a step backward—toward lower, co-operative forms of socialist property."[11]

Also in December the mouthpiece of the MTS, *Machine Tractor Stations* (No. 12, 1957), reiterated Stalin's argument that the proposal would put the collective farms in an exceptional position, a position which Stalin had said would divide collective from public property and lead away from communism. Even more strikingly the journal *Oktyabr*, which had earlier published articles endorsing the idea, now carried criticism of it shortly before Khrushchev's January speech recommending the reform. A writer named N. Lyskin, while supporting the less radical notion of subordinating MTS functions to collective farm management, objected to the sale of MTS machinery to the collective farms on the grounds that it would weaken the state's control over collective farm production.[12] A similar point was made even more forcefully at the same time in an article in the journal of Moscow University that invoked Stalin's precept that the means of production can be rationally used in the public interest only when they are in state hands.[13]

Either Khrushchev had not made his position on the proposal clear or the controversy in the press indicated that the issue had not yet been resolved in the leadership. The former was quite unlikely; proponents of such a radical plan would not have broached it in public without the sanction of high authority, and this must have been fully apparent to those voicing opposition to it. By this time also, after the plan already had been in the political hopper at least since early 1957, there must have been a general awareness among regime circles of the identity of its sponsors.

[11] *Voprosy Ekonomiki* [*Problems of Economics*], No. 11, 1957, p. 17.

[12] *Oktyabr*, No. 1, 1957, pp. 161–69.

[13] The article by M. P. Osadko appearing in the issue of the *Herald of Moscow University*, No. 4, signed to press on January 11, 1958, declared that "with the transfer of the MTS to collectives, we will be abolishing the strong points of the state in the economic administration of the collectives, and the state's economic form of control over the activity of each collective, without infringing on the proprietary right of the collective."

Various signs soon appeared that the divergent lines in the press indeed echoed persisting differences within the leadership over the reform. Khrushchev moved to force the issue to a conclusion by publicly proposing the reform in his speech in Minsk at the end of January,[14] and his theses on the reform released at the end of the next month mirrored the intense controversy that surrounded its birth. He engaged in an extensive defense of the theoretical and practical soundness of the reform against the criticisms of "some comrades, chiefly economists."[15] Like the attack on Malenkov's consumer policies in 1954–55 Khrushchev's real target was not the "economists" but the high figure or figures whose views they echoed. While it was, as usual, difficult to identify such figures, a warning from party secretary Pospelov against misrepresentations of the character of the reform clearly indicated Suslov as among the critics. In his Supreme Soviet pre-election speech in March, Pospelov warned that it was "incorrect" to view Khrushchev's reform as a mere "practical" measure instead of a project of great doctrinal and political import developing Marxist-Leninist theory on the transition to communism.[16]

Suslov, just two days earlier in his Supreme Soviet election speech, had treated the MTS reform precisely in the manner Pospelov condemned.[17] He had briefly praised the sale of the MTS but only as a practical measure designed to increase efficient use of machinery and to raise labor productivity. He was distinctly less laudatory toward Khrushchev's other major measures and more cursory in his treatment of them than were other election speakers. And, unlike the other top speakers, he failed to make even a single mention of Khrushchev in his speech.[18] Suslov's failure to note

[14] Khrushchev's speech was delivered in Minsk on January 22 but was not published in *Pravda* until January 26.

[15] *Pravda*, March 1, 1958.

[16] *Ibid.*, March 14, 1958.

[17] *Ibid.*, March 12, 1958

[18] Three leaders—Pospelov, Brezhnev, and Korotchenko—referred to Khrushchev three times; nine others—Voroshilov, Mukhitdinov, Belyaev, Mikoyan, Furtseva, Aristov, Ignatov, Kalnberzin, and Kirilenko—mentioned him twice, and all the other leaders at least once. Most of the references to Khrushchev were linked to major measures initiated by him. Since the pre-election speeches review party policies Suslov's failure to mention the First Secretary was most remarkable.

the theoretical import of Khrushchev's reform, while citing only its practical aspect, sounded like a faint echo of the anti-party group's complaints against Khrushchev's "practicism" and neglect of theory. Thus there was reason to believe that he had taken exception to the reform on doctrinal grounds, and the only possible objections to the reform on such grounds would be in terms of Stalin's dogmas.[19]

A measure of the heat that had been generated around the issue of the reform was provided by the speech of another high figure two days before Pospelov gave his warning. Kalnberzin, the Latvian party chief who had won candidacy in the Presidium in June, 1957, lashed out at the critics of the reform in the strongest terms. He indicated that, even at that late date after the February plenum had adopted Khrushchev's theses on the reform, critics of the measure were still vocal in the party. He charged that "some woebegone critics" and "shouters" were trying to picture the decision of the plenum as anti-Leninist—strong language in the

[19] The evidence that Suslov and Khrushchev had been at odds on the MTS reform was followed by a Khrushchev maneuver in June, 1958, that appeared designed to implicate Suslov in one of Stalin's excesses. On June 8 *Pravda* published a Central Committee decree dated May 28 exonerating several Soviet composers whose operas had been condemned at Stalin's instigation. The decree corrected "mistakes" in Zhdanov's 1948 music decree and in 1951 *Pravda* editorials that had condemned the operas for ideological errors. The attack on the 1951 editorials was the most suggestive in regard to Suslov. It inevitably reflected on Suslov, who was *Pravda* editor at the time and perhaps even drafted the editorials in question. While the decree put the main blame on Stalin and on Malenkov, Molotov, and Beria for egging Stalin on, it also laid the basis for Suslov's guilt by association.

The action was not linked with any new policy moves in party policy in the cultural field and appeared gratuitous. It in fact came in a period when the party was pressing efforts to discipline dissenters in the literary and artistic field. However, it seems hardly accidental that the decree appeared shortly after L. F. Ilichev became chief of the Central Committee's agitation-propaganda department in May. Ilichev as we shall see was groomed by Khrushchev as a counterpoise to Suslov in the ideological field and would later emerge as a rival of the latter. Shortly after the Twenty-second Congress a Central Committee *apparatchik* in the literary field, A. B. Rurikov, revealed that the May 28 decree had been issued on the "initiative of N. S. Khrushchev" and explained that the decree was an "example of how we overcome mistakes which are connected with the personality cult of Stalin and the activities of conservatives and dogmatists" (*Literary Gazette*, Jan. 4, 1962).

lexicon of party debate.[20] Kalnberzin was alluding to the main conservative criticism that had been openly expressed in the press: giving the MTS machinery to the collectives was a move away from Communist goals and that, instead, policy should aim at converting the collectives to fully state-owned farms.

However, it was also evident from the statements of party spokesmen at the time that Khrushchev's pro-consumer orientation was an interlinked issue in the behind-the-scenes debate. Khrushchev also explicitly defended the MTS reform as a means to an economy of abundance. He rebutted the idea that the reform was a step backward from Communist goals—one of the effects of the reform at least from the orthodox view was to strengthen the influence of market forces in the economy. He explained that abundance was the prerequisite of communism and it could only be attained through the lower costs that the new system in the countryside was designed to produce.[21] Other strong proponents of the reform pressed similar arguments. Ignatov in his Supreme Soviet election speech stressed that the reform's goal was to increase food for the population and to boost the output of the food and light industries. He specifically sought to refute the idea that the emphasis on agriculture in Khrushchev's policy meant that "the problem of further development of heavy industry has been relegated to second place."[22] Mikoyan at the same time engaged in an outspoken defense of Khrushchev's consumer orientation. He recalled how "a number of well-known and old workers of our Party" had wrongly opposed Khrushchev's meat-milk-and-butter program as a retreat from communism because it put steel in second place. Despite his support for Khrushchev's policy, Mikoyan's allusion was a notably "comradely" reference to Khrushchev's enemies.[23] Half of them, of course, at this point were not yet exposed and still held high posts—Voroshilov, Bulganin, Pervukhin, and Saburov—and

[20] *Pravda*, March 13, 1958.

[21] Khrushchev's arguments in defense of the MTS reform can be found in his "theses" on the reform (*ibid.*, March 1, 1958); in his Supreme Soviet speech of March 27, 1958 (*ibid.*, March 23, 1958); and in his speech on the new price and procurement system under the reform on June 17, 1958 (*ibid.*, June 21, 1958).

[22] *Ibid.*, March 9, 1958.

[23] *Kommunist* (Yerevan), March 12, 1958.

Mikoyan was among those who would resist plans for new vendettas against them. His ambiguous reference to opposition to Khrushchev's policy left room, however, for the possibility that there were those outside the "group" and still in the leadership who had questioned it.

In any case, Mikoyan's argument, though ostensibly addressed to a past issue, was applicable to the issues aroused by the MTS reform. He concluded that opposing steel to food was a dogmatic approach having "nothing in common with Marxist theory and with life." He declared, "If we are able, at the present stage of our development, to assure the people an abundance of food products during the next few years, then why should we postpone this . . . until we match the United States in steel production; further, does the question not concern food products, that is, food for the labor forces, which are after all the basic production force in society?"[24]

The raising of the consumer goods-versus-heavy industry question in Mikoyan's and Ignatov's speeches was one of the gathering signs that the matter was coming to the fore in leadership councils. It was implicated in the debate over the MTS reform but was inevitably assuming a central place in the leadership's consideration of Khrushchev's new Seven-Year Plan, which was to be ready in draft form during the summer of 1958. The question was how much rein should be given to Khrushchev's consumer line in the new plan.

Khrushchev's search for ways of freeing more resources for his economic program during this period was mirrored in his flirtation with another radical scheme. In March he raised the possibility of a gradual conversion of the regular professional army into a territorial militia system similar to the one that existed in the early years of the Soviet regime. He saw it as a way of reducing the massive burdens on the national budget of maintaining the large Soviet standing army. The idea never gained headway, however, even though he again referred to it as a future possibility in his January, 1960, speech announcing troop reductions. Not surprisingly the scheme encountered resistance in the defense ministry. It also was subjected to muted criticism in the Leningrad press, an indication

[24] *Ibid.*

that Kozlov took a dim view of it.[25] Here was another sign that the defenders of traditional policy found an ally in the military when the latter's special interests were affected by Khrushchev's initiatives.

CHEMICALS INSTEAD OF STEEL

A key move in Khrushchev's effort to alter economic policy was his unveiling in May, 1958, of a program for the rapid expansion of the U.S.S.R.'s chemicals industry at a Central Committee plenum. Chemicals expansion was to be a prime element of the Seven-Year Plan and a means for undercutting the traditional economic structure. Although he reasserted the priority of heavy industry in regime policy in his report to the plenum, he proceeded to give a new twist to that proposition which modified its traditional meaning. In a long and detailed argument stressing the necessity for the accelerated development of a lagging chemicals industry, he asserted that chemicals was now the "decisive" branch of heavy industry.[26] The assertion clearly challenged the traditional position that steel was the core of heavy industry. In this manner he could now plausibly assert that heavy industrial priority was the basis for stepped-up consumer production. His vision of the multiple consumer applications of chemicals and chemical plastics pointed to the back door through which heavy industry could be increasingly made to serve the neglected consumer.

Khrushchev indicated however that his arguments for chemicals had encountered misgivings from some elements in the regime. Not only did he berate unnamed officials for ignoring the importance of chemicals, but he attacked "some comrades" who questioned his proposal to seek credit and technical aid from the West as a means of rapidly boosting chemicals development. The unnamed comrades allegedly opposed the plan on grounds that it would shore up

[25] A writer in the historical journal of the Central Committee in 1964 alluded to criticism of the militia idea in Leningrad publications in 1957–58 and in the defense ministry's *Journal of Military History* in 1960. See P. S. Smirnov, "O politike partii v voyennom stroitelstve" ["On Party Policy in Military Organization"], *Voprosy Istorii KPSS* [*Questions of CPSU History*], No. 2, 1964, pp. 42–53.

[26] *Pravda*, May 10, 1958.

capitalism. In answer, he said that trade between rival capitalist and socialist economies was mutually beneficial.[27]

Although Khrushchev's chemical program was incorporated in the new Seven-Year Plan, it was destined to lose out to steel and arms for some five years before it was resuscitated. His panacea of aid from the West did not materialize and it was evident at the time the program was introduced that his consumer measures were being kept within narrow confines of existing allocations policy. The program had been accompanied by propaganda fanfare for a series of decrees promising increased output of selected consumer goods, especially synthetic textiles and shoes. However, the decrees did not entail any significant diversion of resources from other sectors of the economy and seemed mainly calculated to maintain Khrushchev's identification with the consumer cause in the popular mind.

Even by the end of 1959 it was already becoming clear that Khrushchev's chemicals program was being short-changed. Kosygin as Gosplan head reported to the Supreme Soviet on the Seven-Year Plan progress and revealed that the goals of heavy industry were being met *except* for chemicals, which was lagging badly, and the report indicated no intention to make up the lag. The plan report allowed for only a 10-per cent increase for chemicals output for the next year of the plan—7 per cent less than was required to meet the threefold expansion of output by 1965 that Khrushchev was seeking.[28]

Here we begin to discern a pattern that would characterize Khrushchev's efforts to implement his policy. He would ask for more and have to settle for less. He would vigorously promote pro-consumer policies but step back whenever resistance began to rise dangerously. And at the same time he would seek to inject new elements in the party line that could be used as the basis for bolder moves in the future.

The signs of high-level conflicts in the first half of 1958 indicated that the image of the triumphant leader moving forward with the united backing of a pliable leadership group was something less

[27] *Ibid.*
[28] Kosygin's plan report was published in *Pravda*, Oct. 28, 1959.

than a mirror of reality. While Khrushchev's primacy was not in doubt, even in this period of consolidation and advance his reforming moves had generated controversy in the leadership. The regime's traditionalists betrayed their disquiet over the leader's policy. The issue of Khrushchev's anti-party foes also lay just under the surface. Mikoyan's reference to them as "old and well-known" comrades in his Supreme Soviet election speech echoed a consensus in the leading group against new purges. Perhaps not accidently the allusion to Khrushchev's foes appeared within a fortnight of Bulganin's removal from the Premiership later the same month and Khrushchev's assumption of that post. The unrest in the leadership was to be strikingly manifested at the Twenty-first Party Congress in January, 1959. It would be the occasion for a reassertion of the common interest of the leadership group, outside of Khrushchev's most loyal confederates, in checking the prime leader's effort to expand his power over it.

5

The DRIVE for SUPREMACY— The TWENTY-FIRST CPSU CONGRESS

THE POLITICAL PLATFORM Khrushchev unveiled at the Twenty-first Party Congress in January, 1959, aimed both at securing his place as the supreme leader of the regime and as the architect of the transition to communism in the U.S.S.R. By the time the Congress convened he had built up impressive political momentum. From his vantage point as head of both party and government he was in a position to assert his claim as the guide of the regime in both theory and practice, and its ubiquitous advisor on matters large and small.

Prior to the Congress Khrushchev's followers portrayed their leader, though he probably never met Lenin, as "Lenin's disciple and comrade-in-arms," as leader of the Soviet "state" and "people," and at the Congress as the leader-theoretician—in short, the classic image of the maximal Communist leader. Yet they could not carry off the massive effort to manufacture a charisma around their leader. The new cult remained a promotional device and an instrument of factional politics within the regime. It was thus not a demonstration of the leader's absolute sway over his colleagues as the case had been with Stalin.

The outcome of the struggle in the leadership over the disposition of the anti-party group at the Congress was visible proof of this. In the months before, Khrushchev renewed the drive against his old foes and indicated his intention to win new punishments against them; but the triumphant leader proved less than a total leader. The drive ground to halt in the face of resistance within the leadership group.

KHRUSHCHEV RENEWS THE ATTACK

Making a prime issue at the congress out of the retention of his defeated foes in party ranks was a key link in Khrushchev's campaign for total control. By the end of 1958 he was pressing for the full exposure of the still hidden members of the anti-party group. To this end his first order of business was completing Bulganin's removal from the top leadership. Khrushchev had replaced him as Premier but Bulganin retained his Presidium membership. The Central Committee was convened in early September and accomplished the dual purpose of scheduling the "extraordinary" Twenty-first Party Congress and effecting Bulganin's removal from the party Presidium. Khrushchev used another Central Committee plenum in November to expose the ex-Premier as a member of the anti-party faction. The stated purpose of this meeting was consideration and approval of Khrushchev's draft report on the new Seven-Year Plan for presentation at the Twenty-first Congress. Khrushchev simply tacked the former Premier's name to a listing of the anti-party group appearing in his report on the new plan. The device looked suspiciously like a ploy to circumvent opposition in the leadership to Bulganin's political disgrace.

Notably Khrushchev tied his exposure of Bulganin with an attack—in the present tense—on unidentified "conservative" elements in the party. He warned that the party "is waging a determined struggle against all who cling to old and obsolete forms and methods of work and who, infected by conservatism, resist the implementation of the Leninist master line of the party."[1]

[1] *Pravda*, Nov. 14, 1958.

The passage was a pointed warning of the dangers of opposition to the leader, Bulganin serving as the object lesson.

The next stage of the attack on Bulganin took place at still another Central Committee meeting in December, when Khrushchev extracted a public confession from Bulganin of his complicity with the anti-party group. It became apparent then that the attack on the ex-Premier was only part of a wider political strategy focused on the issue of the anti-party group's retention in the party. Khrushchev issued a scarcely veiled demand that Malenkov, Molotov, and Kaganovich be expelled from the party. "The tongue is not capable," he said, "of referring to such people as 'comrades,' even though they have remained members of the party."[2] As he had done shortly after the June, 1957, purge and in the June, 1958, opera decree, he once more ominously pictured Malenkov and Molotov as accomplices of Beria, "the rabid enemy of the party and the people."[3] At still another point he referred to his foes as "despicable."[4] The drift of these remarks was unmistakable. The fact that he resorted to the Central Committee forum on three occasions in succession at the end of 1958 was probably in itself a sign that his purposes were being resisted within the Presidium.

Following the plenum and in the weeks prior to the Congress various officials picked up Khrushchev's cue. At the Supreme Soviet at the end of December the U.S.S.R. Prosecutor General raised the specter of a trial of group members for "criminal" violations of "legality" in the past.[5] On the eve of the Congress Spiridonov, the Leningrad party chief, sparked the move for action on the issue by bringing up the Leningrad affair. At the Congress his first move was to openly link Pervukhin and Saburov to the group and demand the group members "give account" then and there.[6] A claque of Khrushchev's most vocal middle-echelon

[2] *Ibid.*, Dec. 16, 1958.

[3] *Ibid.*

[4] *Ibid.*

[5] *Ibid.*, Dec. 26, 1958.

[6] In the issue of *Party Life* (No. 2, Jan., 1957) published on the eve of the Twenty-first Congress Spiridonov charged "some" members of the group with guilt in the Leningrad affair. He raised further charges at the Congress on January 29 (*Pravda*, Jan. 30, 1959).

supporters launched bitter attacks on the anti-party members and made clear their intent to gain Congress support for new punitive action against them. At the same time, however, it became almost immediately apparent that the drive against the group was foundering in the face of resistance from strong forces in the party leadership. The evidences of conflict over the issue at the Congress were manifold and a number of top leaders clearly indicated their opposition to reviving the ritual of the purge.[7] They indicated that they wanted attacks on the group to be limited to their "political" errors—as indeed the June, 1957, plenum resolution had done— and opposed the introduction of "criminal" charges against them.

The Presidium-level speakers at the Congress were clearly divisible according to their stands on the group issue. Those who in varying degrees pictured the issue as closed as far as any further punitive measures were concerned were in the majority.[8] Mikoyan, Suslov, and Kosygin were manifestly moderate while figures like Kirichenko, Ignatov, Belyaev, and Furtseva were harsh in attacking the group. Mikoyan, in particular, virtually declared his opposition to new action against the group members. He pointedly observed that the Congress had been called by the Central Committee to consider the "sole" agenda item of the Seven-Year Plan. Further, he said, he had to explain to American questioners during his trip to the United States just before the Congress that the revival of the group issue at the December plenum did not mean opposition to Khrushchev had developed. And here he further suggested his opposition to efforts to add new members to the group by saying that he told his questioners that the group had not increased by a "single" member.[9]

While Khrushchev did not indicate his position on the issue in his Congress speech as he had in December, he was obviously not a disinterested observer in the matter of his enemies' fate. There is little room for doubt that he was the inspirer of the new purge drive.

---

[7] These evidences have also been discussed in works by Leonhard and Conquest. See: Conquest, *Power and Policy in the USSR*, and Leonhard, *The Kremlin Since Stalin* (London: Oxford, 1962).

[8] Conquest, *Power and Policy in the USSR*, pp. 375–81.

[9] *Pravda*, Feb. 1, 1959.

He had initiated the exposure of Bulganin and undoubtedly arranged for his "confession" at the December plenum as well as Pervukhin's and Saburov's admissions of error at the Congress. He had raised the matter of the continuing membership of Molotov, Malenkov, and Kaganovich in the party and he was clearly not content with the retention of four of his erstwhile opponents in the Central Committee—Voroshilov, Bulganin, Pervukhin, and Saburov. He succeeded in exposing the last three of these four; in the case of Voroshilov there were signs that he had also begun a move against him, but without result at the Congress.[10]

The upshot of the Congress was that Khrushchev settled for considerably less than he had sought. No party expulsions of group members occurred. The trio of Bulganin, Pervukhin, and Saburov were not even removed from the Central Committee, and Pervukhin remained as a candidate Presidium member despite a proposal from the floor asking his expulsion from the Central Committee.[11] Moreover, Voroshilov emerged unscathed with his public standing as Presidium member and Supreme Soviet Chairman still intact.

The evidences of the displeasure of the Khrushchev forces at these results were manifold. Those who pressed the specific indictments against Bulganin, Pervukhin, Saburov, and Shepilov complained bitterly that their confessions of error were inadequate and had simply screened their continuing opposition to Khrushchev. Indeed a close look at the confessions showed there were some grounds for the complaint from the Khrushchevites. Robert Conquest for example has noted that Bulganin in his confession implied that despite his support of Khrushchev's policies he had decided that Khrushchev was unacceptable as a ruler. Khrushchev's Agriculture Minister, Matskevich, complained that Bulganin had "failed to disarm himself completely" and charged that the roots of his subversive work against Khrushchev remained.[12] Saburov

---

[10] *Pravda*'s photographs of the Congress sessions on the first and fourth days showed Voroshilov present but no Congress speech by the elder leader was published. Later when Voroshilov's speech appeared in the stenographic record of the Congress it was explained that it had not been delivered because of illness.

[11] See speech of T. Uldzhabayev (*Pravda*, Feb. 4, 1959).

[12] Matskevich speech at the December, 1958, plenum (see Chapter 4, n. 8).

also subtly indicated that the group had acted against Khrushchev out of fear that he was seeking to impose a dictatorship over them. Despite his rejection of the notion, the point was especially sensitive against the background of the build-up of the leader cult around Khrushchev at the Congress.[13]

It was evident then that Bulganin, Pervukhin, Saburov, and Shepilov—while all having made admissions of error—had refused to sign unconditional surrenders to Khrushchev. Furthermore, the other principals of the group maintained their silence although they too had probably been subjected to severe pressures. One good reason for their behavior suggests itself: they were probably aware that important elements in the leadership were opposed to the effort to renew the purge against them.

One incident shortly after the Congress further underscored the irritation of Khrushchev's forces over the opposition they had met on the group issue and revealed their intent to settle accounts with those who had resisted a new purge. The First Secretary of the Moscow oblast party, I. V. Kapitonov, along with his deputy, N. F. Ignatov, was removed from his post amid charges of malfeasance in the party press. Kapitonov had been a moderate on the group issue at the Congress and in a speech a month afterward he had asserted that the Congress approval of the activities of the Central Committee constituted ". . . a complete and final condemnation" of the anti-party group.[14] He thus openly identified himself with those in the Presidium who had treated the issue as closed. His removal occurred at a Moscow party plenum ten days after his speech, attended by Aristov, Kirichenko, and Churayev, the latter a Central Committee *apparatchik* who had authored a sixty-four page exposé of the anti-party group. Despite his disgrace Kapitonov had reappeared as chief of the Ivanovo oblast party organization by the end of the year, a sign that he had protectors in high places.

[13] Conquest, *Power and Policy in the USSR*, p. 317. Saburov's "statement" to the Congress was not released in full until several months after the Congress when it appeared in the official stenographic record.

[14] *Sovetskaya Rossiya*, Feb. 21, 1959.

THE QUESTION OF THE LEADER'S POWER

The close interconnection at the Twenty-first Congress between the issue of the anti-party group and Khrushchev's effort to expand his power was evident in the speeches of the Congress delegates. The speakers who most vigorously pressed the attack on the group were usually the most zealous promoters of the budding Khrushchev cult. Speakers relatively moderate on the group issue were usually the more temperate in praise of Khrushchev. Particularly striking examples of this tendency were the speeches of Kuzmin and Kosygin. Where Kuzmin boosted both the new cult and the attack against the group, Kosygin avoided adulation of Khrushchev and was a distinct moderate on the group issue. Kuzmin, a Khrushchev protégé, had with remarkable suddenness risen from relative obscurity from the Central Committee apparatus to head Gosplan a few days before the Supreme Soviet approved Khrushchev's sweeping industrial reorganization in May, 1957. Kosygin had for a long time been a high-level figure whose rise to prominence had occurred independently of Khrushchev's patronage.

Kuzmin made the most concentrated attack of the Congress on Pervukhin, who had spoken earlier on the same day. He charged Pervukhin with not owning up to his offenses, a line that associated him with the faction pushing for further action against Khrushchev's defeated opponents. At the same time he referred to Khrushchev's leadership more than a dozen times and went so far as to put his report to the Congress on a par with Lenin's "theoretical studies."[15]

Where Kuzmin had devoted a significant part of his speech to the attack on Pervukhin, Kosygin cited the group in but two brief sentences. He made no mention of Pervukhin or Saburov and noted the group had been "smashed," with the obvious implication that the matter was now past history. Further, Kosygin referred to Khrushchev only twice in connection with his Congress report and without adulatory embellishment. Unlike many speakers, he did not once cite Khrushchev's personal leadership and initiatives. In fact he made fewer references to Khrushchev than any of his Presidium colleagues at the meeting. The striking contrasts between

[15] *Pravda*, Feb. 5, 1959.

the speeches of the two figures thus identified the one as the supporter and the other the opponent of Khrushchev's more far-reaching ambitions.[16]

The Kuzmin speech also provided a particularly clear illustration of how the anti-party group issue was simultaneously being exploited by the Khrushchev forces to inhibit opposition within the ruling group to the current policies of their leader. Kuzmin attacked Pervukhin for past opposition to policies that were still controversial within the leadership. For example he condemned Pervukhin for failure to expand mineral fertilizer production when he was Minister of Chemical Industry. Chemical fertilizers of course were central to Khrushchev's program for chemicals development and he had given them a key place in the Seven-Year Plan. Presumably Kuzmin as Gosplan head was a vigorous promoter of Khrushchev's chemicals policy. He had no opportunity, however, to demonstrate his loyalty to Khrushchev's objectives after the Congress; within two months he had lost the post of Gosplan chief to Kosygin. Under Kosygin's supervision Khrushchev's chemicals program visibly suffered.

As indicated earlier, the question of the old Bolshevik Voroshilov's involvement in the challenge to Khrushchev in 1957 was another focal point of the factional in-fighting behind the scenes at the Twenty-first Congress. Khrushchev apparently attempted unsuccessfully at the Congress to settle political scores with him—the one remaining member of the anti-Khrushchev faction then still unexposed. His retention in the top leadership represented a potential but nonetheless real menace. Voroshilov had lent his considerable political prestige to the attack on Khrushchev's leadership in 1957 and there was always the danger that he might repeat his 1957 performance if Khrushchev were once again subjected to direct challenge in the leadership. The removal of Voroshilov from top posts was therefore high on the order of Khrushchev's unfinished business.

The outward sign at the Congress of a move against Voroshilov was the conspicuous failure of *Pravda* at the time to either report his speech to the Congress or to explain why he had not addressed

[16] For Kosygin's speech to the Twenty-first Congress, see *ibid.*, Jan. 29, 1959.

the meeting, even though his presence in the hall was shown in press photographs.[17] This, combined with Khrushchev's pointed comment at the Congress that young blood should replace the old in important posts, could hardly have failed to bring to the minds of the delegates that the President of the Supreme Soviet was in his seventy-eighth year. *Pravda's* felony was compounded two months later when Voroshilov's Congress speech appeared in the volumes containing the official stenographic record of the proceedings.[18] Voroshilov's speech was juxtaposed with Saburov's, with the editorial note that the Congress Presidium had decided to publish it at Voroshilov's request. The note lamely added that the speech had not been given because of "illness," but this did not explain why the same procedure was not followed by *Pravda* during the Congress.

While the exact sequence of moves and countermoves in the Voroshilov matter at the Congress is not known, it is notable that within a month afterward Mikoyan once again took the lead in maneuvers to block Khrushchev's purposes. In his Supreme Soviet election speech in Rostov at the end of February he placed himself in the way of any vendetta against Voroshilov.[19] He in effect confirmed the fact that Voroshilov had emerged unscathed from the Congress. He gratuitously recalled how Voroshilov had warmed the hearts of the Rostov citizens when he converted military barracks into housing for workers in the Civil War. Also, in an unusual gesture, Mikoyan not only conveyed greetings to the Rostov workers from Khrushchev but also from Voroshilov, Budenny, Shvernik, and Andreyev. While the conveying of Khrushchev's greeting was a method other party leaders had used to pay deference to the prime leader, Mikoyan's extension of the device to include four of the elder leaders of the party constituted more a gesture to collective leadership than homage to Khrushchev. Indeed, Mikoyan strengthened the impression that this was his

[17] *Ibid.*, Jan. 28, and Feb. 2, 1959.

[18] *Vneocherednoi XXI S'yezd KPSS—Stenograficheskii otchet* [*The Extraordinary 21st Congress of the CPSU—Stenographic Record*], Vol. II (Moscow: State Publishing House for Political Literature, 1959), pp. 299–311. The volume was signed to press April 1, 1959.

[19] *Molot* (Rostov), Feb. 28, 1959.

motive by pointedly attacking the notion that the party required the "indispensable man" à la Stalin, the notion that the Khrushchevites had cultivated around their leader at the Congress.

Mikoyan's remarks on indispensable leaders had all the elements of a warning to Khrushchev on the danger of following Stalin's footsteps. He recalled that Stalin shortly before his death expressed doubts that the Politburo would be able to "carry on without him." This apparently was a reference to the same incident Khrushchev had recounted in the "secret" speech three years earlier, an incident that occurred when Stalin was planning a new purge at the top. According to Khrushchev, Stalin offered fabricated evidence of the "Doctors' Plot" to the Politburo members, complaining, "You are blind like young kittens; what will happen without me? The country will perish because you do not know how to recognize enemies."[20] Khrushchev had cited the episode to show to what extremes "Stalin's mania for greatness led." Mikoyan evidently thought that the moral of the story was worth repeating at that juncture of party politics, as the promotion of the Khrushchev cult was reaching a culmination at the celebration of his sixty-fifth birthday in April and his receipt of the Lenin Peace Prize in May.

In sum, the issue of the anti-party group at the Twenty-first Congress exposed the political tight rope on which Khrushchev was poised. He had to contend with the constant danger that his drive for power would provoke his Presidium colleagues into counteraction, and they had good grounds for fearing that the purge campaign against his fallen foes might eventually be turned against them.

The Leader's Program Unfolds

Khrushchev's drive for power at the time of the Twenty-first Congress—mirrored in the anti-party group issue and the new leader cult—corresponded with the unfolding of his political program of détente and reform. In the last half of 1958 Khrushchev

[20] Russian Institute, *The Anti-Stalin Campaign and International Communism*, p. 64.

pressed ahead with his strategy despite political obstacles at home and abroad. Neither the grumblings of conservatives over the MTS reform and economic policy nor the Lebanon and Taiwan crises in the summer and fall of the year altered his intent.

He continued to prepare the ground for limited détente with the West as the basis for his effort to reorient internal policy in favor of agriculture and the consumer. Khrushchev's caution in the Lebanon crisis and his failure to support Peking at the crucial stage of the Taiwan crisis in part reflected his intent not to permit crisis situations outside of his direct control to undermine his broader strategy. Of course in November, 1958, Khrushchev himself would play the aggressive militant with the issuance of his first ostensible ultimatum on Berlin.[21] It was soon evident, however, that his menacing behavior on Berlin, while aimed at forcing the West to retreat there, was part and parcel of an effort to bring the United States to a summit meeting. Summit meetings and reform projects went together in Khrushchev's thinking. This had been shown in his speech in Minsk in January of that same year, which had unveiled his radical MTS reform proposal and also contained his bid for a summit meeting. Moreover, it was in the midst of the crisis atmosphere of Berlin that he was busily preparing a détente-reform program for presentation at the Twenty-first Party Congress. In September the scheduling of an "extraordinary" party congress—unprecedented in CPSU annals—for January was announced, for the purpose of considering the draft of the new Seven-Year Plan.[22]

Khrushchev's aims in calling the Congress went far beyond the formality of ratifying the new economic plan, however. The timing suggested one of the motives. Khrushchev was facing a mounting threat to his leadership in the Communist world from Mao Tse-tung. Mao's staging of the Taiwan crisis and introduction of the commune system as the Chinese short cut to communism in the late summer of 1958 represented an unmistakable challenge. The Congress provided Khrushchev with a vehicle for reasserting Soviet political and ideological leadership; however, it was more than a mere

---

[21] Khrushchev's speech in Moscow on November 10 (*Pravda*, Nov. 11, 1958).
[22] *Ibid.*, Sept. 7, 1958.

reaction to Chinese moves. The Chinese at most were impelling Khrushchev to do more quickly what he already had been intending to do. Soon after the defeat of his challengers in 1957 he had begun to indicate that the U.S.S.R. was being ushered into a new stage of development under his leadership. He had scrapped the last five-year plan with its inevitable associations with the name of Stalin and his economic policies and called for a new seven-year plan. The intention was to emphasize a departure from past policy. The calling of the "extraordinary" congress, the first of its kind in party history, provided him with a platform for dramatizing his claim as a leader who would conduct the Soviet party and the Communist world as well into a new "stage" on the path to communism.

At the Congress Khrushchev assumed the role of the leader-theoretician advancing a "creative" exposition of the new historical stage from the standpoint of Marxist-Leninist theory. O. V. Kuusinen, the elder party theoretician, revealed in his speech the broad purpose behind Khrushchev's excursion into theory. His "many brilliant and new principles," Kuusinen declared, provided a basis for completing the long-stalled project for a new party program. He noted that a new program "should be prepared in time for the next regular party congress," adding that it was his belief that "if the Central Committee will work out the draft of the new program on the basis of the principal propositions of the report of Comrade Khrushchev at this congress, then this will be a good program of the party."[23] Lenin, of course, was the author both of the first program of the party in 1903 and of its revised version of 1919. Khrushchev was setting his sights on acquiring a distinctive attribute of leadership previously held only by Lenin—the authorship of the basic programmatic document of the party.

His theoretical discourses at the Congress provided the philosophical underpinning for his strategy of internal reform and coexistence abroad. He tied to the goal of economic abundance his basic theme that the U.S.S.R. was moving from the lower "socialist" to the higher "Communist" stage of development as

[23] *Ibid.*, Feb. 4, 1959.

envisaged by Marx and Lenin. The process would be complete, he said, when "we shall have provided a complete abundance of everything needed to satisfy the requirements of all the people. Communism is impossible without this", he added.[24] Furthermore a central part of the process, according to Khrushchev, was the realization of the Marxist goal of eliminating the differences between town and country through a "decisive" increase in agricultural output and the "radical" improvement of the living conditions of the rural population. In this connection he revived his idea of the *agrogorods*, saying, "The party is aiming at the conversion of the collective farm villages into urban-type communities with all the latest communal, cultural, and service facilities."[25]

Khrushchev's portrayal of the institutional changes to be brought on by the transition process suggested a declining role for the coercive state. Thus he pressed forward with the idea he had introduced in late 1957 that the "withering of the state process" was underway in the U.S.S.R. While noting that the military establishment must be retained as long as there was an external danger from "imperialism," he pictured a gradual reduction of the internal police functions of the state apparatus as well as some of its administrative duties. He explained that they would gradually be turned over to "public" organizations like the trade unions and the Komsomol. To show that the process was actually occurring he referred to the allegedly spontaneous initiatives of workers and youth in various parts of the country who, on the eve of the Congress, were setting up volunteer militias and informal "comrades' courts" to assist in maintaining public order. At the same time he stressed the idea of a permanent relaxation of the internal political atmosphere, announcing that there were no longer any cases in the U.S.S.R. of persons being tried for political crimes.

Khrushchev here was expanding on his theme from the Twentieth Congress three years earlier that the class struggle was on the wane in the U.S.S.R. He had cleared the way then for developing

[24] *Ibid.*, Jan. 28, 1959.
[25] *Ibid.*

the withering-of-the-state notion by rejecting the Stalinist dogma that class struggle intensifies as socialism develops, requiring a magnification of the role of the coercive state. The Twenty-first Congress theses in turn provided the prelude for his announcement at the Twenty-second Congress that there was no longer a "dictatorship of the proletariat" in the U.S.S.R. but that it had been replaced by a "state of the whole people." He was careful to segregate the party itself from the withering process, though at least in classical doctrine it too was destined to wither with the state. Rather than diminish, the role of the party, according to Khrushchev, would steadily grow and the party institution would be retained indefinitely under communism.

Khrushchev also set forth a series of propositions on the development of the international situation in harmony with his internal theses. He pictured a secure future for the U.S.S.R. in world politics and the steady expansion of Communist power and influence in the outside world without the necessity of major violence. In the new stage, he said, the danger of war with the capitalist world would steadily recede. He further elaborated his Twentieth Congress doctrine that war was no longer "fatalistically inevitable" and added that conditions were developing in the new stage for "excluding world war from the life of society even before the complete triumph of socialism, even with capitalism existing in part of the world."[26]

Tied to these statements was Khrushchev's declaration that the U.S.S.R. was henceforth secure from outside dangers and that there was no longer any possibility of the overthrow of the Soviet regime by enemies foreign or domestic. He announced that the "capitalist encirclement" of the U.S.S.R.—that dogma so basic to Stalinism—was at an end and that "the triumph of socialism in [the U.S.S.R.] is not only complete but final."[27] He indicated also that Stalin's doctrine of "socialism-in-one-country," the corollary of the encirclement doctrine, was also obsolete since a system of "socialist" states had now emerged. Reasserting his

[26] *Ibid.*
[27] *Ibid.*

Twentieth Congress line Khrushchev indicated there was no chance of a reversal in the progress of revolution since the balance of forces in the world was shifting in favor of the Communist world.

Khrushchev's discourse also pictured the countries of the Communist world entering the higher stage of communism "more or less simultaneously." The thesis was at once designed to reaffirm Soviet ideological leadership and to offer a basis for a *modus vivendi* with the increasingly assertive Chinese. In the discussion of the transition to communism he had engaged in a thinly veiled criticism of the Chinese attempt to take the lead in showing the way to Communist society through the introduction of the communes in the Chinese countryside. He stressed that there could be no sudden leaps to communism which bypassed the two-stage process stipulated in Soviet doctrine. Here Khrushchev added the sugar coating. He explained that other Communist states could follow the U.S.S.R. into communism "more or less" at the same time. This was possible, he said, because these countries would not be going it alone but could depend on the combined resources of the U.S.S.R. and the rest of the Communist bloc to accelerate their own transitions.

This rather feeble attempt to find a basis for restoring harmony within the Communist world, however, proved utterly ineffective in overcoming the incompatibility between the Khrushchevian and Maoist prescriptions for Communist policy. Khrushchev's "contributions to theory" at the Twenty-first Congress exposed the widening gulf between the two lines, a gulf that could not be bridged simply by minor concessions on points of doctrine. The propositions he advanced were an extension of the line he had introduced at the Twentieth Congress and they, in turn, set the stage for the Twenty-second Congress. This continuity and consistency of purpose belied the notion that Khrushchev simply made policy *ad hoc*.

Against the backdrop of the new stage outlined at the Congress, Khrushchev was engaged in practical moves calculated to produce the atmosphere of détente with the West that was so neccessary to the success of his plans for reorienting internal policy. Mikoyan returned from his visit to the United States where he had acted as Khrushchev's advance agent for U.S.-Soviet détente in time to give the Congress a rosy report on the possibilities of reducing tensions. His return was followed appropriately by Khrushchev's statement at the Congress that he was lifting the six-month deadline on Berlin he had set just two months earlier.

The message behind Khrushchev's statements was that the time was safe for moving regime policy away from the emphasis on steel and guns. Accordingly, he keyed the new Seven-Year Plan to the goal of surpassing the United States in living standards. He asserted, with the inbred optimism of the sloganeer, that this ambitious goal could be achieved within five years after the completion of the new plan. Despite his promise to the Soviet consumer, the preamble to the Seven-Year Plan itself nonetheless placed the task of strengthening the "economic and defense capacity" of the U.S.S.R. ahead of satisfying welfare needs, and in his speech Khrushchev noted that the "preponderant development of heavy industry" remained the basis of regime policy. At this point he avoided directly challenging heavy industrial priority—the stumbling block to his plan. But the long-term program he outlined at this time provided the basis for major initiatives he undertook in the year following the Congress.

A Point of Order

The propaganda fanfare for the Congress proceedings conveyed a picture of the triumphant and unhindered adoption of Khrushchev's program and the unhindered consolidation of his personal power. The picture was of course marred by the signs of conflict in the leadership over the anti-party group issue and by a strong indication that at least one top Presidium figure held reservations about the program being introduced—once again Suslov would hint at misgivings about Khrushchev's doctrinal and policy innovations.

Suslov began his speech at the Congress with a unique characterization of Khrushchev's report. He declared that since the meeting

was not a "regular" party congress "no report of the Central
Committee has been heard at the congress."[28] He thus imputed
sole personal responsibility to Khrushchev for the contents of his
report. Others at the Congress had also stressed Khrushchev's
personal role in drafting the report but rather portrayed it as the
very embodiment of high party policy.[29] Despite Suslov's subsequent
reference to the "brilliancy" of the report, he also betrayed a distinct
lack of zeal for its doctrinal aspects. Unlike a legion of speakers at
the Congress, he stopped short of saying that Khrushchev had
introduced innovations in Marxist-Leninist theory. He simply stated
that it provided "some important principles of Marxism-Leninism
on the transition from socialism to communism."[30] And to
Khrushchev's announcement that a "new, very important period"
in the U.S.S.R.'s movement toward communism had begun, he
restricted himself to the point that this was in accord with the
classics of Marxism-Leninism on the progression toward communism.
Suslov, in effect, was cautiously indicating that Khrushchev had
added little that was new to theory and furthermore that his statements had something less than the official stamp of approval of the
party. Other than mentioning Khrushchev in connection with the
report, he moreover did not follow the example of other speakers in
praising Khrushchev's personal leadership of the party and Central
Committee. This was consistent with a similar reticence he had
displayed previously on the subject.

Some months later another incident re-echoed the presence
of sentiment in the Central Committee that Khrushchev's program
entailed a neglect of theory. At the June, 1959, plenum Khrushchev
commented on a note he had received from a "comrade" asking
what had happened to "party work" in the party policy. The note
was in reference to the focus on economic problems in Khrushchev's
domestic program and represented a barely concealed complaint

[28] *Ibid.*, Jan. 31, 1959.
[29] Presidium member Belyaev conveyed the latter notion for example in
saying the Seven-Year Plan was worked out "by the party under the leadership
of N. S. Khrushchev (*Ibid.*, Jan. 29, 1959); *Izvestia* (Jan. 25, 1959) declared
that the Khrushchev report was a "programmatic" document for the party and
one of "the greatest works" of Marxism-Leninism.
[30] *Pravda*, Jan. 31, 1959.

that ideology was being subordinated to economics. His reply in brief was that theory could wait while the party tended to the business of solving the U.S.S.R.'s practical economic problems.[31] Notably, Khrushchev's protégé, I. I. Kuzmin, in his Congress speech had revealed in his attack on the anti-party group that they had accused "our party's Central Committee and also Comrade N. S. Khrushchev of practicism and of being too engulfed in the practical tasks of economic construction."[32] It appeared that such criticism had not been silenced in the party even after the Twenty-first Congress.

This Congress, in any case, was Khrushchev's launching point for a political offensive that reached full tide toward the end of 1959 with his visit to the United States. The planned return visit by President Eisenhower in mid-1960 was calculated to provide the atmosphere of East-West détente in which his plans for reorienting domestic policy could prosper. The Spirit of Camp David now replaced the long defunct Spirit of Geneva as the herald of reform. However, the resistance to Khrushchev on the issue of the anti-party group and Suslov's implied reservations over his program at the Congress were two of many signs that the Soviet leader had entered dangerous political territory where snares lay hidden.

[31] Khrushchev's speech to the June, 1959, plenum (*ibid.*, July 2, 1959).
[32] *Ibid.*, Feb. 5, 1959.

6

A COSTLY SETBACK—
The U-2 AFFAIR and AFTER

DESPITE THE SCATTERED signs of discontent within the leadership, Khrushchev's strategy gained momentum throughout the rest of 1959 and by January, 1960, the radical nature of his political intentions by Communist standards were laid bare. He had set in motion a series of major moves at home and abroad to clear the way for his domestic program. In September, 1959, he toned down the picture of major military threat from the West with his trip to the United States and Camp David and underscored his refusal to tolerate Chinese Communist sabotage of his détente strategy with the Soviet government's neutral stance on the Sino-Indian border conflict. Camp David set the stage for his easing the military burden on the Soviet economy through major troop reductions and reliance on a "cheap" rocket deterrent strategy. Military costs were the main stumbling block to Khrushchev's plan to redirect the Soviet economy away from its lopsided focus on heavy industry in favor of a more broadly based economic growth relying on "material incentives." A major departure from traditional party policy, such actions produced violent reactions in Peking— the Chinese dated the radical worsening of the Sino-Soviet conflict from the Camp David phase of Soviet policy[1]—visible discontent among the Soviet military, and counteraction by conservative forces within the Soviet party itself.

The dramatic events of the spring of 1960 exposed the fragile props of Khrushchev's Camp David strategy; the downing of the U-2 over Sverdlovsk on May Day marked its collapse. Whatever the exact circumstances behind the Soviet decision to exploit the U-2 affair, Khrushchev's prestige and political strength within the Soviet party suffered visibly. The episode coincided with major leadership changes. Most of the coterie Khrushchev had brought into the top leadership in 1957 departed or lost ground.

Although these shifts in leadership seemed designed to avoid the implication that Khrushchev's position as such was being challenged, he was now under strong pressure to reshape his policy. The U-2 incident provided his critics with a weapon for attacking his policy of less guns and more butter. They now could argue effectively that the time was not ripe for "consumer communism" in the U.S.S.R. now that Soviet vulnerabilities in the face of the imperialist enemy had been exposed to the world. It is hardly coincidental that a sharpening of the on-going debate in the regime over allocations policy can be dated from this period—a debate deeply implicating Khrushchev's strategy of dovetailing limited détente abroad with consumer-oriented internal reforms.

The Balance in the Leadership Shifts

Khrushchev had gone into combat with an Achilles' heel. His tactics for winning limited détente abroad through summitry by the spring of 1960 were tending to produce diminishing returns. His alternating threats over Berlin and conciliatory gestures, if intended to produce a defeatist psychology in the West, were only conditioning the Western powers to take Khrushchev's menacing behavior with a grain of salt. At home top party leaders and the military undoubtedly were painfully aware that Khrushchev's

[1] Editorial entitled, "The Origin and Development of the Differences between the Leadership of the CPSU and Ourselves," NCNA, Sept. 5, 1963; *Hung ch'i* and *Jen-min jih-pao* [*Red Flag* and *Peoples' Daily*], Sept. 6, 1963.

missile-rattling and intimations of Soviet rocket superiority over the United States in this period contained a large dose of bluff. What was worse they had increasing reason in view of the U-2 flights to believe that the United States was in possession of the same knowledge. The malaise and vulnerability of the regime on this score was echoed in the rising hue and cry in Soviet propaganda after the Twenty-first Congress over "irresponsible" U.S. generals, U.S. bomber flights, and border incidents involving U.S. aircraft.

Danger signals that Khrushchev's developing political strategy was running into trouble accumulated even before the U-2 incident. The plan he introduced at the Supreme Soviet in January for a major troop reduction, tied to a new military doctrine of rocket-nuclear deterrence, had provoked visible opposition. Behind their professions of enthusiasm for the boldness of Khrushchev's military thinking, various top military figures, beginning with Malinovskiy himself, intimated that he had gone too far. While ostensibly engaging in exposition and elaboration of Khrushchev's text, they subtly conveyed their reservations in the form of qualifying statements and counterpoints to the main premises of Khrushchev's arguments.

In bold and sweeping terms Khrushchev had asserted in his speech to the Supreme Soviet that large standing armies, surface navies, and fleets of bomber aircraft were becoming obsolete as a result of the development of rocket-nuclear weaponry. He stressed that the U.S.S.R. with its rocket-nuclear forces now had sufficient means to totally destroy any enemy and argued that rocket-nuclear "firepower, not the number of troops," now determined the military power of a state. He not only said nothing about developing Soviet conventional arms but even envisaged the replacement of the surface navy and air force with rocket forces.[2] Despite his apparent endorsements of this position, Malinovskiy in his speech

---

[2] Khrushchev outlined his position as follows:

"Our state has at its disposal powerful missiles. The air force and the navy have lost their former importance in view of the contemporary development of military technology. This type of armament is not being reduced but replaced. Almost the entire air force is being replaced by rockets. We have now cut sharply, and will continue to cut sharply, even perhaps discontinue, production of bombers and other obsolete equipment. In the navy, the

clearly sought to temper the more radical implications of Khrushchev's argument. He reaffirmed the continuing validity of the traditional "combined arms" tenet of Soviet military doctrine, the notion that war could be won only by the combined efforts of all arms and branches of the armed forces. And he stressed that not all the requirements for the conduct of war could be met by a single branch of the armed forces, that only the unified employment of all types of armed forces could bring success in military operations.[3] Such assertions became the stock-in-trade of the agitation in military literature aimed at Khrushchev's line on military policy. Just below the surface of such arguments was the implicit charge that his radical formulations of the new military doctrine endangered a sound Soviet military posture.

Along with the pressure from the military there were indications in the month prior to the U-2 affair that Khrushchev's détente strategy toward the United States was being undercut by elements within the party leadership itself. Pressures for a hard line were registered in the sharp reaction in the Soviet press to Undersecretary of State Douglas Dillon's speech in mid-April asserting a firm American stance in the face of Soviet pressures on Berlin. A *Pravda* "Observer" article on April 27 charged the speech revealed that high-level circles in Washington were attempting to scuttle the forthcoming summit meeting between Khrushchev and Eisenhower. Also, quite conceivably, a successful overflight of the U.S.S.R. by a U-2 on April 9 may have been exploited by those favoring a change in Khrushchev's policy.

---

submarine fleet assumes great importance, while surface ships can no longer play the part they once did. In our country, the armed forces have to a considerable extent been transformed into rocket forces" (*Pravda*, Jan. 15, 1960).

[3] Malinovskiy's statements, while conceding the great importance of rockets, were more cautiously balanced than Khrushchev's:

"The rocket troops are indisputably the main arm of our armed forces. However, we understand that it is not possible to solve all the tasks of war with any one arm of troops. Therefore, proceeding from the thesis that the successful conduct of military operations in modern war is possible only on the basis of the unified use of all means of armed struggle, and combining the efforts of all arms of the armed forces, we are retaining all arms of our armed forces at a definite strength and in relevant, sound proportions" (*ibid.*).

Even Molotov decided it was a good time to fish in "muddy waters" and submitted an article to *Kommunist* for its Lenin Day issue at the end of April.[4] At the same time Khrushchev's most enthusiastic supporter of the Camp David Spirit, Mikoyan, suffered a sudden decline. *Party Life* in its late April issue—signed to press some two weeks late on May 3—omitted Mikoyan's name from the standard list of leaders credited with leading the Bolshevik take-over in Azerbaidzhan in 1919.[5] At an anniversary celebration in Baku on April 25 the Azerbaidzhan party chief, Akhundov, conspicuously omitted mention of Mikoyan in his speech, though he cited a number of lesser figures involved in establishing Bolshevik power in the region after 1917. The omission was the more notable since Akhundov had duly mentioned Mikoyan in an anniversary article in an issue of the Central Committee journal *Kommunist* dated earlier that month, April 14. Mikoyan's fall in standing was further registered in the line-up of leaders on the May Day reviewing stand in Red Square, usually a reliable indicator of the ranking of top leaders. His standard position next to Khrushchev was taken by Suslov and he moved down to seventh place in line.[6]

These danger signals were a prelude to the series of major leadership shifts begun at a party plenum on May 4 and completed in the July plenum by the formal removal of Brezhnev from the Secretariat as a result of his transfer to the Supreme Soviet Chairmanship in May. The principal losers were figures who had been among Khrushchev's closest supporters in the leadership crisis of June, 1957. Most of them had moved into the Central Committee Secretariat as a consequence of the purge of the anti-party group, creating a Secretariat heavily staffed with Khrushchev appointees. They were in a position to exert powerful influence in the Presidium by virtue of their foothold in both bodies.

Their departure from the Secretariat in May–July, 1960, thus deprived Khrushchev of one of his key levers over those Presidium

---

[4] Ilichev at the Twenty-second Congress asserted that Molotov in the unpublished article represented himself as a comrade of Lenin and betrayed his dogmatism on various issues (*ibid.*, Oct. 26, 1961).

[5] *Partinaya Zhizn'* [*Party Life*], No. 9, 1960, pp. 8–13.

[6] *Pravda*, May 2, 1960.

members who were not merely his political dependents. The Secretariat was cut by half—from ten to five members. Brezhnev, the Khrushchev protégé who had moved into the Presidium as a result of the June purge, soon lost his place in the Secretariat. He was transferred to the chairmanship of the Supreme Soviet, a prestigious but not politically powerful post.

Aristov, Ignatov, and Furtseva, all vigorous defenders of Khrushchev against his challengers in 1957, also left the Secretariat for lesser posts. Presidium candidate Pospelov, a long-time ideological specialist, also left the Secretariat for a smaller position. His role in June, 1957, was obscure, although he was evidently a Khrushchev backer. Notably, he was a critic of Suslov's view of Khrushchev's MTS reform in 1958 and an enthusiastic booster of Khrushchev's theoretical accomplishments in his report to the Twenty-first Congress. Mikoyan once more displayed his staying power, losing no posts, although, as it has been noted, someone in the leadership had mounted a move against him.

The fall of Kirichenko, Khrushchev's former deputy in the Secretariat, was formalized. His *de facto* removal from the Secretariat had already been revealed some months earlier in a brief *Pravda* announcement (January 13) that he had been sent to the minor post of party Secretary in Rostov. Belyaev's departure from the Presidium was also confirmed, and later in January he was downgraded to the Secretarial post in Stavropol. However, he had not been active in the affairs of the CPSU Secretariat since he had been sent to Kazakhstan as that republic's First Secretary in December, 1957. In December, 1959, he became the scapegoat for agricultural failure in Khrushchev's virgin lands and was subjected to withering criticism from Khrushchev himself. While Belyaev's disgrace had an apparent explanation, the sudden fall of Kirichenko—the most powerful member of the Secretariat next to Khrushchev himself— was and remains a political mystery. Khrushchev had groomed him as his right-hand man in the Ukrainian apparatus over many years before he brought him to Moscow. Along with Mikoyan he apparently had been the only Presidium member to stand by his chief in the initial stage of the confrontation in the Presidium in June, 1957. On the face of it, a serious political conflict involving

Kirichenko had evidently developed in the Presidium and Secretariat but had been successfully kept under wraps. It is quite possible his fall in January was somehow linked with Khrushchev's own developing political troubles and was the precursor of the leadership shake-up in May, 1960. In any case, his fall paved the way for Kozlov, a representative of the Leningrad party machine, a counterweight to Khrushchev's Ukrainian machine, to take over the number two position in the Secretariat.

The major effect of the changes in the Secretariat was that Kozlov and Suslov emerged in relatively more powerful positions. Kozlov moved into the Secretariat, replacing Kirichenko as an overseer of the party apparatus. At the same time Kozlov's other natural rival, Brezhnev, was transferred to the ceremonial post of Chairman of the Supreme Soviet. The latter's loss of his Secretarial post as a result, however, was not formalized until the next plenum two months later. Khrushchev, Mukhitdinov, and Kuusinen were now the only other Presidium members in the Secretariat. Mukhitdinov was a loyal Khrushchev protégé who had taken a conspicuous role in boosting the new leader cult prior to the Twenty-first Party Congress,[7] and Kuusinen was an elder Bolshevik brought into the top body in June, 1957.

Kosygin, Khrushchev's independent-minded ally in June, 1957, moved to full Presidium membership from candidate status at the May plenum. Notably, the 1960 changes did not affect Pervukhin's status as a Presidium candidate.

The turnover in the Secretariat was by far the most significant aspect of the leadership changes in the top executive bodies in mid-1960. If we keep in mind that the Secretariat was the most important of these bodies outside of the Presidium itself, the point becomes obvious. Neither the Council of Ministers or the Central Committee Bureau for the Russian Federation equaled it as a base of power. This was true despite Khrushchev's effort to build the Bureau as a counterpoise to the Secretariat after the Twentieth Congress. It would soon become apparent that Khrushchev was

---

[7] Mukhitdinov in a speech in Cairo on September 25 went beyond the customary references to Khrushchev's formal titles and hailed him as a "leader of the people." *Ibid.*, Sept. 30, 1958.

dissatisfied with the new line-up in the Secretariat and would seek every opportunity to restaff and expand that body. In addition the reduction of the Secretariat made it more difficult for the First Secretary to dominate the proceedings of the Presidium and correspondingly enhanced the political weight of the latter body.

However, the pattern of the 1960 changes also indicated that Khrushchev's right to lead the regime had not been directly challenged. In fact an effort seemed to be made to avoid conveying such an impression, although the intrusion of harsher notes in regime policies soon after did suggest that the new voices in the leadership were urging a change in policy. The unfavorable effects on Khrushchev's position were obscured by the fact that Khrushchev, while neither gaining or losing any posts, emerged as the only Presidium member sitting on the three executive bodies of the regime below the Presidium—the Secretariat, the Council of Ministers, and the Central Committee Bureau for the RSFSR. In addition, some of Khrushchev's losses were balanced by some gains in the shifts. His hidden enemy Voroshilov was finally bumped from his post as Supreme Soviet Chairman by Brezhnev. The movement of Podgornyy and Polyanskiy into the Presidium seemed to represent net gains. Podgornyy had come up in the Ukrainian party, but he had not been under Khrushchev's direct supervision for an extended period as Kirichenko had been. Polyanskiy was less closely associated with Khrushchev than Podgornyy but had been a notable booster of the Khrushchev cult at the time of the Twenty-first Congress. The over-all effect of the mid-1960 changes, however, was to raise the political stock of high-level figures who—while Khrushchev allies in 1957—were not simply his political dependents.

The Rise of Kozlov and Suslov

Kozlov and Suslov emerged as the principal beneficiaries of the changes, and Kosygin also appears to have gained considerable ground and a larger voice in economic policy. Their increased role in the leadership was duly registered at the time of the next party plenum in July. Kozlov gave the plenum report on

Khrushchev's activities at the gathering of bloc leaders in Bucharest and Kosygin reported on industrial technology, while *Pravda* mentioned no Khrushchev speeches at the plenum. Ordinarily, Khrushchev could have been expected to speak on both topics.[8] That same month Suslov made an unprecedented series of speeches on regime policy and set the party line for literature and art at a leaders' meeting with Soviet intellectuals. Khrushchev's speech on the occasion was not published and it was some ten months before an abridged version of it was released. In the months following, Suslov was frequently cited as a guide to the party line in literary and cultural periodicals.[9] Although Khrushchev regained the political limelight after July, 1960, the signs of Kozlov's and Suslov's influence persisted. The events of that month—occurring amid a marked emphasis on the collectivity of the party leadership in the Soviet press—distinctly suggested that Khrushchev was subject to constraints under the new balance of forces in the leadership.

While there had been a natural impulsion in the wake of the U-2 crisis for the leadership to face both Washington and Peking with a united front, cleavages were already discernible under the surface of "collectivity." Two episodes in the summer of 1960 indicated that something less than harmony existed between Khrushchev and his two ranking secretaries. On the eve of the July plenum an unmistakable slight was administered to Suslov

[8] *Pravda* reported Khrushchev's presence at the plenum and published a photograph of Khrushchev and other Presidium members during a recess between plenum sessions. Subsequently, an article in *Party Life* (No. 17, dated Sept. 2, 1960) by V. Karpov referred to remarks Khrushchev made at the plenum. Also the official stenographic record of the plenum dated Dec. 2, 1960, showed Khrushchev presiding over the opening session on July 13. The record also carries a speech by the Kazakh official, Kunayev, in which he referred to Khrushchev making some remarks on the first day of the plenum, but no references to a formal speech were made.

[9] Notably, Suslov's expanded role in the arts could be traced back to the changes in the Secretariat at the May 4 plenum. *Sovetskaya Kultura*, organ of the Ministry of Culture, on May 5 in effect signaled the expansion of Suslov's influence in the cultural field as a result of the changes and pictured him as a defender of ideological orthodoxy. Alongside the Central Committee decree announcing the new leadership arrangement which made Suslov's greater voice in a diminished Secretariat manifest, the paper carried an article invoking Suslov's Twenty-first Congress speech in calling for a crackdown on "liberalism" and ideological laxity in Georgian publishing houses.

in the press that bore the imprint of Khrushchev's handiwork. Suslov was mentioned in neither *Pravda*'s nor *Izvestia*'s listing of the top leaders attending the U.S.S.R. Teachers' Congress in early July. The rest of the press, however, duly reported his presence. And even *Izvestia*, while failing to list him, carried a photo of the leaders in the Congress podium showing Suslov present.[10] The episode was the more notable since only a few weeks before a special effort was made in the press to display an amiable relationship between Khrushchev and Suslov. The two leaders, along with Voroshilov, made a well-publicized appearance together at a "workers'" picnic at Pitsunda in the Crimea.[11] If Khrushchev had intended to sidetrack Suslov, the latter's public prominence during the rest of July indicated that he had failed in the effort.

The other sign of disharmony came from Kozlov's bailiwick in Leningrad. Kozlov had given the July plenum report on Khrushchev's trip to Bucharest, evidently in part a calculated display of unity between the two secretaries in the face of the sharp Chinese attack on Khrushchev at the Bucharest meeting. Yet a month later the Leningrad party organ hinted that it was not fully in accord with Khrushchev's hard line against the Chinese. *Leningradskaya Pravda* failed to endorse the first unmistakable Soviet warning that Communist China might face exclusion from the bloc if it persisted in its course, which was contained in an article widely carried in Soviet regional newspapers. The Leningrad paper alone among the regional papers deleted that passage in the article most threatening to the Chinese—a passage referring to China's dependence on Soviet military protection and the dangers to which the country would be exposed if it were "isolated."[12]   174495

Suslov also introduced into one of his speeches in July a point of doctrine that may have been calculated to provide a better ground for reconciling Soviet and Chinese positions. Suslov asserted that "the dictatorship of the proletariat" had now turned from a

---

[10] See *Pravda* and *Izvestia*, July 10, 1960.

[11] *Pravda*, June 13, 1960.

[12] See S. Titarenko, "Lenin's Teachings on the Victory of Socialism and the Present Day," *Leningradskaya Pravda*, Aug. 23, 1960. The article also appeared in *Bakinskii Rabotchii*, Aug. 16; *Sovetskaya Latvia*, Aug. 16; *Sovetskaya Litva* and *Kommunist Tadzhikstana*, Aug. 24; and *Sovetskaya Kirghizia*, Aug. 27.

"national force, meaning a force existing only in one country, and therefore unable to determine world politics, into an international force, that is, a dictatorship of the proletariat in many countries, which will be able to exercise a decisive influence on world politics."[13] This proposition carried with it the suggestion of militant pursuit of revolution on a world scale that bore some kinship with the Chinese political line. The doctrine, as it will be noted later, apparently became involved in a controversy over the theory of proletarian dictatorship in the drafting of the new party program during the coming year.

The Chinese themselves provided another strong indication that both Kozlov and Suslov represented more accommodating positions toward the Chinese leadership in late 1960. It appeared in the first of the series of *Red Flag*'s detailed attacks on Khrushchev's policies in September, 1963.[14] *Red Flag* said that meetings between Soviet and Chinese negotiators working on the preparation of a mutually acceptable statement for adoption at the conference of eighty-one parties in November, 1960, had actually produced agreement on most points. Although the Soviet side had held out on a number of questions, *Red Flag* said, "many" important changes of "principle" in the draft the Soviets initially proposed were made.[15] With Khrushchev's return to Moscow from the United Nations meeting in New York that fall, however, the Soviet side, *Red Flag* asserted, "even scrapped the agreements which had already been reached on some questions."[16] The *Red Flag* revelation left the clear implication that Kozlov and Suslov—the senior Soviet representatives on the drafting committee for the Moscow conference while Khrushchev was at the United Nations—had displayed a greater willingness to compromise than their chief.

It is probably not accidental that these signs of Kozlov's and Suslov's resistance to forcing the split with the Chinese began accumulating after the Bucharest meeting of bloc leaders in

[13] *Pravda*, July 30, 1960.
[14] "The Origin and Development of the Differences between the Leadership of the CPSU and Ourselves."
[15] *Ibid.*
[16] *Ibid.*

June, 1960. Khrushchev's head-on collision with the Chinese at Bucharest, which precipitated a downturn in Sino-Soviet relations, undoubtedly influenced the course of Soviet leadership politics in the aftermath of the U-2 incident.

The external pressure mounted against Khrushchev and his policies by the Chinese had become a very real threat to the Soviet leader with the collapse of his Camp David strategy in May. Indeed on the eve of the Bucharest meeting Peking had real grounds for expecting that Khrushchev's vulnerability could be exploited. One move by the Soviet party less than two weeks after the U-2 episode must have raised Chinese hopes: in a speech on May 11 Khrushchev virtually canceled the invitation to Eisenhower to visit the U.S.S.R. and on May 12 the CPSU Central Committee dispatched a letter to Peking inviting Mao Tse-tung to Moscow. Moreover, the harsher notes intruding into Soviet policy after the U-2 episode must have been read in Peking as a sign that the pressures on Khrushchev for a turnabout in policy were intense. In fact, in the polemics with Moscow the Chinese have said as much by stating they had entertained hopes then that the Soviet leaders had seen the light after the U-2 incident and would adopt the Chinese viewpoint.[17] Moreover, the Chinese have pointed out in their account of the dispute that the CPSU Central Committee proposed in early June that the bloc parties meet in Bucharest during the Bulgarian party congress to discuss the international situation resulting from the collapse of the summit meeting "caused by the United States."[18] The Chinese further said that they counterproposed and the Soviets accepted the project for a world meeting of all Communist parties, whose purpose would be to work out a common Communist strategy after careful preparation. Also, according to the Chinese accounts, the Soviets agreed that Bucharest should be used as an occasion for a provisional exchange of views on the date and place for the world meeting.[19]

[17] Editorial, NCNA, Feb. 26, 1963, and *Jen-min jih-pao,*, Feb. 27, 1963.
[18] "The Origin and Development of the Differences between the Leadership of the CPSU and Ourselves."
[19] *Ibid.*

Khrushchev had every personal political interest in heading off any genuine movement toward rapprochement in Sino-Soviet relations. The greater the rapprochement with the hard-line Chinese the more cramped his own strategy for détente and reform would be. At Bucharest Khrushchev took drastic action aimed at preventing any such development. He unexpectedly initiated an attack on the Chinese which by its very scope and violence apparently overturned the strategy the CPSU Presidium had agreed to pursue at the meeting. The Chinese journal *Red Flag* in its account of the Bucharest affair has suggested that this was just what did happen. *Red Flag* made much over the point that at Bucharest the Soviet leaders "went back on their word" and "to our amazement" launched a "surprise assault" on the Chinese party.[20]

The Chinese account broadly jibes with the detailed description of the Bucharest meeting Edward Crankshaw has pieced together on the basis of reports on the meeting that filtered out from Communist sources.[21] On the eve of the Bucharest meetings the Soviet delegation, led by Khrushchev and including Ponomarev and Andropov, distributed a letter of information from the CPSU Central Committee to the other delegates, containing a systematic critique of Chinese positions. While Peking would later depict the document as a prelude to Khrushchev's own unrestrained vilification of the Chinese at Bucharest when Sino-Soviet polemics later became intense, the CCP delegation at Bucharest apparently had instructions from home to make "Khrushchev's behavior" at the meeting a *casus belli* rather than the CPSU letter of information as such. Thus the Chinese statement distributed to the delegates asserted that it was Khrushchev who "completely violated" the rule that issues be settled among the parties through prior consultation; who "has completely broken" the CPSU-CCP agreement made prior to Bucharest for a provisional exchange of views; and who introduced a draft communiqué, characterized as a "surprise attack," to the meeting without prior discussion of its contents.[22]

[20] *Ibid.*

[21] Edward Crankshaw, *The New Cold War, Moscow v. Pekin* (Baltimore: Penguin, 1963), pp. 97–110.

[22] Appendix II at end of editorial, "The Origin and Development of the Differences between the Leadership of the CPSU and Ourselves."

Hence the Chinese made it abundantly clear at that stage that their complaint was with Khrushchev personally and not with the Soviet leadership as a whole. The Chinese purpose seemed clear: to zero in on Khrushchev as the prime dismantler of the Sino-Soviet axis and Communist unity and to drive a wedge between him and his Presidium colleagues.[23] The statement of the CCP delegation notably treated the CPSU Central Committee letter of information as a separate matter deserving "careful study," saying that a serious reply was in preparation as a basis for "earnest and comradely discussions" between the parties.[24]

In the latter connection, Crankshaw's reconstruction of the Bucharest meeting is illuminating. He says there was no indication that the Bucharest meeting would turn into an open slugging match even after the CPSU letter of information had been distributed and arguments had been exchanged in closed meetings between the pro-Soviet delegations and the Chinese. According to Crankshaw, the "speakers at the first closed meeting had taken their tone from this (the CPSU) letter: they were engaged in a seemly debate."[25] He says the letter "had been composed to carry conviction with the fraternal parties; . . . it was . . . a dignified and reasoned statement . . . and, though sometimes surprisingly blunt, it was nowhere abusive."[26]

Then, however, the Chinese made a move—not mentioned in Peking's accounts of Bucharest—obviously aimed at putting the heat on Khrushchev personally. They released to the delegates copies of an eighty-page private CPSU communication sent to

[23] This purpose seems especially apparent in such passages of the CCP delegation's statement as the following:

"We shall be ready to carry on serious discussions with the CPSU and other fraternal parties on our differences with Comrade Khrushchev when the occasion arises.

. . . .

"Comrade Khrushchev's way of doing things at this meeting is entirely detrimental to the unity of international communism. But, however Comrade Khrushchev may act, the unity of the Chinese and Soviet parties and of all the Communist and workers parties is bound to be further strengthened and developed" (CCP statement, June 26, 1960).

[24] "The Origin and Development of the Differences between the Leadership of the CPSU and Ourselves."

[25] Crankshaw, *The New Cold War*, p. 105.

[26] *Ibid.*

Peking sometime earlier which bore the trademarks of Khrushchev's authorship. It denounced the Chinese in earthy, unadorned language and loosed a flood of charges against them picturing them as no more than crass power seekers. The letter, Crankshaw says, shattered the Soviet self-portrayal as the plaintiff before a high party forum with a case based strictly on grounds of doctrine and principle. Khrushchev responded to this tactic with a speech denouncing the Chinese with unprecedented violence. His no-holds-barred attack at the closed session of the Congress helped turn the fissure in the Sino-Soviet alliance into a crevasse.

Khrushchev's action at Bucharest, it should be recalled here, was followed by another headstrong move that even more deeply aggravated the Sino-Soviet conflict. In July the Chinese were notified that Soviet technicians were being recalled en masse from China where they had been giving major aid in their industrialization drive. This hurried and provocative action was completed within a month's time. While the precise circumstances leading to the decision are not fully known, Khrushchev was undoubtedly its prime instigator. It admirably accorded with his effort to scuttle the possibility of Sino-Soviet détente after the U-2 incident.

Although the Soviet leadership sought to present a united front to the Chinese at the July plenum in the weeks after Bucharest, Khrushchev's Presidium colleagues were probably deeply disturbed by their leader's heavy-handed tactics at Bucharest. His violent action at Bucharest evidently was not based on a prior consensus in the Presidium. Judging by the signs of Kozlov's and Suslov's demurral from Khrushchev's headlong vendetta against Mao Tse-tung, the Chinese were not wholly unsuccessful in exploiting cleavages among the Soviet leaders. Indeed it was even possible that Kozlov rather than Khrushchev gave the report on Bucharest at the July plenum, a report never made public, as the representative of the counsels of caution in the Presidium. While it outwardly served to convey an impression that the leadership approved Khrushchev's conduct at Bucharest, it also prevented him from pressing further extreme attacks on the Chinese before the Soviet party assembly.

"Some Comrades" Object to Pro-Consumer Policy

There were, however, other critical and even more persistent signs of the disharmony within the leadership in the aftermath of the U-2 crisis. Notably, it was on May 5, the day Khrushchev announced the downing of the U-2, that he also divulged the fact that "some comrades" had raised arguments against his pro-consumer moves.[27] These comrades, according to Khrushchev, feared heavy industry and defense would suffer under the plans he had announced in the Supreme Soviet for abolition of income taxes, the shortening of the workday, and additional investment in light industry and agriculture. In view of the narrow scope of Khrushchev's welfare program in any real economic terms the criticism of it must have stemmed from a deeply ingrained orthodox viewpoint. His reference to "some comrades" came the day after both Kozlov and Suslov had gained ground in the party Secretariat at the Central Committee plenum.

More traditional themes on resource allocations now began to intrude in regime statements and actions in the following months. In July a major move toward recentralization of industrial management was among the signs of a more conservative approach to economic policy and was notably out of tune with the philosophy of Khrushchev's 1957 industrial reorganization.[28] Both Suslov and Kozlov appeared associated with the over-all trend. Both betrayed more orthodox viewpoints on resource allocations than Khrushchev's. Both indicated a preference for continuing the favored treatment of the heavy industrial defense sector over any basic reorientation of the economy toward increased consumer production.

In particular a key statement in Kozlov's October Revolution speech in November, 1960, appeared to betray his disagreement with Khrushchev. Though ambivalent on key domestic economic

[27] Khrushchev's speech to the Supreme Soviet on May 5, in *Pravda*, May 6, 1960.

[28] New central organs were established to direct the hundred-odd regional Councils of the National Economy that were the creatures of Khrushchev's 1957 reform. This was the same month that Kosygin gave the report at the July plenum on industry.

issues, he asserted that "everyone knows" steel production is a "basic" index of a "country's economic strength."[29] Not two months later, as if in response, Khrushchev asserted at the January plenum that the strength of a state is determined not only by the "metal" index, but by "the amount of products a man receives and eats."[30]

Also in the latter half of 1960 Suslov conveyed an even more evident preference than Kozlov for heavy industry and defense over consumer welfare. His speeches in July of that year had already stressed a need for increasing military strength to support Soviet policy, contrasting with Khrushchev's earlier reassuring estimates of the adequacy of the Soviet military position. And in late December he betrayed a bias in favor of heavy industry over civilian welfare when the issue of economic priorities was under high-level review in advance of the January, 1961, plenum. He clearly highlighted the role of heavy industry, especially steel and machines, in contrast to Mukhitdinov, Khrushchev's protégé in the Secretariat, during the same period.[31] Mukhitdinov in a speech in early January strongly emphasized the concern of the party for civilian welfare while completely skirting reference to heavy industry.[32] The influence of the more orthodox views of Kozlov and Suslov would evidently play a role in blunting Khrushchev's renewed initiatives in economic policy in January, 1961.

KHRUSHCHEV VERSUS THE "METAL-EATERS"

It was against this background that Khrushchev unveiled his program for a "revolution" (povorot') in Soviet agriculture in favor of the consumer at the January, 1961, agricultural plenum. He revealed that conflict over resource allocations in the party had been sharp, and he took to task "some comrades" whose "appetite

[29] *Pravda*, Nov. 7, 1960.
[30] Khrushchev's speech to the January, 1961, plenum, in *ibid.*, Jan. 21–22, 1961.
[31] See the account of Suslov's speech in *Pravda Vostoka*, Dec. 25, 1960.
[32] *Turkmenskaya Iskra*, Jan. 6, 1961.

for metals" could only unbalance the Soviet economy to the detriment of pressing consumer needs.[33] He warned that failure to close the widening gap between consumer supply and demand would be "fraught with dangerous consequences."[34] In support of his position Khrushchev now promoted a new doctrine for Soviet economic development asserting that consumer production should always exceed demand.[35] He thus overturned the tenet of Stalin's "law of socialism" that growth of production always lags behind the growth of demand under socialism, providing a "stimulus" to production. Despite his arguments, no revolution in Soviet agriculture emerged from the plenum. In fact the plenum resolution failed to adopt the key points of Khrushchev's over-all program and only some of his individual proposals for agriculture were accepted. And despite his seeming domination of the proceedings by his constant interruptions of plenum speakers, including Presidium members, the drive he had mounted at the plenum for his program had been visibly slowed.

From the January plenum to the Twenty-second Congress in October, 1961, the party debate over resource allocations intensified and became increasingly overt in the pages of the party press. Soon after the plenum Khrushchev strongly indicated that the controversy was not limited merely to the issue of domestic economic policy but touched on the basic orientation of Soviet foreign policy itself. In a series of speeches in the U.S.S.R.'s agricultural areas in the two months after the plenum he vigorously defended his emphasis on consumer-oriented economic development as the best "politics" not only at home but abroad as well. According to Khrushchev, overtaking the United States in levels of consumption by 1980 was crucial to winning the economic competition with the United States—the decisive sphere of the East-West conflict. He pointedly warned that anyone not understanding this could not be a "real leader."[36] Anyone opposing his line, he made it clear, would be a dogmatist and a conservative "divorced from life" and destined to be left behind by the party.

[33] *Pravda*, Jan. 21–22, 1961.
[34] *Ibid.*
[35] *Ibid.*
[36] *Pravda*, Feb. 19, 1961.

Following Khrushchev's tour *Kommunist* denounced anti-consumer "theorcticians"[37] and made it clear they opposed Khrushchev's program as "consumer" or "petty bourgeois" communism and allegedly favored "production for production's sake."[38] While the shoe fit Khrushchev's antagonists in Peking among others, the journal's criticism—appearing in an editorial pegged to the January plenum—applied also to those in the Soviet party whom Khrushchev had accused of wanting to push steel output to the limit and let the consumer go begging.

Not deterred by his critics, Khrushchev continued to press his line and at the British Trade Fair in Moscow on May 20, 1961, revealed how far he was willing to go in overturning traditional economic dogma. He openly asserted that the primacy of heavy industry would in time be replaced by equal rates of development for the consumer and light industrial sector.[39] Significantly the Soviet press did not report Khrushchev's remarks and, though he implied his advocacy of the equal rates line in a speech later that month, he did not raise the subject again during that period.[40]

The Debate over the Dictatorship

During the same period the depth of the cleavage developing between the reform forces led by Khrushchev and the more orthodox elements was revealed in a high-level doctrinal controversy, which had come to a head in the drafting of the new party program in 1961. It centered on the traditional doctrine that the U.S.S.R. was a state of the "dictatorship of the proletariat," long the theoretical justification for the maintenance of a massive apparatus of internal repression and a large military establishment; the

[37] *Kommunist*, No. 4, 1961, p. 4.

[38] *Ibid.*

[39] *The New York Times*, May 21, 1961.

[40] In a speech in Alma Ata on June 24 Khrushchev said "*Side by side* [*naryadu s*] with heavy industry, the light and foodstuffs industry will be rapidly developed, that is, the industrial branch which is directly meeting the requirements of the population" (*Pravda*, June 25, 1961).

dictatorship was portrayed as the prime instrument of militant pursuit of the revolutionary class struggle both at home and abroad. While little developed in the works of Marx and Engels, the concept had been made the foundation stone of Lenin's theory of the party and became a central dogma of Stalinism.

Khrushchev's announcement at the Twenty-first Congress that the U.S.S.R. was now in the transition stage to full-fledged communism had forced the question of whether the dictatorship doctrine was becoming obsolete. According to the Marxist prognosis, the dictatorship fades away as the Communist society comes into being—the state "withers away."

During the drafting of the new program, however, Khrushchev's withering thesis encountered objections within the party on the grounds that it involved premature disposal of the apparatus of the state. The resulting conflict was no mere squabble over fine points of abstruse theory among party ideologues. The concept of withering, however abstract in its projection of a stateless society with no need of police or military power, gives doctrinal expression to assumptions regarding the future of Soviet political institutions, the pace and character of internal development, and party political strategy abroad. Khrushchev's formulations on the subject were tailored to support his strategy of détente and reform and the objections raised against them mirrored the orthodox criticism of Khrushchevian strategy.

By the time of the Congress the parties to the controversy had reached something of a compromise regarding the formulations on the state in the new program, but it was in any case an uneasy amalgam of the Khrushchevian and orthodox positions. The result was reflected in the announcement at the Congress that a "state of the whole people" had replaced the dictatorship of the proletariat in the U.S.S.R. At the Congress however Khrushchev disguised the fact that a compromise had been struck but not the fact that there had been an argument. He said that "dogmatic" comrades in the party had lost the argument in the pre-Congress debate over the theory of the state in the transition to communism. He chided "some comrades" for their "dogmatic attitude" in objecting to the replacement of the dictatorship by the state of the whole people.[41] These comrades, according to Khrushchev, had argued that the dictatorship must be retained in the U.S.S.R. up to the "complete victory of communism," i.e., until the world Communist revolution is victorious. [42]

What Khrushchev failed to mention however was that the new program did not contain his own proposition that the withering away of the state was currently underway on a large scale. This was the more notable in view of his assertion in January that his thesis would be reflected in the party program.[43] The fact of the matter was that the new party program had taken a middle ground between the Khrushchev and the orthodox arguments. On the one hand the new program did not adopt the Khrushchev thesis on withering, but preserved the traditional concept of the retention of the state until the complete victory of communism. The latter notion was preserved in the assertion that the "*state* of the whole people" would remain until communism's final victory. On the other hand, the concept dear to the orthodox, the dictatorship of the proletariat, was also declared at an end inside the U.S.S.R.

Although the details of the controversy were largely concealed from the outside observer and only some of its aspects were reflected in the party journals at the time, the drift of the orthodox complaint was fairly evident. Khrushchev's approach to doctrine on the state in terms of internal policy would encourage a dangerous trend toward the watering down of the coercive and repressive functions of the state. From the standpoint of external policy, the role of the state in promoting Communist revolutionary goals abroad would be depreciated before the world revolution was won.

There was already one prime suspect in the party Presidium who was most likely the leading critic of the Khrushchev approach.

[41] *Ibid.*, Oct. 19, 1961, p. 9.

[42] *Ibid.*

[43] The objections to the Khrushchev plan were echoed in a *Party Life* article in May. An article by Romashkin, a Soviet legal theorist, denounced "authors" in the party who asserted that the state's withering could only occur *after* the complete victory of communism. Here he noted that Khrushchev had "directly" asserted withering was already going on in the country (*Party Life*, No. 9, 1961, pp. 10–11).

This was Suslov, who, aside from Khrushchev, was one of the few top figures who had dwelt on the dictatorship issue in his speeches in the year or so prior to the Twenty-second Congress. As already noted, he offered the thesis that the dictatorship had spread from the U.S.S.R. to many countries and had become the decisive force in world history; thus he projected an expanding, not a declining, role for the dictatorship concept. The Suslov thesis conveyed the image of militant prosecution of the class struggle on a world scale that was out of tune with Khrushchev's détente strategy. Suslov reiterated the doctrine in his January, 1961, speech on the Moscow meeting of the world parties, which had ended the month before and where the abortive effort to paper over the Sino-Soviet conflict had been made.[44] And although Khrushchev also tersely mentioned it the same month in his own report on the Moscow meeting,[45] the doctrine was not subsequently developed by the top leaders and did not appear in the new party program, either in the published draft or the final version.

While we can only infer what Suslov may have argued inside the leadership, the trend of his thinking was apparent. Furthermore, he alone among the top leaders at the Twenty-second Congress spoke of the theoretical "difficulties" that had occurred in the discussion of the program draft.[46] While he professed his enthusiasm for the "brilliant" solution of the difficulties reflected in Khrushchev's report to the Congress, the reference to "difficulties" was curiously cryptic and seemingly gratuitous. It must have raised eyebrows in the congress hall even though he went on to give the impression that he vigorously supported the doctrinal innovations in Khrushchev's report.

While he did not say what the difficulties were, it is notable that Suslov was the only Congress speaker to dwell at length on the withering away of the state. He even appeared to endorse Khrushchev's earlier position in saying the process was already taking place, although it "must not be understood" as transforming

[44] *Pravda*, Jan. 23, 1961.
[45] *Ibid.*, Jan. 25, 1961.
[46] *Ibid.*, Oct. 23, 1961.

the state to nothing.[47] He subsumed this statement, however, to the passage in the party program emphasizing that full withering can occur only when two conditions are met—when the Communist society is built in the U.S.S.R. and when socialism has won a world victory.[48] He noted that the passage had "shed clear light" on the question, a passage which effectively made the withering concept a matter for the more or less remote future.[49]

Suslov also added two other points in his comment on the subject which sharpened the suspicion that he had been the leading "dogmatic" comrade in the pre-Congress debate. He attacked the "Yugoslav revisionists" for demanding the withering of the state immediately after the revolution. He labeled the Yugoslav position "anti-Marxist" and said it "would disarm the proletariat in the face of its external and internal enemies and undermine its victory."[50] He stressed, moreover, that the state of the whole people must insure the country's defense and "without hesitation" use its punishing "sword" internally against "anti-social" elements.[51] Here he warned against the "unjustified liberalism . . . often allowed by officials in our administrative organs."[52]

While the controversy over doctrine on the state had been settled more or less for the purposes of the program, the ingredients that produced the conflict remained and continued to animate leadership politics after the Congress. One of these was the tension between the party and the state bureaucracies; Khrushchev's doctrines involved the proposition that the party would grow while the state withered. His withering doctrine did not promote its corollary that the party as a political institution must also wither under communism. In fact he projected an expanding role for the party that looked very much as if he intended it eventually to take the place of the state itself. His radical reorganization of the party at the end of 1962 appeared to be a major step in such a direction. Both the leaders of the state bureaucracy as well as the orthodox ideological functionaries of the party would see a threat to their interests in Khrushchev's line—the former because it impaired the position of the state bureaucracy in meeting incursions of the party

[47] Ibid.   [49] Ibid.   [51] Ibid.
[48] Ibid.   [50] Ibid.   [52] Ibid.

machine into its province, and the latter because it impaired the traditional concept of the party, which requires that it remain separate and aloof from the purely administrative activities of the state. To overly involve the party in such functions harms its political-ideological function, this orthodox argument would run, and to make the party into a state would menace its identity as a missionary agency dedicated first of all to the world revolution.

Molotov's reputed criticism of the new party program apparently embodied something of the latter complaint. Judging by the attacks on Khrushchev's old enemy at the Congress, Molotov charged that Khrushchev's line added up to the party's absorption in domestic affairs and disregard of its revolutionary mission—a line Molotov apparently intimated was a policy of "communism in one country."[53] Notably Molotov's view was not too far from the one Suslov had taken and may help explain some of the violence of the attack on Molotov by the Khrushchev forces at the Twenty-second Congress.

The controversies over economic policy and doctrine on the state faithfully echoed the unabating struggle over Khrushchevian reform within the party in the prelude to the Twenty-second Congress. Although Khrushchev relentlessly pressed the offensive, the indications in the field of policy in the summer of 1961 did not bode well for the prospects of his strategy. In terms of actual policy moves that summer, other counsels seemed to prevail.

The month after Khrushchev flirted with the equal rates concept in economic policy the Central Committee met to approve a draft of the new party program to be ratified at the upcoming Twenty-second Congress. The plenum did not mention the equal rates notion, but it did adopt Khrushchev's thesis that a "new stage" in industrial development had begun.[54] Important changes in defense policy soon after the plenum, however, indicated that the pro-consumer policies the Khrushchev thesis was designed to support were not prospering. The subsequent announcements of a series of

[53] See former *Pravda* editor Satyukov's speech to the Twenty-second Congress in *Pravda*, October 27, 1961.

[54] The draft of the new program approved at the June plenum was published in *Pravda*, July 30, 1961.

regime actions—a one-third increase in the military budget, suspension of the 1960 troop cuts, deferment of the release of servicemen to the reserve, and the dramatic resumption of nuclear testing—hardly augered well for the pro-consumer campaign.[55]

The inherent dilemma of Khrushchev's policy was laid bare by these events of the summer of 1961. His policy of economic reform could prosper only if there were hope for lessening tensions abroad. A measure of détente with the West was necessary, but to pursue détente unambiguously, especially in the wake of the U-2 episode and the repeated failure of his tactics over Berlin, would have laid Khrushchev open to the charge of weakness in the prosecution of the struggle against the "capitalist" adversary in the West. He was under powerful pressure to show that he was a tough and effective Communist leader who could win victories in power-political struggles with the leading power of the "capitalist" world, the United States. This motive was undoubtedly behind his bellicose displays in the summer of 1961. But even the seemingly tough line he had adopted ended in a series of dramatic gestures and stopped short of provoking a genuine confrontation with the Western powers. The raising of the Berlin Wall, the rocket-rattling, and the violation of the moratorium on nuclear testing amounted to diversions concealing the failure to budge the United States and its allies in Berlin.

Yet there was no disguising the fact that these actions were in conflict with the goals of Khrushchev's political program at home. This was perhaps nowhere more apparent than in the cancellation of the troop reduction policy he had introduced just a year and a half before as a means of freeing more resources for his economic program. He had heavily committed his personal prestige to the troop reduction and presented it as part and parcel of a new strategic doctrine authored by himself. However, the U-2 affair and the subsequent collapse of the summit meeting in Paris had

---

[55] See Khrushchev's speech to graduates of the military academy announcing a one-third increase in the military budget and cessation of troop reductions (*ibid.*, July 9, 1961); the Central Committee-Council of Ministers' statement extending terms of military service of servicemen due to be released to the reserve (*ibid.*, Aug. 30, 1961); and the Soviet government statement announcing the resumption of nuclear testing (*ibid.*, Aug. 31, 1961).

severely weakened the props of his political program, including his new military doctrine; following these events he gradually began to soft-pedal the more radical aspects of his military doctrine, as he found himself under continuing pressure from military quarters. Various spokesmen continued to press the "combined arms" concept as the tacit counterpoise to Khrushchev's lopsided focus on nuclear missiles. As the crisis atmosphere gathered around Berlin in the spring of 1961, Khrushchev formally yielded to military opinion and explicitly endorsed the "combined arms" doctrine. Donning his lieutenant general's uniform, he declared in his June 22 speech on the twentieth anniversary of the Nazi invasion that strengthening Soviet defenses "depends on the perfection of all services of our armed forces—infantry and artillery, engineering corps and signal corps, armored tank divisions and the navy, the air force, and the missile forces."[56] The speech, which probably was discussed in the Presidium beforehand, undoubtedly had the blessing of those leaders who sympathized with military opinion and backed a hard line on the Berlin question. In any case it served as an appropriate prelude to Soviet belligerence in foreign affairs during the summer.

The suspension of the troop cuts in the summer logically followed Khrushchev's concession to the "combined arms" view and clearly registered a retreat for him, not simply a sudden or basic change in his political outlook. That this was the case would be borne out by his subsequent efforts to revive the policy of reducing military costs and manpower.

The timing of the nuclear test resumption which scuttled the Geneva test-ban negotiations was another sign of pressure on Khrushchev from within the leadership. The supermegaton explosions came in the midst of the nonaligned conference in Belgrade and amounted to a bald and gratuitous affront to both the Yugoslavs and the neutralist leaders whom Khrushchev had sought to cultivate. Later Khrushchev himself would allude to the resistance he encountered in the leadership to the idea of a test

[56] *Ibid.*, June 22, 1961.

ban in a private talk with Norman Cousins a few months before the test-ban treaty was signed in Moscow in 1963.[57]

The Soviet press explained that Soviet defenses had to be strengthened because of a step-up in the West of military preparations and the increase of international tension to a "white heat." The fact of the matter remained, however, that most of the heat had been generated by actions originating within the Soviet leadership itself. These actions underscored the death of the Spirit of Camp David in the period after the collapse of the summit meeting in Paris in May, 1960, and must have been satisfying to the defenders of traditional policy.

In sum, Khrushchev's erratic behavior during the summer of 1961, stoking the Cold War one day and dampening it down the next, was more a sign of weakness than of strength. He was not in so secure a position that he could pursue a single and consistent course; he could not ignore the powerful pressures and cross pressures of the internal politics of the Soviet ruling group. During this period, however, Khrushchev was careful to portray the shift in the summer of 1961 to an aggressive posture in foreign affairs as a temporary detour from the main line of his program for which he and his supporters continued to work. To have done otherwise would have amounted to an admission that his policy had been completely overturned and his leadership discredited. He looked toward the Twenty-second Congress in October as an opportunity to regain the initiative.

[57] See the revealing account of this interview in "Notes on a 1963 Visit with Khrushchev," *Saturday Review*, Nov. 7, 1964, pp. 16–21.

7

The UNSTABLE BALANCE—
The TWENTY-SECOND CPSU
CONGRESS

By the time the Twenty-second Party Congress was convened in October, 1961, Khrushchev needed a formula for restoring the momentum of his leadership. The record since 1957 was spotty. Despite Soviet achievements in rocketry and space, something less than a picture of uninterrupted advance had been provided by the U-2 incident, the repeated failures to budge the Western powers in Berlin, the break-up of the Sino-Soviet partnership, and even dust storms in the virgin lands. Further, his political program had been hobbled by obstruction from domestic forces opposed to radical departures in policy either at home or abroad. On the eve of the Congress Molotov boldly sent a letter to the Central Committee membership criticizing the draft of the new party program. At the same time the external attack from the Chinese and Albanian militants was increasing in intensity. Even the Khrushchevian vista held out in the draft program of long-term coexistence and declining war danger had been clouded by the crisis atmosphere over Berlin.

Few events in the post-Stalin period so clearly exposed the gulf between the outer appearances and the inner realities of Soviet politics than the amazing proceedings of the Twenty-second Party Congress of October, 1961. According to advance billing its main business was the solemn ratification of a new party program, the first since 1919, giving the blueprint for the "transition to communism" in the U.S.S.R. The usual image of a united and unerring party leadership leading the way to Marxist Utopia was projected in the party press. With little forewarning, however, the meeting's focus was abruptly shifted from the prospects of a happy Soviet future to a lurid recounting of the horrors of the Stalinist past.

At the Congress Khrushchev turned once again to the anti-Stalin weapon to break the fetters on his leadership and with the aid of his confederates generated a new wave of de-Stalinization. This time the recital of the damning details of Stalin's political atrocities was made in full public view and not in a secret speech as in the case of the Twentieth Congress five years earlier. While the dead dictator was pictured as originator of the past evils the party had suffered, Khrushchev's old foes—Molotov, Malenkov, Kaganovich, and, for the first time, Voroshilov—were condemned as the chief executors of Stalin's criminal repressions and the living bearers of the Stalinist legacy in the party. Molotov bore the brunt of the attack. He was portrayed both as Stalin's chief henchman in the great purges of the thirties and the epitome of conservative opposition to Khrushchev's policy. Further, a close correspondence between the views of Molotov and the Chinese-Albanian opposition was implied, and at the same time the Congress became the stage for an intensified assault on the opposition to Khrushchev in Tirana and Peking. For the first time he openly pointed to the Chinese as the abettors of the Albanian Stalinists.

In its broadest terms the renewed anti-Stalin campaign served to dramatize the idea that the Khrushchev regime had broken wholly with the past. It underscored Khrushchev's claim that his program, domestic and international, was inaugurating a new era in Soviet history. It conveniently pushed all the blame for past evils on Khrushchev's former associates in Stalin's Politburo while implying that Khrushchev himself was free of taint, and it aimed at eliminating the defeated leaders as potential rallying points for opposition to Khrushchev in the party. The most urgent motive behind Khrushchev's action, however, was the destruction of all the points of resistance his power and policy had produced within the leading group since 1957. His associates in the Presidium had good reason to fear that he had set out to take by storm a position of unchallengeable power which so far had eluded his grasp.

The Congress of the Second De-Stalinization

In the weeks prior to the Congress there were virtually no indications that the party forum was to be converted into a stage for the unprecedented vilification of Stalin and the anti-party group. Only scattered and routine references to the group appeared in the Soviet press. In the accounts of the provincial party congresses preceding the Twenty-second Congress only a few speakers mentioned the group. By contrast, in the weeks prior to the Twenty-first Congress, it will be recalled, the groundwork for an attack on the members of the group had been laid in advance by various regime spokesmen including Khrushchev himself.

The absence of any such preparation may indicate that the decision to raise the Stalin and group questions at the Congress was taken as late as the Central Committee meeting just three days before the meeting opened. The Soviet press gave few details of the one-day plenum but did note that it confirmed the Central Committee report to the Congress "submitted for the plenum's study" and which Khrushchev would deliver.[1] The convoking of such a plenum on the eve of the Congress was unusual. Judging by the subsequent course of events it quite conceivably was the scene of debate over how the Stalin and group questions should be treated.

In any case, Khrushchev's report on October 17, much like his opening report to the Twentieth Congress in 1956, provided no clear forewarning of the coming onslaught. In fact, it still registered

[1] *Pravda*, Oct. 15, 1961.

the balanced view of Stalin which reflected the consensus that had prevailed within the leading group since the Twentieth Congress. Khrushchev referred to Stalin's misdeeds but also mentioned his merits as a leader of the party and the Communist movement. However, the speech did strike one ominous note. He exposed Voroshilov for the first time as a ringleader of the anti-party group along with Molotov, Kaganovich, and Malenkov; further, he included Voroshilov in the charge that these figures were personally responsible for mass repressions during the Stalin era. This was out of tune with an earlier action of the Congress honoring Voroshilov by electing him to the Presidium of the Congress.

Khrushchev however left the prosecution of the attacks on Stalin, Molotov, Kaganovich, Voroshilov, and Malenkov to others during the first ten days of the Congress.[2] Various regional party secretaries recounted the repressions conducted by various members of the group in their localities during the Stalin era. The Ukrainian party chief Podgornyy, the first speaker in the debate after the Khrushchev reports, set the tone of the attacks, portraying Kaganovich as a "true sadist" during his leadership in the Ukraine after World War II. Podgornyy explained that new facts had come to light since the 1957 plenum. The Leningrad party leader, Spiridonov, once more attacked Malenkov for his role in the decimation of the Leningrad party leadership during Stalin's last years, and other regional leaders followed suit.

Other party figures focused on the group's opposition to Khrushchev's policies or told of their political intrigues against Khrushchev personally. Brezhnev, who had been in charge of the virgin lands project in its first years, singled out Molotov and Kaganovich for opposing that project and Khrushchev's agricultural program as a whole. Furtseva detailed Molotov's opposition to all of Khrushchev's major economic reforms from 1953 to 1957.

---

[2] During the first four days of debate on Khrushchev's reports, the great majority of Congress speakers, especially lower-echelon party leaders, responded weakly to the rush of attacks on the group by the Khrushchev forces. In most cases they did not pick up the calls for expulsion of Molotov, Kaganovich, and Malenkov. They simply repeated standard attacks on the group's political errors and did not echo the charges of "crime." This suggested that many delegates had not anticipated the vehemence of the attack on the group.

Speaking on the third day of the debate she confidently predicted that the Congress would be a Congress for settling accounts on the group issue. Mikoyan restricted himself to criticizing the political errors of the group leaders. He decried the "conservatism" and "dogmatism" of Molotov and singled out the latter's opposition to Khrushchev's coexistence policies. The editor of *Pravda*, Satyukov, described Molotov's letter critical of Khrushchev's policies sent to the Central Committee membership before the Congress. According to Satyukov, Molotov had criticized the new party program for its focus on internal construction and de-emphasis on the prospects for world revolution and had characterized Khrushchev's strategy of "economic example" and "peaceful transition to socialism" as pacifism and revisionism. Ilichev recalled Stalin's rejection of Khrushchev's *agrogorod* proposal in 1951 and revealed that Malenkov had prepared a confidential Central Committee letter attacking the scheme as "anti-Marxist." He also spoke of the unpublished article Molotov sent to *Kommunist* in April, 1960, for the Lenin Day edition in which he reminisced about his associations with Lenin.

Polyanskiy also recounted Molotov's opposition to Khrushchev's agricultural reforms, but his speech was notable for its ferocious condemnation of Voroshilov. He depicted Voroshilov as a wholly witting accomplice of the anti-Khrushchev faction. He bitterly complained that during the "critical moments" of the 1957 crisis he opposed demands from Central Committee members for convoking a plenum. Once the plenum was in session, he added, Voroshilov had had the temerity to defend Kaganovich against charges that he was guilty of the repressions in the Kuban under Stalin. Ignatov, as noted elsewhere, delivered a highly detailed account of the in-fighting of the 1957 leadership crisis.

On October 24 Shvernik, the chief of the party Control Committee and the official charged with initiating expulsion actions against party members, began tying up the indictment against the group leaders. He spoke of the growing accumulation of incriminating information in the hands of his committee regarding Molotov, Malenkov, and Kaganovich. He portrayed them as the instigators of some of the worst excesses of the purge era and ended his documentation of charges with the unambiguous assertion that "they cannot remain in party ranks." As if not enough nails had been driven into the coffins of Khrushchev's old foes, the head of the secret police, Shelepin, declared on October 26 that his archives contained numerous documents showing the direct personal responsibility of Stalin and the group leaders for the mass arrests and executions of cadres in every major apparatus of the Soviet regime from the party and the Komsomols to the state administration and the military establishment. Shelepin offered a succession of some of the most lurid revelations the Congress had yet heard, including such details as the cynical inscriptions Molotov and Voroshilov had jotted down in the margins of execution decrees against Soviet military figures during the purges. Shelepin's material was well designed to justify more than mere expulsion of the group leaders from the party.

On the next day Khrushchev himself came forward with his own summation of the indictment of the former Stalinist leadership and even surpassed all those who had gone before in the sensational aspects of his revelations. He said Shelepin had told much but not the whole story. He intimated that Stalin himself was behind the assassination of Kirov in 1934, which provided the prelude to the great purges of the thirties. He linked Molotov's and Voroshilov's names with the affair, saying that they and Stalin were to question Kirov's bodyguard after the killing. He added, however, that the bodyguard had been liquidated on the way to the interrogation because "someone" needed to remove all traces of the Kirov murder. Khrushchev asserted that there was still much to be revealed concerning this and other instances of abuses of power under Stalin. Khrushchev also told how Ordzhonikidze committed suicide after hearing that his brother had been arrested and shot and confirmed reports that Marshal Tukhachevskiy and other top generals were executed as German agents on the basis of fabricated documents planted by Hitler's intelligence service.

Khrushchev tied his revelations into his principal theme, namely, that there was an organic link between the criminality of the former Stalinist leadership and their challenge to his own leadership in 1957. They did not attack him simply on political grounds but because they feared further exposure of the abuses of Stalinism would reveal their own involvement in them. He asserted that if the group had won power the Stalinist past would have been covered over, especially since they "wanted to make Molotov leader."[3] The latter claim, if true, would go far to explain the concentration on Molotov in the attack on the group at the Congress.

Following the Khrushchev speech the anti-Stalin campaign was carried to its climax with the removal of Stalin's remains from Lenin's mausoleum. The action was staged to appear as the result of spontaneous demands from Congress delegates shocked to the core by the revelations. The most amazing episode in connection with the action was the speech of Madame D. Lazurkina seconding the proposal for Stalin's expulsion from Lenin's tomb. An old Bolshevik who had known Lenin personally, she told how she had been thrown into prison in 1937 and, despite a score of years in prison, forced labor, and exile, never wavered in her belief that Stalin was not responsible for her plight. Only Khrushchev's secret speech at the Twentieth Congress had shocked her into the truth. She asserted that she had had a vision the previous evening in which Lenin appeared complaining about his having "to lie side by side with Stalin, who brought so much harm to the party."[4]

At this point Khrushchev's juggernaut seemed unstoppable, yet there were already signs that all was not going as planned for his forces. During the second week of the Congress a note of irritation had crept into the speeches of those demanding further punishment of the group leaders. On October 24, for example, Sholokhov's demand for action from the Congress was peculiarly shrill. Sholokhov, who had become a crony of Khrushchev's, said:

How long will we stand in party ranks hand in hand with those who have caused so much irreparable evil to the party? Are we not too tolerant toward those on whose conscience are thousands of deaths of loyal sons of the country and party, thousands of ruined lives of their dear ones? The Congress is the supreme organ of the party. Let it pronounce its severe but just decision with regard to the factionalists and renegades.[5]

---

[3] *Pravda*, Oct. 28, 1961.

[4] *Ibid.*, Oct. 29, 1961.

[5] *Ibid.*, Oct. 26, 1961

Similarly on October 26 Pospelov betrayed the pent-up rage of the Khrushchevites at the party's dragging its feet on the issue. He exclaimed:

> There must be . . . an end to the patience and generosity of the party, after all! Or can our great party reconcile itself with renegades and dissenters in its ranks, who insolently oppose the most important theses of Leninism, the Leninist policy of our party, this manifesto of the Communist party of our era, which has been generally acknowledged? Many delegates to the Congress rightly said that Molotov, Malenkov, and Kaganovich cannot be members of our great Leninist party.
>
> Doubtless the Twenty-second Congress will unanimously approve the proposals of several delegations to expel these dissenters and factionaries from the party ranks. They must also bear responsibility for their criminal actions during the period of the Stalin personality cult and for the attempt to oppose the Leninist policy with their anti-party, anti-Leninist, and dangerous line, harmful to the cause of communism. [6]

Two other speeches by party figures on the day before the release of the official resolution were striking. As if the massive detailing of the group's crimes during the preceding days was not yet enough, Z. Serdyuk, a First Deputy Chairman of the party Control Committee, added further documentation of the "crimes" of Molotov, Kaganovich, and Malenkov and demanded to know: "What then links these three with the party after this? On what grounds can they remain in the ranks of our Leninist party?" [7] Rodionov, a secretary in the Kazakh party but a figure with connections in high places, was peculiarly insistent on the total unity of the Congress behind the demand for punishment of the group leaders. He said:

> There is not a single delegate at the Congress who would not condemn the anti-party activities of the factionalists. And if some of us perhaps repeat what has already been said, this testifies to the anger and indignation that affects all delegates equally deeply, to the fact that our thoughts are one, that we are all unanimous in the evaluation of the harmful essence of the anti-party group, and that we all demand just punishment of the apostates. [8]

---

[6] *Ibid.*, Oct. 28, 1961.

[7] *Ibid.*, Oct. 31, 1961.

[8] *Ibid.*

Rodionov's claim to speak for "all" disregarded the failure of some Congress speakers even to mention the group and of many others to voice expulsion demands or touch on the group's "crimes."[9]

The truth was that the leadership was divided on the group issue and the divisions were manifest in the speeches. Some speakers, like those noted, dwelt on the "crimes" of Khrushchev's ex-challengers and either demanded their expulsion or indicated support for further punitive action, or both. Others focused only on their political errors and skirted the issue of new punishments. Kosygin, Mikoyan, and Suslov typified the position of the relative moderates on the issue. None used the argument, which was characteristic of many speakers who pressed for punitive action, that the case was being reopened because "new facts" had come to light; instead, they suggested that the "ideological" routing of the group was being recalled to bring home an historical lesson.

Notably, these three leaders virtually repeated the positions they had assumed close to three years earlier at the Twenty-first Congress. Kosygin said the group was being discussed at the Congress because "we want the lessons of history never to be forgotten."[10] Mikoyan, while sharp in his criticism, seemed to draw the line at further punishment, much as he had done at the Twenty-first Congress. "The struggle against the conservative-dogmatist group," he said, "was carried out by methods of internal party democracy, without application of state measures of repression."[11] He referred to the "ideological crushing" of the group and, like Kosygin, treated the

[9] Rodionov's claim recalls an assertion in *Pravda* shortly after the Twenty-first Congress—an assertion similarly at odds with the wide variations in the treatment of the group by speakers at that Congress and by the failure of many speakers to mention the group at all. In an unsigned article (Feb. 2, 1959), *Pravda* said that at the Twenty-first Congress "there was literally not a single speech which did not contain angry condemnation of the false factionalist and dissident activities of the anti-party group of Malenkov, Kaganovich, Molotov, Bulganin, and Shepilov." Rodionov at the Twenty-second Congress was a shade more careful. Where *Pravda* in 1959 said flatly—and with demonstrable inaccuracy—there was not a single speech "which did not contain" denunciations of group members, Rodionov got around the facts of the case by saying only that there were no delegates "who would not" condemn them.

[10] *Pravda*, Oct. 23, 1961.

[11] *Ibid.*, Oct. 22, 1961.

affair as closed.[12] Suslov took a similar tack and, like Mikoyan, spoke of the group's "ideological" defeat.[13]

The ire that the pro-expulsion faction at the Congress felt toward the moderates was mirrored in Rodionov's speech. He was violently critical of the relatively mild characterizations of the group as "conservative" or "dogmatist" that Mikoyan and some other speakers had adopted. Rodionov said:

> The participants in the anti-party group are called dogmatists. This is correct. But what they tried to do in June 1957—this is not dogmatism; this is real banditry, this is robbery in broad daylight. And for robbery it is necessary to answer with the full severity of the law. They were ready to inflict a grievous wound on the party; they aimed at the very heart of the people—at the Leninist leadership of the Central Committee. For this they cannot be pardoned. Molotov, Kaganovich, and Malenkov . . . used their presence in the Central Committee Presidium not in the interests of the party but for satisfying their mercenary, careerist desires. They have no kind of community of principle with the party; the hands of these adventurers are stained with the scared blood of the best sons of the people.[14]

Despite the massive pressure mounted at the Congress, the success of the moderates in containing the drive against the group was apparent. The seemingly inevitable outcome, the official endorsement of the indictment of the group leaders for their "crimes" and of the proposals for their expulsion from the party, did not occur. While condemning the political errors of the anti-party group the resolution conspicuously disregarded the insistent demands of Khrushchev's closest supporters for their expulsions. It took no note of the flood of "new facts" offered to the Congress on the "crimes" of Molotov and company. Moreover, treating the matter as closed, the resolution hardly squared with the damning descriptions of the ex-party leaders as "criminals" and "sadists" guilty of "mass slaughter" of countless innocents.

In any case the pressures and cross-pressures over the group issue on the leading participants at the Congress were powerful.

[12] *Ibid.*
[13] *Ibid.*, Oct. 23, 1961.
[14] *Ibid.*, Oct. 31, 1961.

Numerous high-level figures seemed intent on having it both ways and leaving escape routes open, whichever way events turned. Many made literally incriminating attacks on the group but failed to commit themselves explicitly on expulsions or new punishments.

The effect of the Khrushchev bandwagon seemed to show even in Suslov's speech. He held to his generally moderate position but for the first time made a brief reference to unspecified crimes of "many" members of the group.[15] Kozlov took a good deal harsher line against the group but remained ambiguous on the crucial expulsion issue facing the Congress.[16] He implied he favored new action against the group leaders but conspicuously failed to commit himself on the immediate issue of party expulsion.

But perhaps nowhere in the Congress proceedings was the collision of the opposing forces in the party more manifest than in Khrushchev's own behavior. His concluding speech on October 27 once more revealed the double game he was playing—on the one hand seeking to divide and conquer those forces in the party capable of opposing him and on the other avoiding action that would impel those forces to unite in a move against his leadership. That speech paradoxically mirrored both Khrushchev's own intention to keep the indictment of the group for "crimes" alive and the consensus of the leadership against endorsement by the Congress of new punishments of the group leaders.

Khrushchev made his indictment of the group leaders far more damning than he had when he initiated the attack in his opening speech. He now described their crimes in detail and offset the idea that the matter could be closed by saying that all the evidence was not yet in. Thus he said that the murder in 1934 of Kirov, which he hinted Stalin instigated, and other similar cases needed further investigation and that not "everything" had been told.[17] Such investigations potentially could be used to incriminate Khrushchev's old foes even more deeply in Stalin's crimes. While he did not directly demand party expulsions of his foes, his indictment only made more glaring the prime argument of the supporters of

[15] *Ibid.*, Oct. 23, 1961.
[16] *Ibid.*, Oct. 29, 1961.
[17] *Ibid.*

expulsion, namely that the party must not continue to harbor criminals within its ranks.

Khrushchev's line of attack was glaringly inconsistent with another major theme of his speech—a theme which makes sense only as a lame effort to paper over the failure to bend the Presidium to his will. He referred to Lenin's "magnanimity" toward his Politburo associates, Zinoviev and Kamenev, after they had committed "treason" against the party by publicizing Bolshevik plans for the 1917 uprising. Khrushchev explained that despite their "treason," they were retained in the party and, after they admitted their "errors," were even restored to their posts in the Politburo.[18] In effect Khrushchev renewed the assurance he had given at the Twenty-first Congress that Stalin-style purges were a thing of the past.[19] Yet the gravity and virulence of the charges he and his supporters had raised were reminiscent of the denunciations of politically disgraced leaders in Stalin's purges and forewarned of an effort to lay the groundwork for punishments more dire than party expulsion.[20] In short he raised the specter of a revival of the purge through the instrument of anti-Stalinism—an instrument that could eventually be turned against recalcitrant colleagues in the leadership.

[18] *Ibid.*

[19] It is not unreasonable to conclude that the assurance had been introduced into the speech as a direct result of pressure from Khrushchev's colleagues. That same speech contains an unusually specific invocation of collective leadership. Khrushchev told the Congress that every speech he made was examined and given prior approval by the Presidium and that no major regime policy was undertaken by personal initiative. The point clashed visibly with the leader cult Khrushchev's confederates had attempted to build around him but it did not deter them from claiming that their leader had personally authored the regime's policies.

[20] The internal inconsistency of Khrushchev's concluding speech was particularly apparent in the treatment of Voroshilov's participation in the June, 1957, challenge to Khrushchev's leadership. Khrushchev in his opening speech seemed intent on portraying Voroshilov as a full participant in, and ringleader of, the anti-party group along with Molotov, Kaganovich, and Malenkov. He charged Voroshilov, along with the others, with personal responsibility for the mass repressions of the Stalin era. Polyanskiy developed Khrushchev's line in his October 23 speech. He told Voroshilov directly, "You must bear full responsibility for anti-party activities as much as all the members of the anti-party group," intimating that Voroshilov was trying to escape culpability.

An Uneasy Standoff on Economic Policy

The Twenty-second Congress in October ended in a standoff on the issue of the group and registered an uneasy balance between the pro-consumer faction and the metal-eaters. The new party program that was ratified neither adopted Khrushchev's pro-consumer platform in its more radical formulation nor did it reflect a full reassertion of the traditional dicta on heavy industrial priority. The Congress marked a discernible shift toward economic orthodoxy, however, both in its proceedings and in the increased emphasis on heavy industry in the Soviet future that appeared in the final version of the party program but not in the draft version issued before the meeting.

In his Congress reports Khrushchev continued to press his pro-consumer arguments, but at the same time it was clear that regime economic policy continued to give short shrift to consumer interests in favor of the traditional priorities of military-industrial power. He spoke, for example, of an unspecified Lenin doctrine that production rates should be calculated for the assured "abundance" in consumer goods but also conceded for the first time in more than a year that heavy industry would in the future play the "decisive role" in regime policy.[21] He recalled the metal-

---

In his October 27 speech, however, Khrushchev announced that Voroshilov was deserving of leniency. Although repeating and even expanding on the charges against Voroshilov—his responsibility for repressions and "executions" and his "participation in the anti-party group"—Khrushchev explained that gentler treatment was due Voroshilov because he had left the group and "helped the Central Committee in its struggle against the factionalists."

The Congress resolution duly reflected this gentler treatment by dropping Voroshilov's name from its roster of the anti-party group. It treated Voroshilov separately, saying that he had committed "serious mistakes" by siding with the group but had admitted his mistakes at the June, 1957, plenum and had condemned the group.

Rodionov on the preceding day had sounded almost as if he were seeking to devalue in advance the pardon extended Voroshilov in the resolution. He warned Voroshilov that the gentler treatment accorded him did not mean that his "deeds" had been forgotten. And he even impugned the sincerity of Voroshilov's letter admitting his "errors" to the Congress: "Comrade Voroshilov was in the same den with the anti-party group, and he did not stray there accidentally, as he tries to suggest in his statement to the Congress."

[21] *Pravda*, Oct. 18, 1961.

eaters' demand for more steel, implying that they had been restrained, but played down the fact that the original Seven-Year Plan steel goal had been raised.[22] And he complained of economic "conservatives" still entrenched in the management of the economy.[23]

Despite numerous signs in the press of contention between the orthodox and reformist economic philosophies in the months prior to the Congress, something of consensus leaning toward orthodoxy was generally apparent at the meeting. The top echelon of the party in most cases reflected this leaning in their speeches. A striking sign of the trend appeared in the speech of the ideologist Ilichev. Earlier in the year he had written articles in *Pravda* calculated to counter conservative views and to show that Khrushchev's welfare line was the "main trend" for the party, providing the key to Communist transition at home and victory over capitalism abroad.[24] He radically changed his position at the Congress by fishing up the favorite red herring of the party conservatives—Malenkov's heresy. His repudiation of Malenkov's "anti-Leninist" equal rates concept must have been as sweet for the traditionalists as it was sour for Khrushchev, who had flirted with that very concept earlier that year.

The retreat of the pro-consumer advocates on the issue of economic priorities was mirrored in the reformulated text of the new program on the future tasks of heavy industry. The final version ratified at the Congress excised the concept that "a new stage of development" had begun in party economic policy,[25] even though Khrushchev had earlier succeeded in incorporating it into the Central Committee resolution of the June plenum four months earlier. He had used the idea as the underpinning for

[22] *Ibid.* Khrushchev recalled that "some" in the party had wanted to increase steel output to 100 million tons annually, "but we held back and said that all branches of the enconomy, along with the production of the steel, should be uniformly developed, remembering the building of housing and children's institutions, the production of clothing, footwear, etc." Yet the original Seven-Year Plan steel goal had been raised beyond its upper goal of 91 million tons, which Khrushchev probably originally favored, to 95–97 million tons.

[23] *Ibid.*

[24] *Ibid.*, April 21, 28, 1961.

[25] The draft of the new program appeared in *Pravda*, July 30, 1961, the final version in *Pravda*, Nov. 2, 1961.

his arguments that the time was ripe for redefining the roles of heavy and light industry and for reorienting heavy industry itself more and more toward consumer goals. The omission was the more notable in the light of Mikoyan's assertion during the Congress that Molotov and his dogmatic supporters had refused to accept Khrushchev's "new stage" concept as the party's "basic line."[26] Mikoyan's complaint was another sign of the intimate connection between the frustration of Khrushchev's efforts to win a clear mandate for his consumer line at the Congress and his unexpected renewal of the onslaught on his defeated opponents as hidebound and criminal Stalinists.

THE SIMULTANEOUS ATTACK ON MAO

While Khrushchev's onslaught was aimed at sources of internal opposition, it also served the purpose of intensifying the battle with the opposition in Peking. The attack on Peking's proxies in Albania was launched with as equal suddenness and ruthlessness as the attack on the anti-party group and reflected Khrushchev's rash effort to bring the conflict with Mao Tse-tung to a head. Molotov was appropriately made the symbol of a kinship between the Peking-led external opposition and the conservative resistance to Khrushchev at home. At the Congress he was pictured as having been busily engaged on the sidelines working up an anti-Khrushchev platform and seeking to recruit supporters at home and abroad. According to various Congress speakers, he had even sent a critique to the Central Committee on the eve of the Congress attacking Khrushchev's policies and had taken the role as ideologist of a coherent anti-Khrushchev program echoing the Chinese positions. Khrushchev's strategy was designed to force a showdown both in the internal and external battle on the grounds most advantageous to himself—Stalinism versus anti-Stalinism.

Along with these moves he forced the first public confrontation with the Chinese. Up to the time of his second speech to the Congress ten days after its opening the whole attack on Chinese positions

[26] *Ibid.*, Oct. 23, 1961.

was still conducted by indirection. The Albanian leaders had remained the whipping boys. Khrushchev in his opening speech and other Congress speakers had professed the hope that the Albanians would see their errors and return to unity with the Soviet party; however, on October 27 Khrushchev carried the attack further. He flatly asserted that the Albanians could not correct their errors without the removal of their leaders, Hoxha and Shehu. Moreover, for the first time he openly implicated the Chinese as the real backers of the Albanians. He called on the Chinese "comrades" to show their concern for unity by bringing the Albanian leaders into line, noting that the Chinese party was in a position to make the best contribution to resolving the conflict. In short, he had thrown down the gauntlet to Mao Tse-tung. At the same time he made a virtually open appeal to the Congress to support his action. It was necessary, he said, to expose "the whole truth" about the position of the Albanian leadership; to have kept silent would have been seen as a sign of Soviet weakness, and the Congress "which is empowered to speak in the name of the whole party," he declared, should "define its attitude on this question and express its authoritative opinion."[27]

It was soon apparent that Khrushchev was seeking to go further than his Presidium colleagues were willing to go on the Sino-Soviet issue, just as he sought to do on the issues of the "group" and economic policy. This was duly reflected in the Congress resolution. It failed to second Khrushchev's public exposure of the Peking-Tirana alliance or his condemnation of the Albanian leaders as beyond redemption. Instead it referred to Khrushchev's original call to the Albanian leaders to return to unity, which had explicit Central Committee approval. Further, the resolution did not repeat the defense of the propriety of the public attack on the Albanians given by Khrushchev and others and which was a clear rebuff of Chou En-lai's complaint on this score. Incorporation of this challenge to the Chinese in the resolution would have amounted to putting the whole authority of the Congress behind it. Moreover, the resolution avoided repeating the charges of nationalism,

[27] *Ibid.*, Oct. 29, 1961.

"sectarianism," and "dogmatism" raised against the Albanians at the Congress sessions. It simply criticized them for "erroneous views" and actions counter to the 1957 and 1960 Communist conferences and dubbed these views as "dissident."[28]

Here was a clear sign of disunity among the leaders on future tactics in the dispute and especially over the advisability of intensifying the attack against Peking. Once again the indications were that Kozlov was among the counselors of restraint at the Congress. After the Congress other such indications would appear, implicating Suslov as well as Kozlov, as will be cited later.

During the Congress the Chinese press indicated its favoritism toward Kozlov.[29] The only Twenty-second Congress agenda report that *People's Daily* carried in full was his report on the CPSU statutes, while Khrushchev's Central Committee report was given merely in lengthy summary. The Chinese paper did carry the texts of Khrushchev's concluding speech and Kozlov's report, which enabled Chinese readers to compare the two leader's approaches to Sino-Soviet issues. Though both CPSU leaders censured Albania, Kozlov's criticisms were considerably more temperate and avoided openly chiding the Chinese for questioning the propriety of the public attack on Albania at the Congress as Khrushchev had done.

THE POST-CONGRESS SKIRMISHES

The signs of conflict in the leadership over the same issues that had animated the proceedings of the Twenty-second Congress persisted in the last months of 1961 and into 1962. Demands for expulsions of the "group" leaders from the party continued to appear after the Congress but in declining numbers. By the beginning of 1962 these demands had generally ceased. A sure sign that the issue was very much alive behind the scenes, however,

[28] *Ibid.*, Nov. 1, 1961.
[29] This was in tune with Chou En-lai's snub of Khrushchev at the Congress. According to Western news reports, Chou finished his speech, brushed past Khrushchev, and demonstratively shook hands with Kozlov on the rostrum.

came in January in the episode over Molotov's scheduled return to his post in Vienna. Soviet Foreign Ministry officials did a turnabout. They first told Western newsmen that Molotov would soon return to his post in Vienna—an indication he was still a party member—and later indicated that plans had been changed and that he would remain in Moscow.[30] Evidently efforts to initiate new moves against the "group" were afoot at this time since the episode was followed shortly by issuance of a Supreme Soviet decree ordering that places and streets still named after Voroshilov be renamed.[31]

The next party plenum in early March, which could have provided the occasion for new action against Khrushchev's former challengers, virtually ignored the question. It looked very much as if powerful pressure had been exerted within the leadership to close the matter as a public issue at the time.

During this same period an ill-disguised and running battle between Suslov and Khrushchev's ideological assistant, Ilichev, emerged. The conflict swirled around the Stalin issue raised at the Congress and broke into the open with a transparent attack in *Pravda* on Suslov's credentials as a theorist, which was followed by a riposte also in *Pravda* against Ilichev's disparagement of theoretical work in the party under Stalin at the Congress.

The unsigned *Pravda* article aimed at Suslov on November 21 attacked "certain people who *now* look ludicrous and pitiful," who "cry that we must start 'enriching' theory" although what they were doing was "breaking down an open door" since Soviet theory and practice were "developing furiously" without their assistance.[32] *Pravda* was not attacking the enriching of theory as such; it was heaping ridicule on those who supposedly were tardy in acknowledging that theory could be enriched. The article put quotation marks around enriching and thereby pinpointed Suslov's speech at the Congress, in which he said the party would continue "to

[30] *The New York Times*, Jan. 9–10, 1962.

[31] Ukase dated Jan. 15 in *Vedomosti Verkhovnogo Soveta SSSR* [*Proceedings of the USSR Supreme Soviet*], Jan. 19, 1962.

[32] *Pravda*, Nov. 21, 1961.

enrich and develop the scientific theory of communism."[33] It was
taken from those passages in Suslov's Congress speech on theory
that seemingly seconded the Khrushchevian theoretical concepts.
The reference to certain people now looking "ludicrous and pitiful"
was lifted without attribution from Ilichev's Congress speech.[34]
The use of the term "enriching theory" was a Suslov trademark
and indeed seemed to betray his orthodox attitude to theory—i.e.,
the view that theory cannot be created (unlike Khrushchev's
"creative Marxism-Leninism"), but must be born out of and cling
closely to past theory.

Ilichev was in effect accusing Suslov of conservatism in theory
and of having belatedly attempted to get on the anti-Stalinist
bandwagon at the Congress. He was also probably alluding broadly
to the theoretical dispute inside the party prior to the Congress
in which, according to Khrushchev, comrades with "dogmatic"
attitudes had resisted the decision to announce the end of the
dictatorship of the proletariat in the U.S.S.R. It was evident also
that Ilichev was zeroing in on Suslov in his reference to Stalin's
arbitary suppression of the economic theories of Voznesenskiy—
the young economic expert and Politburo member purged a few
years before Stalin's death. Suslov was the only present leader
implicated in the affair and had delivered the anathema on
Voznesenskiy's views in *Pravda* in December, 1952.

Suslov's riposte came in another unsigned *Pravda* article exactly
one month later, on December 21, 1961, which reasserted the
"enrichment" formula. Even during the period of the Stalin cult,
the article declared, the party had "tirelessly developed and
enriched" theory and argued that without this theoretical enrichment the U.S.S.R. could not have built socialism or survived
World War II.[35] It then sharply attacked, without naming him,
Ilichev's assertion at the Congress that "only one man" (Stalin)
had controlled "all matters of theory" during the period of the cult
and that "no important works on political economy, philosophy,
and history were printed."[36] The article attacked such assertions

[33] *Ibid.*, Oct. 23, 1961.
[34] *Ibid.*, Oct. 26, 1961.
[35] *Ibid.*, Dec. 21, 1961.
[36] *Ibid.*, Oct. 26, 1961.

as "groundless" and stated that whoever took such a position was guilty of deviating from Marxist-Leninist theory on the prime role of the people and the party in building socialism and was slipping into "idealistic positions."[37]

Three days later in a speech to an ideological conference Ilichev implicitly answered the charge.[38] While backing away from the flat assertions of his Congress speech, he reasserted his basic position. Stalin had done "great" service to the party, including service in the area of theory, but not as a developer of theory but merely as a "popularizer" of Marxism-Leninism.[39] When Stalin tried to develop theory, he added, he made one basic error after another. Ilichev concluded his argument by more carefully reiterating the thesis for which he was attacked, namely, that great difficulties had been created for theory when one man had acted as the law-giver in "literally all" questions of theory and ideology.[40]

Ilichev held the limelight at the ideological conference. He was introduced as the keynote speaker by Khrushchev personally and as shown in *Pravda* occupied a seat on the front row of the rostrum with the top five Presidium members—Suslov, Mikoyan, Kozlov, Kosygin, and Khrushchev. The affair must have been galling to Suslov, the senior ideologist of the party. Further, Ilichev had been brought into the Secretariat at the Congress and was not even a Presidium member.

The next month, however, Suslov won an opportunity to give his own discourse on ideology by delivering the main address to a conference of social scientists at the end of January. Khrushchev notably did not attend this meeting. Instead Kozlov was on hand

[37] *Ibid.*, Dec. 21, 1961.

[38] The presence of an intense conflict was so manifest that the issue of *Kommunist* issued on December 26 was apparently constrained to deny that the party was "threatened by any split whatever" and that there could be no "ideological disagreements" inside the party. However, *Kommunist* warned—the article was signed by prominent party editors—that some conservative party members wedded to outmoded outlooks might go counter to the line of the party. *Kommunist* also added that the party retained all the necessary means for preserving the ideological and organizational unity of its ranks (*Kommunist*, No. 18, 1961, p. 24).

[39] Report on Dec. 25, 1961, to the all-union ideological conference in Moscow, published in *Kommunist*, No. 1, 1962, p. 23.

[40] *Ibid.*, p. 13.

to introduce Suslov and was the only other Presidium member present. The conference had something of the aspect of a rival affair to Ilichev's; however, Suslov was in the disadvantageous position of seemingly having to second Ilichev.

The Suslov speech was a replica of Ilichev's in many respects and repeated points on the Stalin cult the latter had made the month before, but Suslov varied his phraseology on the previous sore points. For example he spoke of Stalin's "pretensions" to "a kind of" monopoly on developing theory—rather than flatly saying he held such a monopoly; of Stalin's "striving" to solve theoretical problems by fiat—rather than saying Stalin succeeded in doing so; his proneness to theoretical error especially in his "last years"— rather than saying this had always been the case.[41] Notably Suslov neither spoke of Stalin as a "popularizer" or mentioned the Voznesenskiy case, despite a lengthy discussion of economic science; these latter points had been raised by Ilichev in his ideological discourse.

Suslov also was out of tune with both Ilichev and the anti-Stalin campaign at the Twenty-second Congress on the sensitive question of the knowledge of Stalin's crimes among the top leaders under Stalin. He asserted that crimes which had been "hidden from the party" under Stalin were only discovered with the purge of Beria in July, 1953,[42] seeming to imply that the party leaders knew nothing of these crimes. He stressed that the party "immediately" after Stalin's death began to restore Leninist norms and to correct abuses—i.e., even prior to Khrushchev's Twentieth Congress attack on Stalin.[43] Suslov's position had the effect of insulating the present top leaders from charges of complicity in Stalin's crimes and allowing the surmise that even the members of the "group" had shared in correcting Stalin's abuses.

In any case, the close similarity of Ilichev's and Suslov's speeches had restored the appearance of harmony in the leadership's ideological pronouncements. Its superficiality, however, was revealed by the doctoring in *Kommunist* of an abridged version of the Suslov

[41] *Ibid.*, No. 3, 1962, pp. 19–20.
[42] *Ibid.*, p. 22.
[43] *Ibid.*, p. 22.

conference report. The *Kommunist* version, as compared with a prior *Pravda* version, significantly altered the text in three places dealing with matters all in some degree relevant to issues in the Sino-Soviet dispute. Whether the changes were made with Suslov's approval or not, their effect was to indicate that Suslov was associated with a more hospitable view of Chinese positions and favored a less intractable approach in the bloc quarrel.[44] These changes, quite possibly a provocative ploy of the Khrushchev forces, completed the identification of Suslov as a Stalinist ideologist in disguise harboring sympathies toward his political kindred in Peking.

---

[44] Suslov's speech, delivered on January 30, was first carried in the form of an "abridged stenogram" in *Pravda* on February 4. A longer version was published in *Kommunist*, No. 3, signed to the press on February 17. *Kommunist*'s version included the passages that had been in the *Pravda* version but with the following excisions:

1. The reference to "export of revolution" was cut from the passage reading "Peaceful coexistence . . . means . . . a renunciation of *the export of revolution and* the export of counter-revolution." This was an obvious last minute change, since the type had been reset to spread the letters and fill the space made by the excision. Thus a stock formulation that had been used in the Moscow declaration of the world parties in 1960 was altered apparently to suggest that Suslov did not oppose forceful Communist intervention in support of Communist revolution abroad but did oppose "imperialist" efforts to retain or extend their positions— a stand in line with Chinese views. Notably the formula renouncing export of both revolution and counter-revolution combined in capsule form warnings against "adventurism"—a charge aimed at the Chinese—and an answer to Chinese charges that the Soviet party was passive toward "imperialist aggression."

2. The term "spirit of compromise" was deleted from the passage: "The great majority of the fraternal parties resolutely condemned the faulty, anti-Leninist line of the leadership of the Albanian Workers Party. They stressed that nothing is more alien to the spirit of Leninism than a *spirit of compromise* [*primirenchestvo*] *and* an approving attitude toward the anti-Leninist position of the present Albanian leaders."

Thus Suslov is pictured as simply saying that an "approving attitude" should not be taken toward the Albanian leadership with the deletion suggesting that he was not averse to seeking some kind of accommodation with the Albanians and their Chinese allies.

3. The phrase "most important" was changed simply to "important" in the following: "A (or the) *most* important task of our theoretical front and of all social science workers is the thorough unmasking of revisionism and dogmatism in the Communist movement." The toning down of the emphasis on theoretically unmasking revisionism and dogmatism could have been designed to suggest

The presence of sentiment against aggravating the Sino-Soviet quarrel also seemed to be echoed the next month in a speech by Kozlov shortly after the March plenum. He betrayed his wariness toward a policy of intimacy with Tito, whom the Chinese were flaying as the ringleader of "modern revisionism." Thus in his Supreme Soviet pre-election speech in mid-March he criticized Yugoslav "revisionism" as well as Albanian "dogmatism".[45] His critical reference to the Albanians was routine, but according to all available accounts of the Presidium members' pre-election speeches Kozlov was the only leader to cite Yugoslav revisionism. In contrast to the *Kommunist* episode with the Suslov report, an effort was made to conceal rather than broadcast the Kozlov position. *Pravda*'s abridged version of the Kozlov speech—the speech was printed in full in *Leningradskaya Pravda*—deleted the sentence referring to Yugoslav revisionism and Albanian dogmatism.[46] It replaced the passage which stressed the necessity of fighting revisionism and dogmatism "no matter what their source"[47] with a sentence calling for "unity of action by Communists in all countries."[48] Although the season for anti-Yugoslav criticism may not

---

that Suslov was averse to an overly vigorous prosecution of the attack on dogmatism. Although he puts revisionism on a par with the dogmatic danger in this passage, elsewhere in the speech he tended to treat revisionism as the more serious of the two deviations.

The implication of the changes taken together—that Suslov favored greater militancy in support of revolutions abroad, was disposed to compromise with the Albanians, and downgraded the drive against dogmatism if not also against the revisionists—described an outlook that had been subjected to attack by Pospelov the month before. Pospelov in a *Pravda* article on January 18 on the fiftieth anniversary of the organizational split between the Bolsheviks and Mensheviks drew an analogy with the present in saying that Lenin also had to fight compromisers who obstructed his drive to oust his enemies from party ranks. Pospelov implied a parallel between Khrushchev's political situation and Lenin's in 1912. Pospelov's sharp attack on Stalin's vacillation and other "compromisers" allegorically applied to those in the Soviet and other parties loath to pursue the attack on the Chinese and Albanians to a point of final rupture. Pospelov's warnings—in view of *Kommunist*'s treatment of the Suslov report—could have well been meant to apply to Suslov in particular.

[45] *Leningradskaya Pravda*, March 16, 1962.

[46] *Pravda*, March 16, 1962.

[47] *Leningradskaya Pravda*, March 16, 1962.

[48] *Pravda*, March 16, 1962.

have been quite closed, Kozlov's dig at the Yugoslavs was out of tune with Khrushchev's major move for rapprochement with Tito in the next two months.

These signs of the cleavage between Khrushchev and the Kozlov-Suslov axis were accompanied by another encounter between Khrushchev and the defenders of traditional economic policy at the agricultural plenum held March 5–9. By any criterion Khrushchev came out second best. In his opening speech he once again vigorously defended a policy of promoting consumer welfare and depicted the goal of an economy of abundance as the noblest ideal of communism. He challenged the "dangerous attitudes" of "some leaders" who wished to divert funds from agricultural investment into other branches of the economy.[49] He also warned against those who would oppose "moral incentives" and "ideological education work" to "material incentives."[50] Reminiscent of his warning at the January, 1961, plenum Khrushchev asserted that failure to act to overcome the lag in agriculture in time could "wreck" the economy.[51]

His inability to gain ground on the allocations issue was echoed in the First Secretary's remarks at the close of the meeting. In striking contrast to the clarion call in his opening speech for major efforts to surmount the agricultural lag with new investments, he told agricultural functionaries that the measures of the plenum did not foreshadow any "immediate" transfer of resources to agriculture at the expense of the growth of industry and defense.[52] Rather weakly he declared that the party and government would "find" enough funds for agriculture and sought to counter the notion that the dim prospect for new investment in agriculture he had offered meant that "I sound the retreat to any extent."[53]

The plenum did not come up with the funds for agriculture Khrushchev wanted; the resolution merely stated that investments for agriculture would be sought. The defenders of heavy industry and defense had held the line, and the new investments were

[49] *Ibid.*, March 6, 1962.   [52] *Ibid.*, March 11, 1962.
[50] *Ibid.*   [53] *Ibid.*
[51] *Ibid.*

obtained some weeks later from the consumers' pocket as prices were raised.

THE SPIRIDONOV AFFAIR

The March plenum registered the stalemate on economic policy that Khrushchev faced. The issue of the expulsion of the anti-party group leaders had been sidetracked and there were the signs that Suslov and Kozlov represented roadblocks to Khrushchev's intentions. He apparently decided strong action was needed. Shortly after the plenum he struck out at Kozlov's organizational base in Leningrad and moved to increase his own support within the Presidium. He went out of his way to convey the meaning of his actions, namely that he was moving against Kozlov, who had just gained recognition at the Twenty-second Congress as second in command in the Secretariat.

Thus Khrushchev identified himself personally with the sudden removal of I. V. Spiridonov from the Secretariat in late April and subsequently on May 3 also from the post of First Secretary of the Leningrad party organization. Khrushchev went to Leningrad to be on hand at the local plenum removing Spiridonov as party chief and delivered a speech there that was never published. This provided a display of the Soviet leader's political strength but at the same time raised the question of why he decided to become publicly involved in a purge action which normally was a chore given to lesser leaders. At the same time that Spiridonov moved out of the Central Committee Secretariat, A. P. Kirilenko—a Khrushchev appointee—moved into the Presidium as a full member. The salient feature of the Kirilenko-Spiridonov shifts was that they overturned actions taken by the Congress only six months before: at the Congress Spiridonov had moved into the Secretariat and Kirilenko had lost his candidacy in the Presidium. The reversal of these decisions under Khrushchev's personal aegis revealed his disapproval of them and approval of the new actions. It was difficult to miss the impression that the Spiridonov affair stemmed from serious conflict between Khrushchev and Kozlov.[54]

The Spiridonov-Kirilenko shifts were also important because of the questions they raised regarding the circumstances under which demotions of other former Khrushchev protégés and supporters, in addition to Kirilenko, had taken place at the Congress. These included Mukhitdinov, Furtseva, Ignatov, and Pospelov. These changes carried further the trend of the 1960 leadership shakeup.

Mukhitdinov's departure from the Presidium and the Secretariat was especially notable; his fall completed the reduction begun in 1960 of Khrushchev protégés with membership in both bodies. Khrushchev thus seems to have been reduced at the Congress to one fairly strong Presidium supporter of his policies in the Secretariat —Kuusinen, who also held Presidium membership. The latter had, among other things, backed the expulsion demands at the Congress. Thus the result appears to have been an equilibrium of the Presidium members in the Secretariat: Khrushchev and Kuusinen on the one side and Kozlov and Suslov on the other. The addition at the Congress of five new secretaries—without Presidium standing— forewarned of moves on both sides toward upsetting the balance in that body whenever the opportunity presented itself. During the rest of 1962 Khrushchev worked toward that goal.

[54] The issue of the anti-party group may have been involved in the Spiridonov affair. Spiridonov failed to demand party expulsion of the group leaders at the Twenty-second Congress. Kirilenko, by contrast, did not fail on this crucial point. Spiridonov's sin of omission was the more glaring because he once more led the attack on Malenkov for his alleged role in the Leningrad purge under Stalin and introduced the proposal for Stalin's removal from Lenin's tomb. Spiridonov may have been in the dilemma of choosing between loyalty to Khrushchev or Kozlov and had tried to straddle the fence, but had leaned too far in the latter's direction.

Another related issue in the conflict may have been Kozlov's divergence from Khrushchev's pro-Yugoslav line. Notably, in the month after the Spiridonov-Kirilenko shift Khrushchev initiated major moves for rapprochement with Tito. Agricultural policy may also have been implicated. In December, 1961, Khrushchev had launched an attack on the Leningrad leadership for its alleged failures in agriculture (*Pravda*, Dec. 16, 1961) and under the pressure of the attack Spiridonov subsequently acknowledged his region's faults on this score (*ibid.*, March 7, 1962).

The Spiridonov affair, in any event, pointed to sharp in-fighting in the leadership and indicated that Khrushchev had gained strength in the Presidium, but not enough to assure his dominance over the forces that had engineered the key leadership changes at the Twenty-second Congress.[55] His battle with the Kozlov-Suslov forces reverberated in the various spheres of Soviet life during the remainder of 1962 prior to the Cuban crisis and its echoes could be heard now here and now there. Two episodes—one a heated controversy over a novel by the literary arch-conservative Kochetov and the other an incident involving a quack cancer cure—showed traces of the behind-the-scenes political battle among the leaders.

In the first months of the year a sharp controversy among literary critics broke out over Kochetov's novel, *The Obkom Secretary*, which portrayed a conflict between a member of the old Stalinist guard and a young party secretary who ostensibly has cast off the old ways. In January, 1962, a critic in the liberal literary journal *Novy Mir* (No. 1) denounced the work as a camouflaged neo-Stalinist tract. He proceeded to strike a sensitive political nerve, declaring that it was "impossible to imagine" that Kochetov's hero "with all his doubts, complaints, and emotional experiences" would have been found among the oblast secretaries who supported Khrushchev against his challengers in 1957.[56] Kochetov's literary followers heatedly countercharged that the attack was politically inspired. The debate had entered into dangerous territory and *Kommunist* itself intervened in an effort to dampen the dispute.[57]

[55] Spiridonov's transfer to the largely ceremonial post of Chairman of the Supreme Soviet Council of the Union symbolized the limited character of Khrushchev's victory and suggested that Spiridonov had protectors among the Presidium members. In this connection, an unusual effort was made at the time to offset the impression that Spiridonov's demotion, together with Kirilenko's unexpected promotion, signified a serious rift among the leaders. A contrived display of unity among the principals in the affair was evident in *Pravda*'s publicity for successive appearances of Spiridonov first with Kozlov and Kirilenko and then with Suslov and Grishin at bloc embassy receptions within days of his ouster as Leningrad party chief.

[56] *Novy Mir*, No. 1, 1962, pp. 219–39

[57] See the article by B. Ivanov, *Kommunist*, No. 4, 1962, pp. 58–68. Ivanov criticized the article in *Novy Mir* and another in *Literaturnaya Gazeta* for trying to show error in Kochetov's political line.

The attack in fact really had raised the question of Kochetov's own loyalty to Khrushchev and by indirection of his political patrons in the party leadership. Suslov almost certainly and Kozlov apparently were among the latter. Kochetov's novels were political hack works manifestly designed to defend political orthodoxy against the tide of de-Stalinizing in Soviet literature under Khrushchev. The flareup over *The Obkom Secretary* clearly echoed the conflict within the regime itself between the rival Khrushchevian and orthodox conceptions of the party functionary. The attack on a fictional party secretary as a Stalinist in disguise foreshadowed the appearance of a Yevtushenko poem in *Pravda* later in the year saying that such figures were at large in real life as well.

The other episode revealing the political threat to Kozlov bordered on the bizarre. A Central Committee decree appeared in August concerning a complaint lodged by certain Leningrad writers against Health Ministry officials. It contained an obviously contrived reference to the "Doctors' Plot." The writers charged that a new cancer cure had been withheld from Leningrad hospitals due to the obstructionism of the officials. The Central Committee decree upheld the officials and likened the accusations against Leningrad medical officials to charges brought against doctors of high officials in the sinister "Doctors' Plot" of 1953.[58]

The relevance of the episode for Kozlov derived both from his identification with Leningrad, the seat of his organizational power, and from his association with the "Doctors' Plot." He alone among the Presidium group had left a public record which could be used to implicate him in this notorious conspiracy. Just a few days before the Soviet press announced the arrest of the nine doctors in 1953, Kozlov had published an article in *Kommunist* which referred favorably to the mass purges of the 1930's and which called for sharply increased vigilance against the danger of subversion in the party. The arrest of the doctors, it is generally believed, signaled Stalin's intention to conduct a new purge of the party apparatus— an intention which was cut short by his death in March, 1953.

[58] *Pravda*, Aug. 1, 1962. In addition to the decree the letter of complaint was accompanied by a reply from Leningrad medical officials denouncing the alleged cancer cure as worthless.

The Ilichev-Suslov debate, the Spiridonov affair, and the other signs that Khrushchev was turning his fire on Kozlov and Suslov were only a prelude to dramatic events to come in the fall of 1962.

8

ATTACK and RETREAT —
To CUBA and BACK

AT THE TWENTY-SECOND CONGRESS Khrushchev had fought to
overwhelm the forces of resistance he had encountered in the regime
after 1957 in a second de-Stalinization campaign. His effort fell
short of success and ended in something of a stalemate. The
Spiridonov affair after the Congress was a sign that Khrushchev
was building his strength for another try against his long-term
opponents. On the eve of the Cuban crisis in September and October
of 1962 he launched a co-ordinated attack on many fronts: a new
wave of anti-Stalinism broke into the open and was soon turned
against "Stalin's heirs" in the party, and a vigorous drive was
initiated to promote Khrushchev's "economics-over-politics" line
as inviolable Leninist dogma. The line prepared for a major
restructuring of the party according to the "production" principle
and its bifurcation into separate hierarchies of agricultural and
industrial committees.

These moves at home were complemented by bold action in the
foreign field. *Kommunist* and the *World Marxist Review* printed a new
Khrushchev plan for bloc economic integration under Soviet
leadership. Rapprochement with the Yugoslavs was vigorously
promoted through Brezhnev's visit to Belgrade in September,

which was designed to pave the way for an exchange of visits between Khrushchev and Tito. This move was aimed not only at Khrushchev's opponents in Peking and Tirana but also served to undermine those in the Soviet party favoring a cautious approach in the conflict with the Chinese.

The masterstroke of Khrushchev's unfolding strategy was the plan to install intermediate-range nuclear missiles in Cuba. Success in this boldest and riskiest of all his foreign ventures would have won for him not only a momentous political victory over the United States but also would have given him a powerful handle for subduing his critics both in Peking and Moscow. Its failure, however, removed the linchpin from the broad political offensive he had been developing toward the end of 1962.

In the months following the Soviet backdown in Cuba, Khrushchev's offensive began to lose momentum. The de-Stalinization drive ground to a halt and went into reverse. Strong counter-pressures against key aspects of Khrushchev's economic policy became visible amid signs of sharp debate over his party reform and the "economics-over-politics" line. Without prior warning a major recentralization of industrial management in the state apparatus was undertaken in March, 1963, which paralleled a similar reorganization after the Hungarian revolt in 1956. The action clearly clashed with Khrushchev's past approach to the organization of economic management. Though he would survive his time of troubles in the Cuban aftermath, the heavy blow his prestige suffered from that affair must be counted as one of the causes of his political demise two years later.

THE ATTACK ON STALIN'S HEIRS

The far-reaching aims of Khrushchev's renewed offensive in the fall of 1962 were revealed in a Yevtushenko poem published in *Pravda* on the very eve of the Cuban crisis.[1] Through the poem, entitled "Stalin's Heirs," Khrushchev raised the threat of a purge of those in the leadership who had obstructed his purposes. The

---

[1] *Pravda*, Oct. 21, 1962.

political content of the poem was manifest. It called for vigilance in the party against alleged Stalinists still hidden in high places and intimated that these sinister figures at home were the tacit allies both of the retired members of the anti-party group and of the anti-Khrushchev opposition in Peking and Tirana. Thus it divided the heirs of Stalin into those in retirement who viewed their inactivity as temporary, and others who cursed Stalin from the rostrums but secretly yearned for a revival of Stalinism. It ominously pictured their involvement, along with their political kin abroad, in an intrigue against Khrushchev's de-Stalinizing policies.

It is quite possible that Khrushchev personally commissioned Yevtushenko to write the poem for use in his anti-Stalin campaign at the Twenty-second Congress. Yevtushenko says in his autobiography that he wrote the poem at the time of the Congress but could not get it published because of the opposition of dogmatists who, he said, had spread rumors that it was anti-Soviet. He explains, however, that he sent the poem directly to Khrushchev, who had it published in *Pravda*.

This political bombshell in literary wrapping was immediately followed by another. The companion piece of Yevtushenko's poem, Solzhenitsyn's celebrated novel on Stalin's prison camps, was also published under Khrushchev's sponsorship. According to numerous reports in the Western press at the time and since, Khrushchev had pressed for the release of the novel against opposition in the Presidium, specifically from Suslov and Kozlov. If the report was true, we can be sure, these figures were acutely aware that Khrushchev was using the novel as a political weapon that could be turned against them.[2]

In September Khrushchev combined with his new anti-Stalin

---

[2] Notable, in this respect, was the Yevtushenko poem's allusion to heart attacks the secret Stalinists had suffered presumably under the shocks of de-Stalinization—an allusion which perhaps was a swipe at Kozlov who apparently was incapacitated for a time by an attack just before May Day in 1961.

Also, according to the account of the indictment of Khrushchev at his ouster in 1964 in the Communist-backed Italian paper *Paese Sera*, Khrushchev was charged with personal responsibility for the publication of Solzhenitsyn's novel (*Paese Sera*, Oct. 30, 1964). Reportedly, Suslov delivered the main attack on Khrushchev at his ouster.

drive an "economics-over-politics" campaign to clear away political obstacles to his policy. In addition to a poem and a novel, he had in hand a newly "rediscovered" work of Lenin which, according to the Soviet press, had been recovered from the party archives.[3] The press explained that the forty-four-year-old document, like the Rosetta stone, had baffled attempts to decode the obscure shorthand in which it had been recorded. *Izvestia* asserted that a bright young archivist had cracked the code during the summer.[4]

While it was difficult to judge the authenticity of the story, there was no difficulty in deciphering the political import of the document. It was designed to remove a stumbling bloc to Khrushchev's over-all strategy, namely, the long-established tradition that *politics*, the conduct of the revolutionary struggle, takes priority over the party's concern with economic problems. As far back as the Twentieth Congress Khrushchev asserted that Lenin had said the reverse was true after the Bolshevik revolution, although it was a claim difficult to support from Lenin's known writings. Indeed, his challengers in 1957 reputedly had accused Khrushchev of violating Leninism on the point.[5] He now had a somewhat belated answer from the scriptures. The rediscovered Lenin—said to be the unpublished chapters of his well-known 1918 article "Immediate Tasks of Soviet Power" — conveniently dropped Lenin's pre-revolutionary insistence on the supremacy of politics in party policy. The immediate political value of the document, however, was not in the reply it gave to the challenge five years earlier by the defeated anti-Khrushchev faction or even to the thinly veiled complaints of more recent vintage voiced in Peking against the focus on economics in Khrushchevian strategy. More pertinently it was used as the doctrinal buttress for a major move in domestic politics.

THE PARTY REFORM

The economics-over-politics line provided the rationale for a sweeping reorganization of the party apparatus. At a Presidium

[3] *Pravda*, Sept. 25, 1962.
[4] *Izvestia*, Sept. 30, 1962.
[5] See N. Ignatov's speech to the Twenty-first Congress in *Pravda*, Feb. 3, 1959.

meeting on September 10 Khrushchev introduced a plan for restructuring the party apparatus from top to bottom on the "production" principle.[6] The reform, formally presented at the Central Committee the next month, split the party apparatus into separate hierarchies of industrial and agricultural bureaus reaching into the Central Committee itself and replaced the traditional "territorial" organization of the apparatus. The reform was the logical outgrowth of Khrushchev's view that the party must increasingly become a functional element in the management of the Soviet economy and the party officialdom must be increasingly devoted to the practical affairs of industrial and agricultural production.

The contents of the new Lenin document were admirably suited as a prop for the plan. For example, it stressed an argument that Khrushchev had advanced on numerous occasions in line with his focus on "economic tasks": that "economic organizers" and not "political agitators" were needed in the leadership positions in the regime.[7] In this connection the document contained an explicit proposal, not in the 1918 published version of the article, that leadership changes should be made to meet this need. Thus in the new document Lenin advocated that "in accordance with this need for economic leaders, a certain re-evaluation of leaders should be carried out, a certain reshuffling of them so long as it is possible for them to adapt themselves to new conditions and to new tasks."[8]

Lenin's call for a change in leaders had a distinctly familiar ring. It echoed repeated warnings by Khrushchev and various party spokesmen since early 1961 that those who do not "understand" the party's emphasis on agricultural and consumer economics cannot be "real leaders." Such warnings, furthermore, had been often linked with polemical defenses of the Khrushchev economic line against the criticism that this line subordinated ideology and politics to pragmatic economics.

---

[6] N. S. Khrushchev, *Stroitel'stvo Kommunizma v SSSR i Razvitiye Selskogo Khozyaistva* (*The Construction of Communism in the USSR and the Development of Agriculture*) (Moscow: State Publishing House for Political Literature, 1963), Vol. 7, pp. 163–77.

[7] *Pravda*, Sept. 28, 1962.

[8] *Ibid.*

The target of the reform was apparent. Ostensibly designed to promote cadres with skills in technical and economic work, it more importantly struck a blow at the natural opponents of the primacy of economics line within the party: the top- and middle-echelon party *apparatchiki* whose careers were in the realm of political-ideological work. It also struck at the powers and influence of the regional party bosses—they were to be converted from the chief political executives in the provinces into managerial overseers of the local industrial or agricultural economy.

As it took shape at the November plenum, the reform effected significant changes within the party's key executive organ, the Secretariat. Four new non-Presidial secretaries were added, two of which headed the new Central Committee Bureau for Agriculture and the Bureau for Industry. Three of the four other non-Presidial secretaries that had been added to the Secretariat at the Twenty-second Congress also received assignments that were the apparent outgrowth of the reform. These changes made obvious inroads into the spheres of influence of those Presidium members in the Secretariat apart from Khrushchev. Khrushchev's evident aim was to restore the leverage he had lost when the Secretariat had been reduced to four Presidium members in 1960—Suslov, Kozlov, Kuusinen, and himself. Although they retained their clear seniority over the new non-Presidial secretaries, the reform impinged on their spheres of influence in the Secretariat. Khrushchev had obviously designed the reform to enhance his own position as well as the prospects for his program. Further, the expansion of the Secretariat to twelve men raised a threat to the integrity of the eleven-man Presidium as the top executive body of the party and to its incumbent membership as well.

Aside from the elder figure Kuusinen, the Presidium's senior ideologist, Suslov, was particularly menaced by the change. In addition to the diluting effect that the influx of new secretaries could have on his own influence in the Secretariat, Suslov's rival, Ilichev, was made chief of the new Central Committee Ideological Commission established at the plenum.[9] Though without Presidium

[9] In presenting his reform proposals to the plenum in his report, Khrushchev made no mention of the new ideological commission. In fact his report virtually disregarded the question of what would happen to the ideological functions of the party under this reform.

status, Ilichev had long been groomed by Khrushchev as a counterpoise to Suslov.

Yet those who were threatened by the changes were not without means to resist Khrushchev's purposes. While the momentum behind the party reform project was great enough to carry it through at the November plenum without major hitches, the adverse effects that the Cuban backdown had on Khrushchev's leadership provided them with opportunities for counteraction in various spheres of policy.

THE RETREAT

Khrushchev's hopes of winning a breakthrough both in international and domestic politics collapsed with the failure of the Cuban missile venture. What bypaths of political logic led him to undertake this staggering gamble or what even made him think it could succeed probably will never be known with certainty. He must have had some notion of the odds against success. However, in view of his past tactics, some surmises regarding his calculations suggest themselves.

Clearly, if the plan had worked Khrushchev could have claimed that he had redressed in a single stroke the U.S.S.R.'s strategic inferiority to the United States. He undoubtedly saw the venture as a way of cutting the Gordian knot that entangled his strategy of détente and reform following the U-2 episode. The argument of the defenders of traditional policy that guns and steel could not be sacrificed to butter in the face of a more powerful enemy would have lost force, while Khrushchev's own concept of the inexpensive rocket deterrent would have gained plausibility. This must have been one of the benefits he hoped to obtain.

While the Cuban venture, on the face of it, was in blatant contradiction to his own détente policies, it nonetheless bore the earmarks of the classic Khrushchevian tactic—the sudden and bold initiative aimed at setting opponents off balance and producing a quick and decisive advantage in political struggle. It also aimed at accomplishing much with little, namely, with the fairly limited number of intermediate-range ballistic missiles involved in the operation. While yielding some military advantages, Khrushchev's primary motive in placing the missiles, however, seemed rather more political than military. Missiles in Cuba would have provided him with a powerful negotiating lever for pressuring Washington, especially with regard to Berlin. A new arrangement could have been demanded there in return for withdrawal of the missiles. In Berlin Khrushchev had virtually exhausted every means of pressure on the Western powers and the results had been meager. Any major move against Western positions threatened to produce a direct confrontation, which would have left him little room for maneuver. And any such move would have grossly violated Western rights and branded the U.S.S.R. as the instigator. Sending missiles to Cuba, on the other hand, technically involved no breaches of international law or established arrangements among the powers, but obliged the United States to assume the onus of taking "illegal" actions if it wanted to respond effectively. In addition, the Soviet action could be painted, and was painted, as the defense of a small and threatened ally.

Khrushchev's fatal error was his evident expectation that the United States would react other than by an immediate show of force. One sign that he did not anticipate a sudden military confrontation off the shores of Cuba was the Soviet failure to make any serious effort at concealing the missile operation. He was obviously aware that Washington would quickly discover what was afoot. The signs of confusion in Moscow in the week following President Kennedy's announcement of the blockade of Cuba further indicated that the Soviets were not well prepared to cope with this contingency. On the other hand, if President Kennedy had not forced the issue with such rapidity, Khrushchev would have had various options for exploiting the crisis.[10] Khrushchev's visit

---

[10] Khrushchev's discomfiture at the suddenness of the American action was distinctly conveyed in his speech to the Supreme Soviet in December. He said: "The United States military pushed the development of events in such a manner as to facilitate an attack on Cuba. We received information from Cuban comrades and from other sources on the morning of October 27 directly stating that this attack would be carried out in the next two or three days. We interpreted these cables as an extremely alarming warning signal. And the alarm was indeed justified. Immediate action was necessary to prevent an attack on Cuba and to preserve peace" (*Pravda*, Dec. 13, 1962).

to the United Nations scheduled for November could have been the starting point for a long process of bargaining with the United States. He could have made various demands as preconditions for Soviet withdrawal of the missiles in Cuba, such as a reciprocal withdrawal of missile bases in Turkey or Europe, or, as has been suggested, a new arrangement on Berlin. If Khrushchev gained nothing from such a process he probably assumed he would have still had his rocket bases ninety miles from American shores.

Also he may have reasoned that success would have strengthened his hand both within the Soviet leadership and the Communist movement to the extent that he could have, after tensions subsided and the situation stabilized, worked out a new *modus vivendi* with the United States. However unrealistic such an assumption may have been, the fact of the matter simply may be that Khrushchev believed that he could have his cake and eat it too. The inconsistency was not only part and parcel of Khrushchev the politican but of the political milieu in which he moved. Being a leader who sought to justify reform internally and limited détente externally, he was constantly vulnerable to the charge that he had foresaken the struggle with the "imperialist" adversary. He also needed to show his mettle in battle. He wanted victories against the West, but not at costs that would permanently damage his long-term program at home. Despite the seeming illogic of the Chinese charge that Khrushchev was both an "adventurer" and a "capitulationist" in the Cuban missile crisis, it nonetheless struck close to Khrushchev's dilemma. Fortunately, he was enough of a political realist to recognize when a gamble had been lost and knew how to employ all of his demagogic arts in papering over failure. With notable skill he used the resolution of the crisis as an example of how war could be avoided through a policy of mutual concessions.

Because of the inconsistency of the Cuban missile project with Khrushchev's own détente policies, the possibility has remained that the action was urged or imposed upon him by militant elements inside the regime. However, in addition to the reasons suggested above, it seems unlikely that his more conservative colleagues considered the plan sound. Furthermore the adverse effects of the

Cuban failure on Khrushchev's personal prestige continued to manifest themselves for some months after the crisis. In fact the withering criticism from the militants in Peking must have come close to expressing what probably was in the minds of some of his colleagues in the Presidium. The Chinese accused Khrushchev of committing not one but both of the cardinal errors which must be avoided in Communist political strategy. They charged him with "adventurism" for having advanced against the enemy further than the strength of his position allowed. His subsequent withdrawal of the missiles was "capitulationism," according to the Chinese. He had yielded in the face of enemy pressure. The "hare-brained schemes" Khrushchev's successors accused him of promoting could well have included the Cuban missile venture.

It is also unlikely that Khrushchev received much enthusiastic support from Soviet military leaders for the Cuban project. No mastery of military strategy was necessary to see the risks in placing strategic weaponry in a forward and exposed position where the adversary's military advantages were overwhelming. It was perhaps Khrushchev's tendency to think in terms of political struggle alone that caused him to brush aside the hard facts of the U.S.S.R.'s military inferiority. At the same time, however, once the missiles were in Cuba it would not be surprising if some military leaders and Presidium members as well strongly objected to Khrushchev's precipitate and humiliating backdown without extracting even a face-saving concession from the United States; here the Chinese charge of capitulationism probably struck home. In fact, one of the clearest signs that Khrushchev was under powerful pressure on this score was his last-minute attempt to win a reciprocal withdrawal of American missiles from Turkey, *after* he had agreed to remove the missiles from Cuba without preconditions in his October 27 letter to President Kennedy. On October 28 the Soviet press published another Khrushchev letter demanding a Cuba-Turkey missile trade, a demand hurriedly withdrawn later the same day. On the day before *Red Star* had published an article signed by Leontiev which had pointedly asked, "Why shouldn't American military equipment and troops be removed from hundreds of bases located around the Soviet Union?" Both Kosygin and

Khrushchev in their subsequent public defense of the Soviet backdown sought to answer the question raised in the Leontiev article. In delivering the official address on the October Revolution anniversary November 6 Kosygin noted, "Some may ask: Was it necessary to give in? We feel that both sides had to concede, because where there are mutual concessions, there is sensible compromise." Offering a similar rationale in his Supreme Soviet speech on December 12 Khrushchev said, "Some say that the United States forced us to retreat." The references undoubtedly included more than critics in Peking.

There were other clear indications that dissatisfaction in the military establishment over the Cuban affair was profound, dissatisfaction which led Khrushchev to take strong counteraction. Marshal Chuikov was apparently charged with the task of initiating the campaign in the military press after the crisis to assert the supremacy of the party leadership in the military sphere. In his *Red Star* article of November 17 Chuikov warned against incorrect "attitudes and opinions" among officers and recalled that Lenin had upbraided Stalin in 1920 for asserting that "our diplomacy sometimes most effectively spoils the results achieved by our military victories." The point was obvious. The military should keep out of politics and display unquestioning obedience to the political leadership, Khrushchev in particular. The theme was pressed with vigor in the military press throughout 1963.[11]

---

[11] It is at least noteworthy that signs of intensified conflict between Khrushchev and the military over their respective prerogatives in the realm of strategy first emerged in the summer of 1962 and continued into 1963. The appearance in the late summer of 1962 of the volume *Military Strategy* by a team of military experts headed by Marshal Sokolovskiy apparently aroused Khrushchev's ire. Its assertions of the military's role in formulating over-all doctrine and strategy as well as influence on state policy evidently was viewed by Khrushchev as a challenge to the authority he had claimed in this sphere in January, 1960. Whether by intention or not the volume appeared at a time when the Cuban missile plan had been under discussion. (The actual decision to emplace the missiles had probably been taken either by the time Che Guevara came to Moscow on a military aid mission in August or, at the latest, prior to the TASS statement of September 11 warning the United States that the U.S.S.R. was firmly committed to the military protection of Cuba. Khrushchev in his Supreme Soviet speech in December referred to a Cuban request for aid in the "summer.") The publication of the Sokolovskiy volume at this juncture

However, this was easier said than done. A pamphlet signed by Malinovskiy on military policy also in November putting unprecedented emphasis on party supremacy and Khrushchev's leadership in military matters in the same breath asserted that the Cuban crisis demonstrated that "real reasons exist which force the government and the Communist party to strengthen the Soviet armed forces."[12] While ready to pay public deference to Khrushchev, the Minister of Defense was not reluctant to exploit the Cuban failure to press for increasing the military budget. The force behind post-Cuban pressures for more resources for military purposes was revealed in a major speech by Khrushchev a few months later. Still on the defensive after Cuba, he conceded in his Supreme Soviet election address of February 27, 1963, that the satisfaction of consumer needs would have to be deferred so that the regime could commit the "huge resources" needed to keep Soviet military power abreast of the Western powers.

The general political damage the Cuban fiasco was inflicting on Khrushchev's policy began to be evident soon after the Soviet decision between October 26 and 28 to yield to the American demand for withdrawal of the missiles. It became visible in various spheres of policy but especially in connection with the question of Stalinism, revisionism, and economic policy. First the anti-Stalin drive withered and was replaced by a conservative, not to say neo-Stalinist, counterattack against de-Stalinizing writers and artists. The development gave almost a prophetic quality to the warning in the Yevtushenko poem. Signs of pressure against Khrushchev's policy of ever greater intimacy with Yugoslav

---

would have been especially galling to Khrushchev if military spokesmen had been warning of the dangers entailed in the missile venture.

The evidence of political-military tension in the 1962–63 period is comprehensively covered in Thomas Wolfe's *Soviet Strategy at the Crossroads*, (Cambridge, Mass.: Harvard University Press, 1964). Also, the impact of the Cuban crisis on Khrushchev's relations with the military as well as the evidences of the conflict between them at the time is discussed in detail by Roman Kolkowicz, *Conflicts in Soviet Party-Military Relations: 1962–62*, RAND Research Memorandum, RM–3760–PR (Santa Monica, Cal.: RAND Corporation, Aug. 1963).

[12] R. Malinovskiy, *Bdityelno Stoiat Na Strazhe Mira [Vigilantly Stand Guard over Peace]* (Moscow: Voyenizdat Ministerstva Oborony SSSR [Publishing House of the Ministry of Defense], 1962).

revisionism emerged and the influence of forces urging retrenchment in economic policy and economic management became felt. There were also evidences of a running debate within the regime over Khrushchev's argument that economics rather than politics and ideology had become the basic criterion in the formulation of over-all policy.

The Stalin issue was the most sensitive and immediate barometer of the effect of the Cuban crisis on Khrushchev's political fortunes. A countertrend against the new anti-Stalin campaign became apparent within days after the backdown in Cuba. On November 1 *Pravda* reprinted a weeks-old Mongolian account of the purge of a top-level Mongolian leader who had ruthlessly exploited anti-Stalinism as an instrument of factional struggle.[13] The analogy to the Soviet political scene and Khrushchev's own uses of anti-Stalinism was difficult to miss. Two days later the same paper resurrected Voroshilov from the political disgrace to which he had been condemned by Khrushchev at the Twenty-second Congress. In a signed article the old Bolshevik voiced support for Khrushchev's actions in Cuba, but the price of his support seemed evident in his treatment of anti-Stalinism as a dead issue for Soviet politics. Briefly alluding to the "errors and distortions" of the Stalin cult, he pointedly asserted that "now all this lies behind us."[14]

But it was with the strike at the Soviet literary and artistic avant-garde, the most vulnerable element in Khrushchev's de-Stalinization movement, that the conservative counterdrive displayed its full power. The attack originating at the November plenum was clearly predicated on the accusation that the anti-Stalin drive had given free rein to "revisionist" influences among Soviet intellectuals and had even emboldened them to challenge the legitimacy of party authority over them. "Artists" addressed a letter to the plenum asking the Central Committee why the party allowed "revisionism" in the arts access to the public media.[15] The move almost certainly had Presidium-level sponsors. These may

[13] *Pravda*, Nov. 1, 1962.

[14] *Ibid.*, Nov. 3, 1962.

[15] See L. Ilichev's December 17, 1962, speech to writers and artists (*ibid.*, Dec. 18, 1962).

well have included Suslov, who had raised similar questions at the Twenty-second Congress, insisting on unequivocal dominance of party ideology in Soviet literature and art. Clearly perturbed by the increased freedom of access to the Soviet public that was enjoyed by heterodox writers and artists, Suslov complained of "large state funds" spent on "ideologically barren" literary and artistic work. He had pointedly asked, "Is it not time to stop subsidizing artistic waste?"[16] The question implied a lack of ideological vigilance and failure to keep a tight ideological rein on Soviet intellectuals, a lapse for which Ilichev carried prime responsibility as agit-prop chief. The "artists'" letter at the November plenum also landed on Ilichev's doorstep, demanding to know why the press, radio, and television had been let out to purveyors of "revisionism" and "alien ideology" in art and asking why the party line was not being enforced in this regard.[17] Moreover, the charges implicated Khrushchev himself. He not only had groomed Ilichev but in May, 1959, enunciated the line that had given leeway to heterodoxy in the arts. At the writers congress that month he declared that the party would remain aloof on literary and artistic questions; he advised writers and artists to settle their own disputes and not call for party intervention.[18] Khrushchev's line had been clearly to the advantage of "liberalizing" elements in Soviet culture.

On the defensive now, Khrushchev hastened to identify himself with the crackdown in the arts by going into a tantrum over abstract paintings at the Moscow art exhibition on December 1. This was evidently a put-up affair staged by the leadership to dramatize a reversal of party cultural policy and, more important, to put a halt to the anti-Stalin offensive Khrushchev himself had launched. As if to underscore the change in the wind, party Secretary Ponomarev told Soviet historians later the same month that "we admit, as N. S. Khrushchev has again emphasized, the services of Stalin to the party and the Communist movement."[19] He was

---

[16] *Ibid.*, Oct. 23, 1961.
[17] Ilichev's speech (*ibid.*, Dec. 18, 1962).
[18] *Ibid.*, May 24, 1959.
[19] *Voprosy Istorii* [*Problems of History*], No. 1, 1963, p. 10.

referring to a brief passage buried in the Soviet leader's speech to the Supreme Soviet on December 12.[20] At the Twenty-second Congress Khrushchev had made a mockery of the earlier party line that Stalin had "merits" despite his abuses—the two positions were incompatible. Only the strongest political pressures could have caused Khrushchev to back-track.

Also in the months after the November plenum exposés of Stalin's tyranny went out of style; the young writers who had rejected the Soviet literary heritage as tainted with Stalinism were castigated, and those of the older generation who had served Stalin were vigorously defended. Predictably, Yevtushenko and even Solzhenitsyn became the targets of the conservative attack.

Under the pressure of the conservative counterattack, Khrushchev in the first months of 1963 had retreated further on the Stalin issue than he had at any time since the aftermath of the Hungarian revolt. His speech on March 8 to writers and artists, in which he surrendered major elements of his own de-Stalinization policies, gave a measure of that retreat. And, most significant in terms of leadership issues, he even undermined his own charge at the Twenty-second Congress that the leaders of the anti-party group had been witting accomplices to Stalin's crimes. In response to Ehrenburg's admission that he had known about Stalin's misdeeds, Khrushchev now claimed that party leaders had been unaware "at the time" that most of the victims of terror in the Stalinist era were innocent.[21]

Though Malenkov and Kaganovich were mentioned in derogatory contexts, Beria was made the main culprit under Stalin—the line the ruling group had originally adopted after Stalin's death. Only after Beria's trial and execution, according to Khrushchev, did the full story of the abuses under Stalin become known to the leadership. At the same time Khrushchev's references to Stalin's repressions were outweighed by his heavy emphasis on the dead leader's political merits. His focus on Stalin's services to the cause was distinctly reminiscent of his earlier restoration

[20] *Pravda*, Dec. 13, 1962.
[21] *Ibid.*, March 9, 1963.

of the dictator's image in the aftermath of Hungary when his policies were under fire in the Presidium.

In this speech to writers and artists he joined the attack on Yevtushenko and Ehrenburg, but his admonishment of these writers was mild in contrast to the old-line literary watchdogs who were pressing for punitive measures against the offenders. Moreover, while complaining of the "flood" of dangerous anti-Stalinist works that had been sent to editorial offices in the wake of the release of Solzhenitsyn's novel, he was careful to note that the "Central Committee" had approved the release of the novel.

The Danger of Yugoslav Revisionism

The attack on revisionist tendencies in the Soviet arts was accompanied by signs after Cuba that there were reservations about Khrushchev's active rapprochement with the "Yugoslav revisionists," reflected in Brezhnev's visit to Belgrade in September paving the way for Tito's visit to Moscow in December. The Chinese and Albanians had reacted violently to the latter move and were making the Yugoslav question their main bone of contention with the Soviets.

Thus, in November, one day before the CPSU November plenum, a *Pravda* article struck a discordant note by flatly asserting that revisionism remained the main danger for the Communist movement and that Yugoslav revisionism was "its fullest expression."[22] The article followed the appearance of an editorial earlier in the month in the *World Marxist Review*, the Soviet-controlled journal of the world Communist movement, which treated revisionism as a dead issue and focused on the possibility that dogmatism could become the main danger.[23] In any event, party secretary Ponomarev, author of the article, appeared to fall in the category of the "people" who—as Khrushchev complained in his Supreme Soviet speech a few weeks later—"one-sidedly" stress the revisionist danger, and who in this connection name the Yugoslavs, "whether to the point or not,"[24]

[22] *Ibid.*, Nov. 18, 1962.
[23] *World Marxist Review*, No. 11, 1962, pp. 31–38.
[24] *Pravda*, Dec. 13, 1962.

It was not likely that Khrushchev was merely referring here to Peking's anti-Yugoslav vituperation. His chiding of "some people" on the point was pale in comparison with the scathing denunciation elsewhere in the speech of Peking's positions as a whole.

Khrushchev's evident intent was to show that dogmatism was the greater danger, yet his appraisal of the two deviations was tortuous and seemed to echo the crosscurrents on the issue in the Soviet leadership. In fact, he was transparently urging that dogmatism rather than revisionism be declared the main danger—the necessary prerequisite for marking out the Chinese as a full-fledged "deviation" in the Communist movement. This was the obvious conclusion to be drawn from his withering attack on Chinese positions at the Supreme Soviet in Tito's presence. Indeed, a few days after the speech *Pravda* revealed moves in the party to push the Soviet position over to the line that dogmatism was now the main danger. A French party resolution flatly saying dogmatism was now the main danger was printed and was followed by a *Pravda* editorial saying that "Communists of all continents" see that dogmatism is becoming a "more and more serious danger."[25] The move aborted, however, and gave way in January to the standard formula equating the dangers of revisionism and dogmatism—a formula more in line with the shift to conciliatory tactics toward the Chinese by the Soviets that month.

Ponomarev's November *Pravda* article thus had evidently echoed the presence of a more conservative position in the CPSU on the revisionism-dogmatism issue than Khrushchev favored. There indeed was a seeming lack of co-ordination on the point at the series of European party congresses at which leading Presidium members spoke in the fall of 1962 after Cuba. Although the congresses provided the platform for a sharpening attack on the Chinese there were also discordant attacks on Yugoslav revisionism. The Yugoslavs reacted sharply to these. They had already on November 14 criticized the revised CPSU history released at the end of October under Ponomarev's chief editorship for its justification of the ideological grounds for Stalin's attack on the Yugoslavs in

[25] *Ibid.*, Dec. 21, 1962.

1948.[26] The Bulgarian congress resolution, which included condemnation of Yugoslav revisionism, evoked immediate expressions of displeasure from Belgrade.[27] Suslov, who addressed the latter congress, was remarkably restrained on Sino-Soviet issues and did not so much as mention the Albanian "dogmatists" who were then the focus of Moscow's proxy attack on Peking. Nor did he mention the rapprochement in Soviet-Yugoslav relations. As anti-Yugoslav sallies continued to appear the Yugoslavs began to see in them echoes of efforts to conciliate "Stalinist forces" in the U.S.S.R. and the bloc and indications that there were still hopes within the Soviet camp of a "compromise" with the Chinese.[28]

Kozlov in his speech to the Italian party congress the first week of December seemed in tune with Ponomarev's assessment of revisionism as the prime danger. He praised the Italian party for its fight at the 1960 Moscow meeting, and since, against "revisionist splitters and opportunists of every brand"—a phrase that logically would include the Yugoslavs.[29] Here Kozlov was undoubtedly alluding to the fact that the 1960 meeting made revisionism the main danger. This passage preceded his sharp criticism of the Albanians but curiously enough he refrained from using the "dogmatist" epithet against them. His handling of the revisionism-dogmatism issue contrasted with Brezhnev's at the Czechoslovak congress the next day: in citing the 1957 and 1960 Moscow documents Brezhnev reversed the order of reference to revisionism (first) and dogmatism (second), which Kozlov had duly employed, referring instead to "dogmatists and revisionists."[30] Kuusinen, who addressed the Hungarian congress at the end of November, had avoided the issue of Yugoslav revisionism. In sum, there seemed to be less than complete harmony on the issue within the Presidium.

[26] *Radio Zagreb*, Nov. 14, 1962.

[27] *Borba*, Nov. 14, 1962.

[28] *Radio Zagreb* attacked the revised CPSU history for favorably referring to the 1948 Cominform resolution against Yugoslavia viewing it as an attempt to conciliate "Stalinist forces" in the U.S.S.R. and the bloc. *Radio Zagreb* (Nov. 22) also commented pessimistically on anti-Yugoslav statements by Kadar and the Chinese delegate at the Hungarian party congress as signs that "both sides" in the Sino-Soviet dispute were hoping to reach a "compromise."

[29] *Pravda*, Dec. 4, 1962.

[30] *Ibid.*, Dec. 6, 1962.

Khrushchev's retreat on the Stalin issue was paralleled by retreats in the economic field. Already at the November plenum he had made his most unequivocal obeisance in years to the doctrine of the primacy of heavy industry. He stated that heavy industry would continue to play the "decisive" role in the U.S.S.R.'s economic future,[31] an assertion notably in contrast with his tentative effort in May the year before to carry his consumer line to the extreme of discarding the primacy of heavy industry line altogether.

Yet he continued to do battle with the metal-eaters by once again challenging the economic dogma that steel production was the criterion of national power and growth. He argued that chemistry now provided metal substitutes that devalued the metal criterion, and he brought in consumer goods through the back door by noting the wide uses of chemical products in consumer goods as well. He vented his frustration at those in the regime who, he said, still cry "steel!"[32] In the process he exposed his past failure to contain the pressures for more steel in his complaint that the Seven-Year Plan steel goal was being surpassed by thirteen million tons.[33] The regime's energies, he said, could have been better spent increasing production of plastics.

Despite his pleas, however, the November plenum did not shift away from the consensus on resource allocations that had emerged at the Twenty-second Congress. Within three months after the plenum, addressing his constituents on the eve of elections to the Supreme Soviet, Khrushchev disclosed that his consumer program had been indefinitely shelved in favor of the claims of heavy industry and defense.[34] In early March he even paid further deference to military needs by introducing a reference to defense requirements in his "economics over politics" doctrine,[35] a qualification that

[31] *Ibid.*, Nov. 20, 1962.

[32] *Ibid.*

[33] At the January 1961 plenum there were various signs that Khrushchev had sought to hold down steel output. In his January 6 speech for example he specifically indicated that he opposed plans for a 100–2 million ton output by 1965—the Seven-Year Plan target had been set at 86–91 million tons—and implied that the original target was sufficient. It would not be until December, 1963, that Khrushchev would appear to win his point at long last.

[34] *Pravda*, Feb. 28, 1963.

[35] *Ibid.*, March 14, 1963.

had not been included when the doctrine was introduced as Leninist writ in September five months earlier. His pre-election speech at the end of February most clearly exposed the unfavorable turn in Khrushchev's political fortunes after the Cuban crisis. The speech contrasted sharply with the one given by Kozlov at the same time: where Kozlov exuded confidence and optimism about the Soviet present and future, Khrushchev disclosed his disappointed hopes regarding his program and could offer nothing more inspiring to the Soviet populace than the prospect of more belt-tightening.[36]

Kozlov conveyed the impression of a leader who knew where he was going, and he appeared to represent himself as a spokesman for the political center of the newly emergent conservative consensus in the leadership. His confident assertions that all was well in the consumer sector, his cautious but weighted views on resources allocation, and his stress on the importance of ideological over material incentives in the productive process, all seemed to be part of a coherent program. He in effect revealed himself as a judicious metal-eater.[37]

[36] At one point Khrushchev's speech read like a post-mortem on the demise of his pro-consumer program:

"Of course, had the international situation been better, had it been possible to achieve agreement and to shake off the burden of armaments, that would have multiplied the possibilities for a further improvement of the economy and for raising the welfare of the people. The national economy of the Soviet Union is growing anyway. But then it could have grown much faster. It should be said quite frankly that when the government has to examine the distribution of means among various branches of the economy and to decide on where the existing material resources are to be directed, and in what proportions, one often has to solve difficult problems. On the one hand, one would like to build more enterprises producing consumer goods: clothes, footwear, and other goods which improve the daily life of people; one would like to invest more money in agriculture and to expand the housing program. We understand that this must be done for the people. The leaders of our party and our government have risen from the people themselves; they know of the needs of the people and share its life. . . . On the other hand, life dictates the need to spend enormous sums on maintaining our military might at a proper level. Naturally, this diminishes—and cannot but diminish —the opportunity for the people to gain direct benefits. But one has to put up with it in order to defend the gains of the October Revolution, the gains of socialism, and to prevent imperialists from attacking our motherland and launching a general war" (*Pravda*, Feb. 28, 1963).

[37] *Leningradskaya Pravda*, Feb. 27, 1963.

The forward momentum of the conservative countertrend was duly registered in the *Pravda* announcement on April 10 of a Central Committee plenum on ideology scheduled for the end of May, the first of its kind in the post-Stalin era. The accompanying editorial reflected the evident intent of the party conservatives to water down Khrushchev's economics-over-politics doctrine. The editorial counterposed ideology to economics as a generator of productivity in Soviet society and emphasized that ideology and Communist "consciousness" played chief roles in boosting production in the U.S.S.R. The argument was visibly at odds with Khrushchev's basic line since the Twentieth Congress that "material incentives" provided the key to expanding the U.S.S.R.'s productive forces in the "transition to communism."

A New "Supreme State Organ"

The shift toward orthodoxy on resource allocations was duly
. reflected in a major economic reorganization in March, 1963, which was sharply at odds with Khrushchev's philosophy on economic management. A new Supreme Council of the National Economy was established as the "supreme state organ" for industrial management.[38] The new agency was well adapted to preside over the new "hard" orientation of Soviet economic policy; it marked a major recentralization of regime planning and renewed emphasis on the military sector of the economy. Dimitri Ustinov, a top manager in the arms industry, was brought in to head the new agency. The move involved a downgrading of Khrushchev's favored chemicals industry, which was placed under a subordinate state committee in Gosplan that in turn had been subordinated to the new agency. This major reorganization was not foreshadowed at the November plenum or in Khrushchev's reorganization proposals at the plenum. In fact the new agency implicitly challenged Khrushchev's concept of party dominance of economic management, which had underlain his restructuring of the party

[38] *Pravda*, March 14, 1963.

according to the "production principle." The new agency reasserted the role of the state apparatus in relation to the party in the direction of the economy.

Also, just a month before the new Supreme Council was created, the party Presidium had openly slighted the non-Presidium members of the Secretariat who had been given major functional authority over the Soviet economy under Khrushchev's party reform. These secretaries were omitted from the formal election letter signed by the Presidium members specifying the electoral districts where each of the top party leaders was to stand for election to the republican Supreme Soviets.[39] On the past six occasions when such letters were issued in the post-Stalin period all the secretaries had been named. The effect of this departure from protocol was to underline the primacy of the Presidium over the Secretariat and to detract from the prestige of the secretaries who had been appointed to administer Khrushchev's reform. It was hard to miss the impression that the arrangement setting up the new centralized state economic agency had been imposed on Khrushchev rather than engineered by him and was the political offspring of a policy orientation at odds with his own.

It was perhaps not coincidental that the new agency was a close replica of a similar one created after the Hungarian revolt when Khrushchev's policy had been under fire. In December, 1956, Pervukhin was made head of a similarly high-powered centralized directing and planning agency, the Gosekonomkommissia, against Khrushchev's apparent wishes. After regaining the initiative in early 1957 he abolished it by an industrial reorganization setting up the decentralized system of regional Councils of the National Economy.

ECONOMICS OR POLITICS ?

This uneasy period for Khrushchev between November, 1962, and March and April, 1963, was also mirrored in signs of inner-party

[39] *Ibid.*, Feb. 5, 1963.

debate on the economics-over-politics line. The line had provided foundation for his political plans on the eve of Cuba and the conservative resurgence afterward was evident in the dispute over it inside the party.

Athough various Presidium members referred favorably to the line shortly after Cuba, two key figures most directly affected by Khrushchev's party reform betrayed their lack of enthusiasm for it: Suslov, who spoke at the Bulgarian party congress in early November, and Kozlov, who addressed the Italian party congress a month later, conspicuously omitted any mention of the primacy of economics formula. The omission was accompanied by their failure—in contrast to other Presidium members at the time—to single out Khrushchev for praise for his conduct in the Cuban crisis.

This hint of division in the Presidium on the economics-politics issue was followed by increasing indications in the press that the party's old-line ideologues and *apparatchiki* were objecting to Khrushchev's economics line and the party reform it justified. Numerous articles appeared answering unidentified critics who saw the party reform as a violation of the traditional concept of the party. The gist of their complaint was that the ancient sin of treating the party as an economic-administrative apparatus to the neglect of its prime political function was being committed.

While *Kommunist* and *Izvestia* complained that the "reactionary" press saw the reform as "depoliticization" of the party,[40] the term more aptly summarized the traditionalist case against it. Specifically articles in the party press took exception to arguments that the reform contradicted "principles of party work," threatened the "worker-peasant alliance" and party leadership of that alliance, and meant separating "town and country."[41] The common denominator of these arguments was that violence was being done first to the party's day-to-day political-ideological activities, second to the party's political dominance over the peasantry and countryside, and third to the ultimate political goal of eliminating the differences between town and country.

[40] *Kommunist*, No. 18, 1962, p. 8, and *Izvestia*, Dec. 19, 1962.
[41] For example, see the articles by Ye. Bugayev in *Pravda*, Dec. 26, 1962; by Ye. Ligachev in *Ekonomicheskaya Gazeta*, Jan. 26, 1963; and by V. Stepanov in *Izvestia*, Feb. 8, 1963.

The agit-prop chief of the Central Committee Bureau for the RSFSR, Ye. Ligachev, entangled himself in an answer to one sharp query whether the economics-over-politics line contradicted Lenin's criticism of Trotsky in the 1920's for his "economic-administrative" approach to the labor unions. Lenin had insisted then that "politics cannot but have primacy over economics."[42] Someone had recalled that Lenin said the opposite of what he purportedly had said in the rediscovered 1918 document and in the context of post-revolutionary domestic policy. Ligachev merely compounded the felony by attempting to reconcile the two Lenins "dialectically."[43]

With one notable exception the press attack on the criticism pictured the critics as dogmatic and conservative. *Soviet Russia*, for example, usually reflecting the unadulterated Khrushchev, declared in its review of the fifth volume of the Soviet leader's statements on agriculture in January that "only hardened dogmatists" could question the reform and the principle on which it was based.[44] The exception, however, appeared shortly after the November plenum in an article by L. Slepov—a high-ranking apparatus expert on party politics—charging that "only revisionists" could scorn the party's focus on economics and stating that the party "sharply" criticizes those who see "some kind of wall between party and economic work."[45] However, Slepov's remarks applied to the orthodox view as well and he may have raised the revisionist bogey precisely to lessen the vulnerability of the party reform to the charge that it was itself revisionist in inspiration.

The signs of controversy persisted into the first months of 1963. As noted, in March Khrushchev for the first time made military needs an explicit and primary element in the exposition of the policy implications of his primacy-of-economics strategy—reflecting the pressures within the regime for more military spending. And the *Pravda* editorial announcing the ideological plenum for May registered the resurgence of "ideology and politics" in contrast to the economics theme.

[42] Article by Ye. Ligachev, *ibid.*
[43] *Ibid.*
[44] *Sovetskaya Rossiya*, Jan. 5, 1963.
[45] *Ibid.*, Nov. 29, 1962.

Other signs of divergencies on the economics-politics issue cropped up in the press later in April. *Ekonomicheskaya Gazeta*, after soft pedaling the subject for several months—devoted an entire issue (April 20) to promoting Khrushchev's favored policies under the theme that "economics has become the most interesting policy in the entire work of the party, to which all other tasks, both organizational and ideological, must be subordinated."[46] But a week later an article in *Pravda* skipped any reference to the primacy-of-economics formula in an article where it was obviously called for. The article, by an A. Motylev, commemorated the forty-fifth anniversary of Lenin's 1918 article without so much as mentioning the new Lenin document or its economics-over-politics line.[47] Motylev only discussed the article as it was originally published in 1918. The omission was made all the more glaring since *Izvestia* on the same day published a similar anniversary article referring glowingly to the new Lenin document and the primacy-of-economics dictum.[48]

Only a few days before the anniversary articles appeared Khrushchev paid unusual deference to the orthodox view of the role of the party. He even went so far as to undercut the rationale of his November reform. In a speech on April 24 he in effect answered the orthodox objection that the reform tended to convert the party into an economic-administrative apparatus by saying that traditional principles of "party work" had not been abrogated. Thus he gave uncustomary stress to the traditional argument that party committees are primarily "organs of political and organizational leadership" and must not replace economic organs. The emphasis was distinctly counter to the philosophy of party work Khrushchev had long advocated and which he had asserted in no uncertain terms at the November plenum. When he had propelled his new Lenin formula on the primacy of economics to the forefront of party work, he had maintained that once the party was in power "the organization of the national economy, stocktaking and control, and production management assume prime importance,"[49] while all other organi-

[46] *Ekonomicheskaya Gazeta*, April 20, 1963
[47] *Pravda*, April 20, 1963.
[48] *Izvestia*, April 28, 1963.
[49] *Ibid.*, Nov. 20, 1962.

zational, ideological, cultural, and educational work would be subordinate.

Although Khrushchev's shift in emphasis was qualified by his typical insistence on "practical and businesslike methods" in the party's operations, his explicit delimitation of party work to "political and organizational leadership" expressed a view that was hard to reconcile with his former position. This switch—which proved temporary—closely corresponded with a view of party work with which Kozlov had earlier associated himself. In his article appearing simultaneously in *Kommunist* and the *World Marxist Review* in mid-1962, for example, Kozlov enjoined party organs "not to act in the place of government, trade union, co-operative, or other public organizations" by "merging the functions of the party with other bodies or by undue parallelism in work."[50] Moreover, in contrast to Khrushchev's repeated emphasis on the need for "concrete" party guidance of economic work, Kozlov said that the party's guidance should be based on "persuasion, ideological influence, and . . . moral prestige. . . ."[51]

He had also strongly reasserted his view in his February pre-election speech, which had boldly contrasted with Khrushchev's speech the day after in its conservative slant. Kozlov referred to fears in the party that the division into agricultural and industrial branches would lead to a split between the urban and rural party. He asserted that such a result "cannot be allowed in any circumstances."[52]

Although Kozlov may have already been out of the political picture due to his "illness"—announced by the Central Committee on May 4—Khrushchev in his April 24 speech, described above, still evidently deemed it expedient to pacify party traditionalists on the question of the party's role at a time when he was striving to recoup his losses.

In any case, at the beginning of May a tenuous compromise seemed to be reached between the differing views of the economics-politics relationship. A major article by Glezerman, a leading

[50] *World Marxist Review*, No. 6, 1962, p. 8.
[51] *Ibid.*
[52] *Leningradskaya Pravda*, Feb. 27, 1963.

ideological expert, was published in *Kommunist* and was obviously calculated to lay the issue to rest.[53] Though the article's main purpose apparently was to show that the Khrushchev position was good Leninism, its elaborate explanation of that position was manifestly defensive and suggested that the criticism of it had carried force. Behind the Marxist-Leninist scholastics of Glezerman's arguments the political arguments that had taken place between the Khrushchevites and their orthodox critics were discernible.

Glezerman's professed purpose was to correct erroneous views and confusions among party workers over Lenin's contradictory statements on the economics-politics issue. In a display of dialectical gymnastics he explained away the fact that not only the pre-revolutionary but also the post-revolutionary Lenin had repeatedly put politics before economics. Though we can only conjecture, someone in the party may have questioned the historical credentials of the new Lenin document. Elsewhere Glezerman seemed to concede the point to the critics when he said that Lenin made the primacy of economics contingent on the absence of "political dangers and political mistakes."[54] The implication here was that Khrushchev's primacy-of-economics strategy was not necessarily sacrosanct in all circumstances. On the other hand he appeared to squelch an attempt to limit the applicability of this line as a general strategy for the Communist world when he labeled "incorrect" the view that it was feasible only in a "socialist state" moving into communism, that is, in the U.S.S.R.[55]

The Glezerman article marked something of a truce in the debate for the moment at least. This impression was strengthened when on May 8 an issue of the Central Committee historical journal went to press with a new article signed by the Motylev who had failed to mention the new Lenin document in commemorating Lenin's 1918 work in his *Pravda* article. The new article now had a co-signer and it contained approving references to the new Lenin document and the primacy-of-economics line.

[53] *Kommunist*, No. 7, 1963, pp. 30–40.
[54] *Ibid.*, p. 35.
[55] *Ibid.*, p. 31.

By this time also Khrushchev's political condition was on the mend and he was regaining his strength. At the June plenum—the ideological plenum had been postponed a month—it was evident that he had weathered the storm of the Cuban aftermath.

9

KHRUSHCHEV'S LAST OFFENSIVE —
TEST BAN and CHEMICALS

DESPITE THE GRAVE BLOW the Cuban setback administered to Khrushchev's prestige, he succeeded in regaining the initiative in the leadership by mid-1963. He mounted what proved to be his last political offensive in the summer and it continued along with characteristic ups and downs and attendant signs of internal conflict until his sudden overthrow in the fall of 1964. The nuclear test ban and a new Spirit of Moscow provided the external props for a sweeping project for chemicals development at home. He pressed for forced draft development of chemical fertilizers as a fulcrum for shifting the economy's center of gravity toward agriculture and the consumer. On the eve of his fall he began unveiling a comprehensive pro-consumer economic plan obviously calculated to embed his program in the foundations of long-term regime policy. Also he sought to develop a decisive drive against the Chinese opposition abroad and renewed at home the pressure on the Stalin and anti-party group issues. In April, 1964, along with the announcement that the Soviet party wanted a world party meeting to deal with Peking's challenge, it was divulged that "Molotov and others" had been expelled from the party.

174

THE INITIATIVE REGAINED

The signs of Khrushchev's recovery from his political slump after Cuba accumulated during April and May, 1963. Though the precise factors aiding his resurgence can only be surmised, Peking's extremism and the windfall of Kozlov's illness must have helped.

Peking overplayed its hand against Khrushchev in early March by raising the issue of the Sino-Soviet borders. The border reference was a riposte to Khrushchev's sarcastic thrust in his Supreme Soviet speech in December that the CPR's tolerance of Macao and Hong Kong on its territory showed that the Chinese did not practice what they preached. Peking's apparent intention was to dramatize to Moscow the danger of pushing Khrushchev's anti-Chinese vendetta too far; instead it gave Khrushchev a powerful argument against sentiment in the leadership favoring restraint in the conflict with China.

Peking at this time had some grounds for thinking it could exploit a weakness in Khrushchev's armor that was revealed in the CPSU letter to the CCP on February 21. That letter had shown signs of Soviet willingness to make limited concessions for the sake of unity, saying that forthcoming talks should seek to bring differing positions "closer" together. It proposed an agenda for talks clearly amenable to the Chinese view of the priorities in Communist policy, namely, the order of discussion should be (1) the anti-imperialist struggle, (2) the national liberation movement, and (3) strengthening unity.[1]

However, in the Soviet party's next letter after the Chinese raised the border issue the Soviets had radically changed their tune. A new agenda was proposed for the talks in a letter on March 30 that was a standard rendition of Khrushchev's view of Communist priorities, giving primacy to strategies to which Peking most strongly objected. Peaceful economic competition and peaceful coexistence were placed ahead of the struggle against imperialism and the national liberation movement. Unity was the fifth item on the revised agenda. At the same time the letter unequivocally stated

[1] *Pravda*, March 14, 1963.

there was no flexibility in Soviet positions and indicated that the CPSU would be ready to face a break if necessary. The new line was in contrast even with Khrushchev's statement at the East German party congress in January that talks would draft joint theses reflecting a common viewpoint.[2] This letter flatly turned down Peking's invitation to Khrushchev to visit Mao in Peking, a proposal in effect that the Soviet leader come to his Canossa.

The March 30 letter to the Chinese party came at a crucial juncture in Soviet politics. It was released a week before Kozlov's disappearance from public view; his last public appearance was at the Second Congress of Soviet Artists on April 10. It is worth noting in this connection that during the remainder of the month Khrushchev appeared to be striking at Kozlov with the "clarification" of the May Day slogan on Yugoslav "socialism" and an unmistakable attack on his views on industrial policy. The failure to note Yugoslavia's "building of socialism" in the May Day slogans occurred when Kozlov was the senior secretary in Moscow and Khrushchev was in the Crimea.[3] One day after Kozlov dropped from public view and three days after the slogans had been published, *Pravda* in an unprecedented action set the record straight by noting that Yugoslavia was indeed "building socialism."[4] *Pravda*'s lapse on the point had been all the more glaring in the wake of the CPSU's assertion, in its letter of March 30 to the Chinese, that "we consider" Yugoslavia "a socialist country."[5] Notably it was the issue of Yugoslavia's "socialist" bona fides that Mao made a *casus belli* in his conflict with Khrushchev in this period.

[2] *Ibid.*, Jan. 17, 1963. In January and February there was also a hiatus in the public quarrel with the Chinese resulting from the Soviet call for an end to polemics at the SED congress. The call was complemented by action. The CPSU at the end of February made an overture to the Albanians for bilateral talks along with the proposed talks with the Chinese.

[3] While Khrushchev was out of town, an unusual gathering of top leaders was publicized on April 3. Eight Presidium members were present—Brezhnev, Kirilenko, Kozlov, Suslov, Mikoyan, Kosygin, Voronov, and Polyanskiy. The decision on the May Day slogan may have been taken with at least the cognizance, if not the agreement, of all these figures. The slogans appeared in *Pravda*, April 8, 1963.

[4] *Ibid.*, April 11, 1963.

[5] *Ibid.*, April 3, 1963.

On April 24 Khrushchev challenged Kozlov's call in February for heavy investment in new machine-building plants to overcome a machine "shortage." He declared instead that existing plants should be more intensively utilized and cited figures showing that such a policy was twice as profitable as new plant construction. This argument fitted in with the thrust of his speech as a whole, namely, that the heavy industry proponents had permitted massive wastage of resources in the metallurgical and defense industries.

During this very same period speculation was spreading that Khrushchev had been slipping. At the end of March Giuseppe Boffa, Moscow correspondent for the Italian party organ *L'Unita*, asserted in a dispatch that Moscow was living through a "delicate . . . political moment" and alluded cryptically to a "difficult struggle underway" within the U.S.S.R. over a wide range of internal and external policy issues.[6] And Khrushchev himself stimulated the rumors in his April 24 speech by saying that he was aging and could not hold his posts indefinitely.[7]

Though it would seem that Khrushchev had gone through his worst days by the end of April, his April 24 speech, despite its swipe at Kozlov on machine-building and complaint against the metal-eaters' wastage of resources, still mirrored a conservative consensus in the leadership. It registered further retreats from some of his favored themes. He gave short shrift to his "materials incentives" theme in favor of "ideological" stimuli and now, without the qualification regarding food consumption, said steel output was the index of national power. Moreover he echoed the traditional view of the role of the party, declaring an injunction against the party "replacing economic organs" and stressed the party's "political and organizational" leadership of the masses.[8] All these points closely corresponded with positions Kozlov had taken earlier. It thus looked as if Khrushchev had back-tracked as part of an effort to buttress his political position. While what specifically had

[6] Giuseppe Boffa, "Moscow in the Hour of Debate," *L'Unita*, March 31, 1963.

[7] However, a month later a different Khrushchev spoke at a Kremlin reception for Castro. He brushed aside rumors that he would resign, saying his position was good and hoped it would remain so to the end of his days (see *The New York Times*, May 24, 1963).

[8] *Pravda*, April 26, 1963.

happened behind the scenes at this time must remain conjectural, the outward signs of troubles within the leadership raised interesting questions. Had there been a clash in the Presidium and had the question of Khrushchev's resignation been broached? Had Khrushchev himself raised the threat of resignation to force a vote of confidence? The smoke suggested that there had been a fire of some kind. But by the beginning of May Khrushchev seemed to be out of the woods. A Central Committee plenum on May 3 took two significant actions—Kozlov's "illness" was announced and the plenum scheduled for May 28 and on which party conservatives seemed to have pinned their hopes for ideological retrenchment was postponed to mid-June without explanation.[9]

At the June, 1963, plenum on ideology Khrushchev reverted to the characteristic political lines from which he had retreated earlier in the year. At the same time, through the appointment of his Presidium allies Brezhnev and Podgornyy as Central Committee secretaries, he seemed to retrieve much of the leverage he had lost in May, 1960, in the Secretariat. The balance of Presidium-level secretaries thus appeared to tip in Khrushchev's favor.[10] The "successor" spot left by Kozlov seemed to be shared by Brezhnev and Podgornyy, a sign that Khrushchev was now acutely aware of the danger posed by a single heir apparent. The addition of the new Presidium-level secretaries advanced his long struggle since

[9] The announcement of Kozlov's illness was published on May 4 in *Pravda*— the third anniversary of his entrance into the Secretariat in May, 1960. The announcement of the postponement of the ideological plenum was held up for ten days but it explained that the Central Committee took the decision on May 3. Six days later Adzhubei gave the correspondent of the Tokyo newspaper *Mainichi* the least likely of explanations for the gyration over the Yugoslav slogan saying it had been "a mere correction of a technical error." The slogans which are among the most sensitive registers of current party policy are gone over with a fine-tooth comb at the highest levels before they are made public. Further, the slogan affair had come against the background of the other signs noted in the last chapter of differences among the leaders over Yugoslavia's "revisionism" in the Cuban aftermath.

[10] In this connection, it was notable that the occasion which prompted official acknowledgment of Kozlov's illness, his absence from the leadership group at the May Day parade, also marked a decline in Suslov's status in the May Day protocol line-up on the reviewing stand. For the first time since 1960, he returned to a place below Mikoyan.

1960 to restore the Secretariat as his prime lever over the Presidium itself and thus return to the situation he enjoyed after his 1957 victory, when his personal appointees to the Secretariat formed a majority in the Presidium. The shift resulted in a 14-member Secretariat that now exceeded the Presidium proper in size; nonetheless, Khrushchev was still short of his goal of installing into the Presidium itself a majority of secretaries whose undivided loyalty he could count on.

Khrushchev's primacy over his Presidium colleagues was underscored when the Central Committee decree issued by the plenum on the Sino-Soviet talks scheduled for July referred to him as "head" of the Presidium—the first time this formula had appeared in a formal party document of this kind.[11] Of course, one effect of this departure from protocol was to rebuff Chinese attacks on his leadership, but it also was a pointed reassertion of his stature among his colleagues.

In his speech to the plenum Khrushchev returned to the attack on Stalinism and the "group" and signaled an easing of the conservative drive against the de-Stalinizing writers. He failed to praise Stalin's virtues as he had done three months before and renewed the charge that his anti-party foes had opposed his attack on Stalin at the Twentieth Congress because of their "great guilt."[12] He portrayed himself as a man who had stood up to Stalin.

In a remarkable speech at the plenum *Izvestia* editor Adzhubei developed the same theme: his father-in-law was personally guiltless in the matter of Stalin's repressions and had in fact been a voice in the wilderness against the excesses of Stalinism. In a defense of Khrushchev's leadership in the post-Stalin decade, he cited a 1937 Moscow party resolution, when Khrushchev was First Secretary of the organization, to bolster the shaky claim that the Soviet leader had resisted the Stalin cult even during the purges.[13]

In the month after the June plenum it looked as if Khrushchev was also intending to launch out on a new campaign exposing the crimes of Stalinism. His general political offensive was in full swing

[11] *Pravda*, June 22, 1963.
[12] Khrushchev's June 21 speech to the plenum, *ibid.*, June 29, 1963.
[13] *Ibid.*, June 20, 1963.

at this point. The test ban was signed in Moscow and his visit to Tito was upcoming, his personal patronage of Tvardovskiy's long poem satirizing the Stalinist legacy was advertised in *Izvestia*, and the sharpest attack so far on the Chinese leaders—in a CPSU "open" letter—had been launched. Amid these moves came Khrushchev's speech at a Moscow rally in honor of Kadar on July 19. After a few minutes he announced that he was digressing from the prepared text of his speech. What followed was a violent diatribe against Stalinism and all its works and an impassioned defense of the notion that consumer welfare was the only real criterion of "socialist" success. In sum, the speech was an emotionally charged defense of his leadership and policies. Though avowedly aimed at his Chinese enemies, it also struck at the forces that were resisting him at home.

Khrushchev accused his Chinese foes of "poking their noses" into CPSU internal affairs and seeking the overthrow of his leadership and charged that the Chinese had engaged in the full-scale rehabilitation of Stalin in early March with that express aim in view.[14] In utter contrast to what he had said about Stalin's merits in early March, he numbered Stalin among the "tyrants in the history of mankind" who stayed in power with the "headsman's axe."[15] Here he made a rare allusion to the innocent citizens-at-large who perished at the hands of the secret police during the purges and cried, "No one is going to whitewash these black deeds (of the Stalin era),"[16] the latter an equivocal reference applicable to the internal scene as much as to the Chinese. And in a reference to that blemish in his political record, the 1956 Hungarian revolt, he declared that Stalinism, not de-Stalinization, produced rebellion and that "clumsy administrative pressure" must give way to "patient explanation and persuasion."[17]

The attack on Stalinism was accompanied by an equally remarkable digression on the necessity of centering regime policy on the

[14] *Moscow Radio Home Service*, July 19, 1963. Khrushchev's speech to the Moscow rally was broadcast live.
[15] *Ibid.*
[16] *Ibid.*
[17] *Ibid.*

material welfare of the public. Here he argued that if socialism did not give people enough bread, clothing, and leisure time to surpass capitalism in this respect "we shall be idle babblers and not revolutionaries."[18] Curiously enough Khrushchev's comments on the consumer theme were his first "digression from the text" and followed on the heels of praise in the prepared text for Hungary's faithful pursuit of the policy of preferential development of heavy industry. This reference to traditional doctrine was not repeated in his speech and the remainder of the extemporaneous passage was studded with references to "bread" and "empty bellies" and expressions of concern over the attractions of capitalist abundance. Elsewhere, in referring to the test ban, he stressed how valuable a reduction of defense costs would be in aiding the Soviet consumers. Here was Khrushchev's vision of a political regime at home unencumbered by the overt terror and coercion of the Stalin era and capable of meeting the material needs of the population at large.

While Khrushchev was at his demagogic best, one got the feeling that he had bared a bit of his inner political soul and perhaps too much of it. *Pravda* heavily edited and toned down the speech which had been originally carried live over Moscow Radio.[19] It blunted Khrushchev's charge that the Chinese were aiming at the Soviet leadership as such by replacing the reference to "leadership" with "system." It toned down the attack on Stalin and completely excised the remarks about the tyrant and the headsman's axe—a passage the Chinese did not overlook in a withering *Red Flag* attack on Khrushchev's anti-Stalinism two months later.[20] *Pravda* also prudently inserted stock phrases about the freedoms and rights men would enjoy under socialism, balancing out Khrushchev's one-sided emphasis on food and consumer goods.

All the signs suggested that Khrushchev was ready to launch out on a new anti-Stalin campaign and the Moscow rally speech probably aroused fears in the Presidium that the leader was once again planning a strike for greater power. Yet such a campaign did not emerge. An arrangement, whether tacit or explicit, seems to

[18] *Ibid.*
[19] *Pravda*, July 20, 1963.
[20] *Jen-min jih-pao* and *Hung Ch'i*, Sept. 13, 1963

have been struck in the succeeding months within the leading group, reflecting Khrushchev's enhanced political strength but at the same time asserting the group's restraining weight. The indicator of the new balance of forces was once more the anti-party group issue. At long last it was announced at a Central Committee plenum that "Molotov and others" had been expelled from the party.

THE IMAGE OF UNITY

It was none other than Suslov, in a long report to the February CPSU plenum on the deepening Sino-Soviet crisis,.who briefly announced that Molotov and other group members—for whom the Chinese leaders had expressed "sympathy"—had been expelled.[21] Suslov gave no further details and the available evidence permits us to assume only that the action had occurred sometime between early 1962 when expulsion demands ceased to appear in the party press and the release of the Suslov report in April, 1964. Khrushchev had achieved his minimal goal, but only after five to seven years of effort. The unobtrusive manner of the revelation in the speech of a figure who had resisted the move in the past raised as many questions as it answered. It seemed evident that the very character of the move was the product of a calculated high-level decision. The decision mirrored Khrushchev's basic political strength and the choice of Suslov to make the revelation emphasized the point since he had been among the moderates on the "group" issue. In his February plenum report he went further than he ever had in publicly allowing that Molotov and other group members were not simply guilty of political mistakes but of crimes under Stalin.[22] Suslov's concession of this point flowed logically from the loss of political ground he had suffered earlier at the June

[21] Suslov's report to the plenum, Feb. 14, 1964, was published in *Pravda*, April 3, 1964.

[22] Suslov made a passing reference to the responsibility for repressions under Stalin of "many" of the group members, whom he did not name, at the Twenty-second Congress, but his remarks on the group as a whole had still put him on the side of the moderates on the issue at that time.

plenum where his influence in the Secretariat had been diluted by the entrance of Presidium members Brezhnev and Podgornyy into that body. Suslov also paid greater deference to Khrushchev's leadership than he had ever done before.

Prior to the February, 1964, plenum there were unmistakable signs that Suslov was under political attack from Khrushchev. The attack was manifest in moves furthering the public rehabilitation of Voznesenskiy, the Politburo member purged and put to death under Stalin in 1949–50.[23] The renewal of the process of reinstating Voznesenskiy began just prior to the June, 1963, plenum when Khrushchev had returned to the political offensive. The political overtones of the development were hard to miss. Suslov was the only top leader of the ruling group linked with the affair. It was he who had delivered the indictment of Voznesenskiy's "anti-Marxist" economic views in *Pravda* in December, 1952—the first public attack made on Voznesenskiy since he had disappeared three years

[23] The rehabilitation of Voznesenskiy—who had been a fast-rising party figure and economic theorist—was unofficially begun by Khrushchev in his secret speech to the Twentieth Party Congress and subsequently he received favorable mention in official biographies. However, despite references to his best-known economic work on the U.S.S.R.'s World War II economy, the question of the political acceptability of his theoretical views was skirted. But coincident with Suslov's loss of ground in the Secretariat, the Central Committee's party historical journal published an article which signaled the restoration of Voznesenskiy's political reputation and respectability as an economic theorist (*Voprosy Istorii KPSS* [*Problems of CPSU History*], No. 6, 1963, pp. 94–98). The article was the harbinger of a rash of articles six months later in the Soviet press marking Voznesenskiy's sixtieth birth anniversary. All protested the injustice of Voznesenskiy's condemnation and all asserted the validity and continuing relevance of his economic views.

The author of the *Pravda* anniversary article was a G. Sorokin, who also was a target of Suslov's 1952 attack. Sorokin raised a sensitive point of regime political history. He asserted that Voznesenskiy had been a victim of the Leningrad purge under Stalin—an assertion first made by Khrushchev in his secret speech in 1956 and reported by Shelepin at the Twenty-second Congress. The claim conceivably could be used not only to link Suslov with Stalin's last major purge but Kozlov as well. At the Twenty-second Congress, Shvernik, chief of the party control commission, had manipulated the dates of the Leningrad purge to make it appear that it had taken place in a period during which Kozlov had held top posts in the Leningrad party organization. Shvernik indicated that the purge spanned the years from 1949 to 1952, whereas previous mentions of the purge had implied it was carried out in 1949.

earlier.[24] Suslov had depicted him as a dangerous innovator whose theories denied the "objective" economic laws of socialism.[25]

Nonetheless, the revelation of the party expulsion of group members in Suslov's report at the February, 1964, plenum also registered something less than a massive triumph for the Khrushchevites. At the Twenty-second Congress they had clearly pressed for a public ritual of confession, purge, and perhaps even a show trial of the group leaders for their "crimes." Suslov's revelation of the expulsions was designed to rid the Chinese of any notion that there were exploitable cleavages within the Soviet leadership or that Khrushchev could be "isolated" from his colleagues. At the same time his remarks implied that the issue of the anti-party group was now passé as far as Soviet internal politics was concerned. However, there was no ground for assuming that the question of the "group" had actually been resolved with the Suslov announcement; in fact, it actually sharpened the issue. It could only increase the other leaders' fears that Khrushchev would seek to use the expulsions as a factional weapon. There was no guarantee that he would not press the issue of the anti-party group's "crimes" for partisan aims whenever he considered circumstances favorable to such action.

In fact, disharmony within the leadership over the matter was suggested in an article appearing in *Pravda* a few weeks prior to the Suslov plenum report.[26] The article, signed by an old Bolshevik, L. Shaumyan, asserted that Kirov and other party leaders on the eve of the purges of the thirties had sought to head off Stalin's drive for absolute power. Shaumyan's underlying message was clear. The leader who strikes for total power may be challenged by his associates and the Stalinist generation of leaders, including Khrushchev, shared responsibility whether direct or indirect for the purges. The article scarcely accorded with Khrushchev's repeated effort to shunt off all the guilt for Stalinist repressions on his enemies.

[24] *Pravda*, Dec. 24, 1952.
[25] *Ibid.*
[26] *Ibid.*, Feb. 7, 1964.

Shaumyan stressed that by the time of the 1934 Congress the party had defeated all its internal enemies and there was no justification for further purges. However, he said that "many" Communists were alarmed by the growth of the Stalin cult and that some Congress delegates, "primarily those who remembered Lenin's testament well," moved to stop Stalin's strike for total power.[27] He said Stalin got wind of the move and "knew that the old Leninist cadres of the party would be a decisive hindrance for the further strengthening of his position and for the concentration in his own hands of even greater sole power."[28] Shaumyan indicated Stalin used the murder of Kirov for "a severe reprisal against all people who did not suit him" and subsequently had over half the delegates to the 1934 Congress and 70 per cent of the Central Committee executed.[29] According to Shaumyan, an irreparable blow against the "old Leninist guard" had been struck.[30] Shaumyan not only quoted from the Congress speeches of a whole list of the victims but also cited innocuous quotes from Khrushchev's and Mikoyan's speeches. The obvious point could not be missed—Khrushchev and Mikoyan were not among the old Leninist guard or among those who "did not suit him (Stalin)."[31] At the least Shaumyan's article complicated Khrushchev's disclaimer of all responsibility.

Shaumyan had entered dangerous political territory and the matters he had raised could be turned against, as well as in favor of, Khrushchev's political interests. This aspect of the article was particularly notable in its reference to Yenukidze's participation at the 1934 Congress and his subsequent purge following a report to the June, 1935, plenum by Yezhov in which he attacked Yenukidze as a political "degenerate."[32] Khrushchev and Zhdanov publicly denounced him in speeches to the Moscow and Leningrad party organizations shortly thereafter, explaining why he had been expelled from the party.

Whether Khrushchev was directly linked with the purge or not, there was a dramatic sign in the party press in May, 1962, that

[27] *Ibid.*
[28] *Ibid.*
[29] *Ibid.*
[30] *Ibid.*
[31] *Ibid.*
[32] Schapiro, *The Communist Party of the Soviet Union*, p. 404.

the question was a sensitive one in party politics. *Izvestia* on May 18 had carried a commemorative article on Yenukidze noting that he had been "calumniated, arrested, and convicted" in 1937.[33] The very next day *Pravda* carried a similar article which corrected the record. It noted that Yenukidze had been "calumniated" starting in 1935 and later had been arrested and convicted.[34] Someone in the party apparatus apparently had sought to counter *Izvestia*'s effort to gloss over the embarrassing fact that Khrushchev had been one of the "calumniators" of Yenukidze in June, 1935! Someone seemed to be warning that the use of rehabilitations for factional purposes was a two-edged sword.

In this connection, it is notable that the circumstances surrounding the announcement of the party expulsion of "Molotov and others" bore earmarks of a consensus against rocking the boat in internal leadership politics. Undoubtedly the increasingly total Chinese challenge after Cuba to Soviet leadership as a whole as well as to Khrushchev personally was producing a strong impulsion toward unity within the top group against the outside enemy. Khrushchev gained a strong tool for demanding a vote of confidence in his leadership, which was symbolized by the announcement of Molotov's party expulsion; he sorely needed such a vote in the face of Peking's relentless abuse. For six long months, from September, 1963, to February, 1964, Khrushchev was vilified in a series of *Red Flag* attacks without any counter-response from the Soviet party. But even the backing for Khrushchev reflected in the expulsion announcement seemed to have a price, one that seemed to be echoed in an unusual emphasis both on the internal stability of the leading group and on the "collective" nature of the party leadership.

The idea of a stable internal leadership situation was conveyed by Kozlov's formal retention of his Secretarial and Presidial posts despite his disability. Although there were obvious grounds for announcing his political retirement, a succession of party plenums passed without such action. Instead his name continued to appear

[33] *Izvestia*, May 18, 1962.
[34] *Pravda*, May 19, 1962.

in official listings of the membership of the Presidium and the Secretariat. The same impression was distinctly conveyed in the celebration of Khrushchev's seventieth birthday in April. Though the Soviet press gave extensive play to the Soviet leader, there was no picture of the Communist "chief" (*vozhd'*) over and above his colleagues, nor even a picture of the indispensable man. And the letter of greetings signed by the Presidium members, in contrast with their greetings on his sixty-fifth birthday in 1959, neither credited him with being the initiator of all the major policies of the regime nor referred to him as "our senior comrade."[35] Part of the motive for the Presidium's not spotlighting him as the prime leader of course was to show a tacit contrast between the cult of Mao in China and the "collective" style of leadership in the U.S.S.R. But then again these images mirrored a political reality. Mao was a genuine communist *vozhd'* while Khrushchev had not succeeded in attaining that exalted status.

THE CHEMICALS PROGRAM

The June, 1963, plenum had also marked Khrushchev's return to the offensive in economic policy. His refurbished chemicals program which he unveiled in the summer of 1963 served as a strategic plan in the renewed attack on the traditional structure of the Soviet economy. The over-all theme of the plan was the priority development of chemicals and it focused on a massive expansion of the output of chemical fertilizers for agriculture. Although it might have been expected that the overhauled chemicals program would enjoy clear sailing after the leadership changes at

[35] The drift of the letter was in tune with an uncharacteristic disclaimer by Khrushchev at the Twenty-second Congress in his second speech that he was not the initiator of any of the policies of the regime but that everything was the product of the joint endeavors of the Presidium—an assertion not only discordant with Khrushchev's conduct before and after the Congress but also in open contradiction to the praises of his leadership by his closest supporters. Compare the Presidium's birthday greetings, *ibid.*, April 19, 1959, with its greetings read by Mikoyan at a Kremlin dinner on April 17, 1964, *ibid.*, April 18, 1964.

the June plenum, the old pattern of controversy over economic policy reasserted itself. Both before and after the approval of a major step-up in the pace of chemicals output at the December "chemicals" plenum, it was once more evident that Khrushchev's renewed initiative in economic policy was arousing resistance.

The plenum's formal approval of the chemicals program did not put an end to the vigorous contention between the Khrushchev forces and the defenders of the status quo in economic policy. Two months later Khrushchev explicitly defended his program against criticism within the regime. That criticism was apparently severe enough to cause him to protest against "hidebound" and dogmatic attitudes that saw his economic policy as a retreat from the "general line" of the party.[36]

Although these critics apparently were in a less advantageous position than they had occupied in the Cuban aftermath, their restraining influence was discernible. At the December plenum a significant scaling down of the original chemical fertilizer goal proposed and advocated by Khrushchev was evidently due to such an influence. Prior to the meeting a call for a lesser program was published,[37] and at the plenum the more ambitious program Khrushchev had outlined in his speeches and a memorandum to the Presidium in July was duly replaced by a more modest one. The fertilizer target for 1970 was set at seventy to eighty million tons at a cost of four and one-half billion rubles. Thus an investment and production cutback of about 25 per cent had been made in Khrushchev's original fertilizer plan.

[36] *Ibid.*, Feb. 15, 1964.

[37] A letter from seven agricultural "experts" on *Pravda*'s and *Izvestia*'s front pages in the month before the plenum challenged the scope and rationale of Khrushchev's fertilizer plan which he had presented in July to his Presidium colleagues in a memorandum. Khrushchev had proposed a goal of 100 million tons of chemical fertilizer for 1970 involving an estimated 5.8-billion-ruble investment and stated that even greater expenditures might be required to meet the goal. Eighty-six of the 100 million tons were specifically earmarked for crops. Although addressing their complaint to the Ministry of Agriculture, the "experts" declared that the 86-million-ton goal for agricultural crops was excessive. They called for "some reduction" of funds for fertilizer investment and a goal "somewhat less" than the 86 million tons. The experts' criticism amounted to an attack on Khrushchev's program as an exaggeration of actual needs (*Pravda* and *Izvestia*, No. 17, 1963).

If he had had second thoughts on his plan, they had developed amid publicly expressed objections to it.[38] The objections to his fertilizer goal had appeared after his commitment of scarce resources for wheat purchases in the West had already aroused dissent in the regime. At the December plenum Khrushchev had lashed out at "some people" who had favored belt-tightening to deal with the harvest debacle of that year—an approach the Soviet leader characterized as an imitation of the "method of Stalin and Molotov" who he said starved the people.[39] It is worth recalling that Khrushchev's campaign for his fertilizer program in the summer and fall coincided with a period when the full impact of the 1963 harvest disaster was beginning to be felt.

The issue of how to deal with the harvest crisis evidently became entangled with the question of the fertilizer program. Khrushchev had argued that his program would prevent such catastrophes in the future. But there were apparently some in the leadership who already felt that the wheat deal with the West engineered by Khrushchev to tide the U.S.S.R. over was an unnecessary extravagance and drain on scarce funds. In fact in an interview on October 25 Khrushchev intimated that the party Presidium had debated which of two "paths" should be followed to cope with the harvest crisis: belt-tightening or purchases of wheat abroad.[40] Moreover, at the end of October the Soviet Trade Union chief seemed to echo the presence of opposition to the wheat deal. Grishin told the trade union council on October 28 that the harvest was "fully adequate to meet the population's needs" and advocated economies in the use of grain and administrative controls on storage and distribution.[41]

[38] The tacit repudiation of Khrushchev's earlier proposals was made the more pointed by the fact that the experts referred to a target of 77 million tons by 1970 as though this—rather than Khrushchev's 100-million-ton goal—were the figure in question. While the whole matter was presented as a mere technical suggestion, the impression was hard to avoid that Khrushchev had been restrained from committing the economy to an unrealistic course. The belated scaling down of the goal, seemingly through the intervention of the "experts," was hardly a political boon to Khrushchev, who characteristically presented himself as the regime's expert par excellence on agriculture.

[39] *Pravda*, Dec. 10, 1963.

[40] *Ibid.*, Oct. 27, 1963.

[41] *Trud*, Oct. 29, 1963.

The ups and downs of Khrushchev's agricultural plan seemed to correspond with fluctuations in Soviet foreign policy during the same period. During the summer when he launched the chemicals drive there appeared to be a general harmony among the various facets of Soviet policy: the test ban and détente with the West, renewed intimacy with Tito, reconciliation with liberal writers, increased polemics with China. With the fall, however, discordant notes intruded, notably incidents on the autobahn and the Barghoorn case. These episodes even led U.S. Ambassador Thompson to ask Khrushchev at a Kremlin reception, "What happened to the 'Spirit of Moscow'?" [42] At the same time, Moscow sought to call off disputes with the Chinese. Whatever the specific motivations behind each of these actions, they were of little help to Khrushchev's argument that the time was safe to embark on expensive domestic programs. As usual the most powerful argument in the arsenal of the critics of Khrushchev's economic policy was that military requirements must hold priorty over other needs. The force of this argument in party councils was echoed in developments both at the December plenum and after.

Rather than a wholly new and expanded chemicals program the plan adopted at the plenum and ratified at the Supreme Soviet later in the month mainly involved a renewed regime commitment to overcome the severe lag in the original program for chemistry established years before. That program had lost out to steel and guns. Indeed the decision to commit the considerable resources to overcome the lag did mark a victory, but a belated and limited one, for Khrushchev in his battle to compel a shift of economic policy toward his favored long-term goals. The victory was characterized by cuts in the arms budget at the Supreme Soviet after the plenum; however, the reduction of the military budget was more symbolic than substantial—some 600 million rubles—and the move was counterbalanced by the equally symbolic cutback in housing construction for the Soviet population.

Once again Khrushchev proposed a troop cut in connection with his program and once again there was an almost immediate

[42] *The Washington Post*, Nov. 8, 1963.

display of resistance to the idea from Soviet military quarters. And once again the military opposition to troop reduction was an early symptom of a more general conflict within the regime among forces which expected to gain or lose from the implementation of Khrushchev's policy. Soviet military leaders conspicuously failed to endorse the troop cut plan. Only Marshals Malinovskiy and Yeremenko mentioned it at all following the December plenum, but without indicating their approval or disapproval. Malinovskiy merely repeated Khrushchev's own tentative phraseology at the plenum that the "possibility" of some reduction of forces was being contemplated and Yeremenko referred to the "forthcoming cut in the Soviet armed forces." Malinovskiy's reference did not appear in the Soviet press but in articles signed by him for the East European press,[43] while Yeremenko's was in a Soviet periodical for foreign distribution, the English-language *Moscow News* (January 11, 1964). Just a week after Khrushchev made his troop cut proposal Marshal Chuikov, the Soviet ground forces commander, not only ignored the proposal but argued vigorously in *Izvestia* in favor of developing the large ground forces, asserting that the Western nations were "not disposing of their ground forces, but on the contrary, were steadily developing them."[44]

The signs of displeasure in the military leadership over the troop cut were amplified by articles in the military press advancing the idea that no relaxation of a broad-gauged Soviet military build-up was feasible or justifiable then or in the future. A two-part article by the military commentator Colonel General N. Lomov in *Red Star* on January 7 and 10, 1964, typified this line of argument. He emphatically reasserted the "combined arms" concept, pointedly

[43] The articles were published in *Zolnierz Wolnosci* (Warsaw), Feb. 22, 1964, and *Neues Deutschland* (East Berlin), Feb. 23, 1964.

[44] *Izvestia*, Dec. 22, 1965. Other aspects of the Chuikov article as well as the evidences of military discontent over Khrushchev's troop cut plan after the December plenum are dealt with in detail in Wolfe's *Soviet Strategy at the Crossroads*. The evidences of tension between Khrushchev and the military establishment over the troop reduction issue from 1960 to 1963 are comprehensively analyzed in Matthew Gallagher's "Military Manpower: A Case Study," *Problems of Communism*, XIII (May–June, 1964), 53–62.

stressing that victory in modern war required "a multi-million-man modern army."

Other similar warnings appeared in the military press during the next few months regarding the continuing growth of Western military budgets, conventional weapons, and manpower strength— materials drawing a particularly threatening picture of Western military power and war preparation. Articles also appearing in *Red Star* spoke of the indispensability of conventional forces in future wars and the necessity of a combined-arms strategy. Such arguments once more betrayed concern in the Soviet military establishment that revival of the troop reduction idea was only the harbinger of further encroachments into the military sphere in Khrushchev's search for resources for his long-term economic program. The arguments also seemed designed to remove the underpinnings of Khrushchev's more confident and optimistic assessments of present and future Soviet strength and the prospects of sustained détente in East-West relations—assessments that supported his argument that heavy industrial and arms expenditures had become disproportionate with the U.S.S.R.'s needs and a threat to Soviet economic development.

Behind such argument lay the resentment of Soviet military leaders against Khrushchev's intrusions into their professional province. In this connection, Malinovskiy's forceful assertion of the military's role in regime decisions relating to military policy in his article in *Red Star* on Khrushchev's birthday (April 17, 1964) seemed hardly coincidental. While favorably referring to Khrushchev, he also pointedly recalled that the party had rejected Stalin's practice of arbitrarily imposing his views on the military and stressed that full-dress consultation of the political leadership with military leaders and experts had become the basis of any regime action in the military sphere.[45] In this manner Malinovskiy

[45] Malinovskiy said:

"Before deciding on any problem and adopting a practical decision on it, members of the party Central Committee and members of the CPSU Central Committee Presidium, make a detailed study of the state of affairs in the army and navy, of the urgent problems in consolidating the country's defense capacity, of urgent problems of military development, and consult leading military cadres. After this a concrete decision is reached."

served notice both that the Soviet military had come to expect a full hearing for its views and that it opposed any unilateral actions by political leaders affecting its interests.

Khrushchev's irritation at the persistent pressures on him from military leaders was betrayed in a remark he made during his trip to Egypt the next month. In a digression from the prepared text of a speech to Egyptian military officers on May 18, he said, "I do not know how it is in the U.A.R., but my esteemed friend the President would be able to tell me whether a military person ever tells him: 'Do not give us any more weapons, there are enough of them.' For with us this is not said." [46] The remark, although offered in a jocular vein, touched a sensitive point.

It was already evident by the time of the Central Committee plenum in February that Khrushchev had met with more than the military's objections to troop cuts: he was contending with broad resistance to his program as a whole from political and bureaucratic forces within the top echelons of the party and government apparatus. His unscheduled speech to the party meeting (the main report was given by Minister of Agriculture Volovchenko) was clearly aimed at the dissenting opinions within the regime and was largely devoted to a polemical justification of his new policy course.[47] The defense of the rationale of his program was the more striking in that its formal adoption at the December plenum just two months before had presumably placed its premises beyond debate. Although Khrushchev at various points attributed criticism to his program to hostile Western commentators, articles subsequently appearing in the Soviet press specifically referred to domestic critics as authors of the type of criticism he sought to refute.

Khrushchev went to unusual lengths to show that his chemicals program would adversely affect neither Soviet economic growth

[46] *Moscow Radio*, May 18, 1964. *Pravda* on the following day changed Khrushchev's words so as to remove the implied complaint and to give a wholly favorable aspect to the military's desire for funds. Further, the remark was recast in terms of "appropriations" rather than "weapons": "I do not know how it is in your country . . . but in our country the military, in their solicitude for the strengthening of the country's defense capacity are in no hurry to declare: 'Enough appropriations for these ends!' "

[47] *Pravda*, Feb. 15, 1964.

nor the U.S.S.R.'s military posture. He heatedly denied the charge —ascribed to "imperialists"—that the chemicals program was a deviation from the U.S.S.R.'s traditional commitment to heavy industry.[48] He explained that chemicals was a part of heavy industry and elaborately demonstrated through statistical data that the bulk of chemical production ranked as "means of production."[49] He was similarly defensive in assuring his listeners at the plenum that the country's defense needs would continue to enjoy top priority even if this required postponements of pressing consumer requirements. In his reference to the reduction of the military budget and the troop cut Khrushchev sought to calm the military's fears that the chemical program would harm the U.S.S.R.'s military power. He offered assurances that "we realize that economizing [on military costs] must be reasonable" and that "it is impossible to reduce the size of appropriations for armaments and the army to a degree that would allow the imperialists to surpass us in armed strength and thus impose their will and policy on us."[50] All in all the speech tried to assure the plenum that no unduly radical turn in Soviet domestic policy was being engineered.

Khrushchev's assertions in February were in sharp contrast to those he had made earlier in campaigning for his chemicals program prior to the December plenum. He had indicated that the huge resources needed for the program would necessitate inroads into the traditionally favored metal and defense industries.[51] He had foreseen a slowdown of other branches of the economy in favor of the priority development of chemicals and had buttressed this idea by advancing the view that the country had already created a "first-class" heavy industry and that the time was ripe for directing

---

[48] *Ibid.*

[49] *Ibid.*

[50] *Ibid.*

[51] In his interview in July, 1963, with the U.S. Secretary of Agriculture Orville Freeman, for example, Khrushchev specifically said he would get the money for chemical fertilizer production from the defense budget (N. S. Khrushchev, *The Construction of Communism in the USSR and the Development of Agriculture* [Moscow: State Publishing House for Political Literature, 1964], Vol. 8, p. 51).

"immense" funds toward chemicals, agriculture, and consumer production.[52]

At the February plenum Khrushchev, as before, put his pro-consumer line temporarily in the background in deference to pressures from traditional opinion on economic policy. Although he displayed his sensitivity to the pressure of conservative opinion, at the same time he kept intact the basic premise underlying his program, namely, that it must entail readjustments of resource allocations patterns. He also added an argument designed to remove the grounds for the complaint that his program upset the proper relationship between heavy and light industry. He argued that the distinction between heavy and light industry was no longer clear-cut and that chemicals, although part of heavy industry, served the needs of both industrial reproduction and consumption. Khrushchev asserted that the question of a conflict between "group A" and "group B"—that is, between heavy and light industry—was not relevant. He had introduced this assertion as long ago as the Twenty-second Congress and it appeared later at various times in connection with debate over economic policy.

Khrushchev went on to pinpoint areas within the regime where stumbling blocks to his policies had been raised. He singled out regime planners and warned state planning officials that departmental interests must be subordinated to the general state interests of developing the most "progressive"—notably chemistry—industrial branches. He attacked the practice of carrying over planning patterns from year to year without change or adjustment. He struck at the state metallurgy committee in particular and warned the officials in charge of the steel industry that they must understand what is new and draw the necessary conclusions.

In an especially revealing part of his plenum speech Khrushchev warned the regime that the chemicals program should not be dismissed as a passing fancy: "I would like to emphasize—and it is necessary that all the comrades understand this—chemistry is not

[52] See, for example, Khrushchev's press conference published in *Pravda*, Oct. 27, 1963, and his report to the December CPSU plenum, *ibid.*, Dec. 10, 1963.

a fad."[53] It should not be assumed, he added, that the program was started for the sake of a "craze."[54] He complained that planning officials treated chemicals as secondary in allocating resources. This he said had been the case despite the fact that since 1958 it should have been "beyond question that chemistry should be given priority."[55] It was not credible that the chronic insubordination with which Khrushchev charged the planners was perpetrated solely on their own initiative against the manifest will of the political leadership. The full explanation of the phenomenon could only be sought in the lack of consensus on the issue within the leadership itself. Only in such a situation could planning functionaries have expected to escape penalties for decisions adverse to the chemicals program. It was also difficult to miss the impression that Khrushchev's protest was aimed at Kosygin, in particular, who held prime responsibilities in regime planning in the period when chemicals had taken second place to steel.

Khrushchev's pro-consumer policy had in fact lost ground in the period between the U-2 incident and Cuba. This outcome was not simply due to the built-in bias of the economy in favor of heavy industry but was also due to the successful resistance of the defenders of traditional policy to Khrushchev's pressures for basic shifts in the economy. By the time of the February plenum he was faced with the problem of how to muster the massive pressure needed to make up for the ground his economic policy had lost.

His effort in this direction after the plenum was reflected in new forays against economic traditionalism in the press. Articles by pro-reform economists appeared attacking "theoretical economists" and "practical workers" who opposed shifts in resource allocations patterns. The most explicit posing of the issue appeared in a major *Pravda* article at the end of February. The economic theorist A. Arzumanyan, head of the Institute of World Economics and International Relations, boldly struck out at the defenders of heavy industrial priority and openly recommended the heterodox doctrine of equal rates of growth for heavy and light industry and

[53] *Ibid.*, Feb. 15, 1964.
[54] *Ibid.*
[55] *Ibid.*

even future priority for the latter. Asserting that the "party" was now engaged in struggle against "dogmatism" in economic policy, he lashed out at economic theorists and working officials who still adhered to Stalinist dogmas on economic growth and opposed increased investments in the civilian economy as a "consumer approach."[56] He tarred them as advocates of Molotov's alleged concept of "production for production's sake."

Arzumanyan was simply carrying Khrushchev's arguments for a shift in economic policy to their logical conclusion, building on Khrushchev's assertion at the February plenum that there were no longer grounds for opposing "group A" to "group B," that is, heavy to light industry.[57] Khrushchev had not taken as forthright a position as Arzumanyan at either the December or the February plenum, but his sympathy for the view was already clear and he held back from openly espousing it only out of political considerations. Indeed he had given it off-the-cuff endorsement as far back as the British trade fair in 1961 and the arguments he had used in support of his program were the kin of Arzumanyan's.[58] The Arzumanyan article was in fact an important ploy in his effort to shift the balance of opinion within the regime in favor of his long-term economic policy.

[56] *Ibid.*, Feb. 24–25, 1964.

[57] Arzumanyan said: "Historical experience shows that periods of more rapid development of group A than group B are possible, but periods of equal development of both groups or even the more rapid development of group B are possible."

[58] At the end of February Khrushchev forcefully pressed another of his key arguments at an unanticipated Central Committee conference, which heightened the impression that the February plenum had left much unfinished business on the docket. The conference was called to "implement" the decisions of the February plenum and was attended by the top leadership. He focused on the need for radical and immediate improvement of material incentives on Soviet farms.

The incentive issue was simply another side of the coin of the resource allocations problem. And within a few weeks after the conference another pro-reform economist, L. Gatovskiy, made the point explicit in an article in *Economic Gazette* (April 16). Gatovskiy pictured the problem of inadequate economic incentives as directly and adversely affected by the existing pattern of resource allocations. Echoing debate in the regime, he attacked the "widespread" view that wage increases should not accompany increases in labor productivity due to technology, arguing that the aim of increasing material incentives requires

By the beginning of the fall of 1964 Khrushchev apparently decided to strike forth on a new campaign to convert the arguments Arzumanyan had presented into fundamental regime policy. At a joint meeting of the CPSU Presidium and the Council of Ministers at the end of September he proposed a virtual revolution in regime planning, calling for a decisive shift in both the structure of the Soviet economy and the future direction of its development.[59] He unveiled a scheme for putting consumer production in "first place" in regime planning.[60] Consumer priority, he indicated, was to be the basis of a new long-term plan. He was reviving the Malenkov heresy and evidently intended to carry it much further than Malenkov himself had ever dreamed of doing. At the same time Khrushchev's proposal flowed logically from and rounded out the strategy he had developed after he regained the political initiative in mid-1963.

His move at the party-government meeting represented his most direct attack on the entrenched economic traditionalism that had hindered his economic program. By contrast with his defen-

---

more funds as well as effective use of wage scales and bonuses. Consumer goods production must, he said, at the same time be accelerated to prevent inflation. Here Gatovskiy attacked the defenders of heavy industrial priority challenging the "dogma" widespread among "economists" and "practical workers" which favor even greater tempos of heavy industry over consumer industry. While careful to pay deference to preferential development of heavy industry, he warned that the policy must not be pursued to the detriment of increasing incentives and consumer production. According to Gatovskiy, "When the high tempo of development of group A and of production accumulation is achieved through holding back the tempo of the increasing production of consumer goods and thereby weakening material incentives, then the growth of all social production will unavoidably begin to be artificially slowed down. . . . "

[59] Khrushchev's new scheme emerged at one of the series of expanded party-government executive meetings held under his chairmanship after June, 1963, devoted to economic policy and planning. Khrushchev appeared to use the meetings as a device for shunting aside the new Supreme Economic Council headed by heavy industrial expert D. F. Ustinov. The latter super-directorate had been created in the aftermath of the Cuban crisis in March, 1963, apparently to preside over the turn to the more traditional economic policy that had begun to emerge in that period. The expanded executive meetings under Khrushchev's direction were clearly calculated to return regime policy to his favored pro-consumer orientation and their agendas were focused on consumer welfare, chemistry, and agriculture.

[60] *Pravda*, Oct. 2, 1964.

siveness early in the year, Khrushchev now made virtually complete his public identification with the proposition that an equal or preferential growth of consumer industries should replace the preferential growth of heavy industry as regime economic doctrine. Khrushchev previously had withheld endorsement of the doctrine in his formal statements, although it had been the unstated premise of his pro-consumer arguments over the years.

Khrushchev's espousal of the heterodox line at the CPSU Presidium-Council of Ministers forum—leaving fewer avenues for tactical retreats on the issue than he had in the past—was a measure of his determination to accomplish the basic reorientation of economic policy he had long sought. In contrast to the previous year, when Khrushchev launched his chemicals drive amid a harvest disaster in the countryside, this move was mounted as a good harvest was being delivered to the state, a point which Khrushchev duly stressed at the party-government meeting.

According to the September 22 *Pravda* account of Khrushchev's speech (the text was never released) he told high party and government leaders that the "main task" of the new economic plan was to insure the preferential development of consumer industries.[61] The substance of his remarks—according to *Pravda*'s edited account —was that heavy industry and defense had now been adequately developed and the pace and focus of future development plans should be shifted in favor of consumer welfare and light industry. The only counterbalance to Khrushchev's call for a consumer plan were statements to the effect that defense would not be neglected under the new plan. Thus at two points he stressed the "constant" solicitude of the regime in "further" strengthening defense. Such statements, however, were clearly tangential to the main thrust and tone of his argument and bore all the earmarks of a perfunctory reassurance to the military.

The Khrushchev position sharply contrasted with his defensive stance on his chemicals program at the February plenum. On that occasion he had assured the plenum that consumer requirements would continue to bow to defense needs in line with traditional

[61] *Ibid.*

policy. Now, less than eight months later, he unequivocally asserted that consumer welfare must come "first" in regime planning. He also declared that the traditionally defense-oriented heavy industries must increasingly contribute to consumer production. "We now have a powerful metallurgical industry, a modern and developed machine-building industry, a highly developed power engineering, fuel industry, and other branches of heavy industry," he said. [62] He concluded that at the present stage of development "our task consists of the further development of the means of production for the broader production of consumer goods." [63]

Khrushchev's new project almost certainly required the scrapping of the existing planning framework and an overhaul of the economic goals set forth as long-term policy at the Twenty-second Party Congress and in the new party program three years earlier. The Congress and the new program had registered a conservative bias that clearly had not met his wishes. He had been persistently trying to break out of the later framework. His new project was probably intended to be a keystone of what in effect was a revised party program to be presented at the Twenty-third Party Congress due to be held in 1965. Khrushchev probably saw the new program as his last and, hopefully, lasting political monument. Perhaps he hoped it would serve as the marker of the U.S.S.R.'s entrance into the "higher phase of communism" and his own claim to fame in Soviet history.

Khrushchev's move on the economic front was evidently a visible portion of far-reaching moves he was initiating on the eve of his fall. As previously, his actions in the domestic policy sphere were being dovetailed with major moves in external affairs. In the bloc and the Communist movement he was engaged in an intensive effort to convoke a world meeting of Communist parties where he hoped to formalize the split with the Chinese. As long as Mao Tse-tung was formally included in the movement Khrushchev's political elbow room at home and abroad was cramped. He also needed the break as a means of stemming the steady disintegration of Soviet control and influence in the Communist movement, within the

[62] *Ibid.*
[63] *Ibid.*

bloc and especially in Eastern Europe, that was taking place. The trend was severely eroding his own prestige.

At the same time he was attempting to broaden the détente policy with the West which he renewed with the test ban. Among the new initiatives in this sphere he was apparently contemplating a visit to Bonn. A shelving of the German problem, at least temporarily, would have contributed to the atmosphere of reduced tension Khrushchev sought. He probably also looked forward to President Johnson's victory over Goldwater in the American elections as another reason for arguing that the time was ripe for fully implementing his program.

Ultimately, the realization of Khrushchev's purposes required the removal of the sources of high-level opposition and resistance he had encountered within the regime. The possibility that he might achieve his goal was abruptly ended in the second week of October by his overthrow at the hands of a Presidium coalition, including a number of his own past supporters.

10

KHRUSHCHEV'S FALL—
The AMBIGUOUS LEGACY

THE FINAL, CLIMACTIC CHAPTER of Khrushchev's reign opened with his political recovery after the Cuban crisis in 1963 and closed with his fall in October, 1964. His restored strength was not a sign of robust health, however; his prestige had suffered a body blow from the missile fiasco at the very time his party reform was producing a profound reaction among the ideologues and political *apparatchiki* of the party. He lost support in the court of appeal, the Central Committee, to which he had resorted in overcoming his challengers in 1957. The Kozlov challenge was a logical outgrowth of the Cuban failure and dramatically exposed the leader's vulnerability to attack; it set the stage for the successful assault on Khrushchev's leadership within the Presidium a year and a half later.

This is not to say Khrushchev had become powerless. Until the eve of his fall his personal power well exceeded that of any individual member of the Presidium and it took a formidable coalition to down him. In fact the issue of his power vis-à-vis his colleagues remained very much alive up to his ouster. After the Twenty-second Party Congress Khrushchev had begun more or less openly menacing those who had objected to his initiatives or had taken independent stands. This had been the import of Yevtushenko's poem in *Pravda* warning the party of the danger from unregenerate Stalinists in high places.[1] It had become clear that top figures were mutually interested in heading off Khrushchev's efforts to assume greater powers and to dispose of a recalcitrant Presidium membership.

Khrushchev was seeking this power to gain a freer hand for implementing his policies. Following his recovery from the Cuban crisis, he had mounted another of his characteristic political offensives. His downfall came with dramatic suddenness while he was rapidly unfolding a refurbished and far-reaching strategy of détente and reform: the test ban, the chemicals program, his new long-term consumer plan, and an intended overhaul of agricultural policy were parts of a new assault on the status quo. Concurrently, he was trying to force a decisive break with his Chinese enemies and was renewing pressure on the question of the anti-party group at home.

Despite this picture of forward movement in the last chapter of Khrushchev's rule, there were continuing signs of resistance to his policy initiatives. Furthermore his successes in getting the Central Committee to endorse his plan for a world party meeting and to announce that "Molotov and others" had been expelled from the party proved to be Pyrrhic victories: the first foundered in the face of opposition from foreign parties; the second only strengthened the resolve of various members of the leading group to prevent him from acquiring purge powers over them.

KHRUSHCHEV'S OUSTER

The precise circumstances and behind-the-scenes maneuvers preceding the confrontation between Khrushchev and the Presidium coalition which overthrew him remain veiled to us. There were, however, indications of high political tension in the leading group during the two months or so prior to Khrushchev's fall.

[1] See pp. 147–48 of Chapter 8 for details.

Togliatti's famous memorandum written on the eve of his death in the U.S.S.R. was an early storm warning. The Italian leader boldly alluded to political conflicts among the Soviet leaders and voiced his disquiet over the internal political situation. The memorandum evidently resulted from his concern over what he learned from talking with Brezhnev and other Soviet leaders shortly after arriving in Moscow on August 9.[2] Khrushchev was touring the provinces then and apparently had no opportunity to meet personally with Togliatti; he soon fell ill and, before Khrushchev arrived at his bedside in Gagra on August 21, he died. While Togliatti professed not to know the nature of the disagreements to which he alluded, he did refer to problems of "economic structure and policy," bloc economic integration, and the fits and starts of de-Stalinization as well as the lag and "resistance" to internal liberalization in the U.S.S.R.[3] Of course the memorandum as a whole was devoted to an apologia of the Italian party's independent stand in the Sino-Soviet hostilities.

On the day before Togliatti's arrival in Moscow Khrushchev himself openly referred to disagreement in the leadership. Speaking during a tour of the agricultural provinces, he mentioned complaints of "some comrades" against advance publicity of the agenda for the Central Committee plenum scheduled for November.[4] The dispute at the least involved Khrushchev's tactic of publicly promoting projects that the Presidium had not yet considered or passed upon.

The delay in publicizing Khrushchev's sweeping proposal for a new pro-consumer plan at the joint Presidium-Council of Ministers meeting toward the end of September was another sign of conflict in the Presidium.[5] Moreover, an extended account rather than the

[2] According to *Pravda*, Togliatti was met by Brezhnev and Ponomarev. At Togliatti's funeral Brezhnev recalled that he had had a "lively" talk with the Italian leader and it was widely rumored in the Italian press that Togliatti had gotten wind of deep troubles among the Soviet leaders. (*Pravda*, Aug. 10, 1964.)

[3] *The New York Times*, Sept. 5, 1964, contains the text of the Togliatti memorandum.

[4] *Pravda*, Aug. 10, 1964.

[5] *Pravda* published an account of Khrushchev's speech on October 2 saying simply that it had been given "recently" at a joint CPSU Presidium-Council of Ministers meeting. A dispatch by *L'Unita*'s Moscow correspondent A. Pancaldi on October 25 reported that the meeting had been held September 20–25, 1964.

text of Khrushchev's speech was released—reportedly before the issues it raised had been resolved in the Presidium.

These signs of conflict, however, were nothing new in themselves. With the notable exception of Kozlov's moves in the leadership after Cuba, conflicts within the top group had not produced a direct and open challenge to his position. Yet the question of leadership was not far below the surface. No doubt Khrushchev was acutely aware that criticisms of his policy in the Presidium could one day develop into a frontal attack; it was therefore the more surprising that he was caught off guard by the coalition of Presidium members that overthrew him. Their control of the channels through which advance warning might have been transmitted to Khrushchev, principally the secret police, seems to have been complete. He apparently was also denied any opportunity to canvass support against his challengers as he did in 1957. Also, unlike 1957, he did not have a Zhukov in the military establishment ready to come to his aid. Evidently the anti-Khrushchev coalition was reasonably confident that the Soviet military would at the very least remain neutral during the confrontation in the Presidium. Brezhnev's special toast to the Soviet military at the Kremlin reception on the October Revolution anniversary a few weeks after Khrushchev's fall may have been an oblique gesture of the new leader's gratitude on this score.

Khrushchev could well have become overconfident of his organizational position as a result of the new arrangement in the top echelon after June, 1963. The entrance that month of both Brezhnev and Podgornyy, the former Ukrainian party chief, into the Secretariat as rival "heirs" may have led him to think that he had reduced the threat to his personal power from any one of his associates. He apparently did not properly gauge the danger of their coalescing in a common effort to depose him. He evidently expected his closest confederates to remain loyal in a crisis. However, Khrushchev's reputed intention to bring his son-in-law, Adzhubei, into the Secretariat shortly before his fall may have indicated that he already had some doubts about the political reliability of even his formerly most trusted fellow secretaries. What seemed to tip the balance in the leadership against him was the desertion of

Brezhnev and other former supporters. He had weathered the Kozlov-Suslov challenge after Cuba but that episode had dramatically exposed the chinks in his political armor.

Ironically the rival "heir" arrangement might have actually helped precipitate the plot against Khrushchev. Brezhnev may have had a special motive for turning against Khrushchev as a result of his rivalry with Podgornyy in the Secretariat. Brezhnev's return to full-time duty in the Secretariat just three months before Khrushchev's fall bore the markings of a move to counter Podgornyy's build-up of political strength in that crucial body. As a full-time secretary Podgornyy had gained a year's march over him, while much of his own time had been taken up by the protocol functions of Supreme Soviet Chairman. Thus Brezhnev may have decided that time was not on his side under Khrushchev and that he could best gain an inside track in a successor regime through Khrushchev's overthrow.

Whatever may have been some of the personal political motives of the principals in the move against Khrushchev, they struck at a time when he was manifestly vulnerable. The steady disintegration of Soviet authority in the Communist movement, in the bloc, and especially in Eastern Europe itself was eroding his personal prestige as a Communist leader. Incidentally, it is worth noting in this regard that Togliatti in his memorandum had transparently attempted to counter the notion that Soviet prestige was slipping, arguing that despite Chinese attacks on the Soviet leaders, especially Khrushchev, it was never higher.[6] The Cuban incident, followed by the harvest debacle of 1963, however, had in fact deeply tarnished the luster of Khrushchev's leadership both at home and abroad. Further, the decline in the growth rate of the Soviet economy belied the image of forward movement so vital for a Soviet leader to sustain—especially one promising decisive results through a policy of reform.

Khrushchev, in short, had been forced into retreat too often and the aura of success around his leadership had faded. This was a serious vulnerability. In this connection his successors cultivated

[6] *The New York Times*, Sept. 5, 1964.

the impression that his erratic style of leadership was a basic cause of his overthrow; yet this was more a pretext than a real reason. Khrushchev's shifts and turnabouts were not so much a sign of political incompetence as they were the outward manifestation of the intense, complex internal battle he had conducted to sustain his leadership. In instance after instance when he retreated from a previous policy line he was doing so under heavy political pressures and not simply because he had changed his mind. All of this provided the occasion for an assault on his leadership.

It also should be emphasized, however, that the opportunity could have soon slipped from the grasp of Khrushchev's adversaries. They had to act quickly and exploit the factor of surprise—just as Khrushchev himself had so often done. For example, had Khrushchev succeeded in formalizing the break with Mao and the Chinese within the movement at a world party meeting, had he succeeded in developing an atmosphere of limited détente with the West and thus gaining a freer hand for pursuing his political plans at home, he would have been in an improved position to move against the recalcitrants in the Presidium. He might then have sought to fulfill his intention of reshaping the leading group in his own image and, if possible, destroying its capacity to act as an autonomous political force.

By the fall of 1964, however, his innovations in policy, his zeal for sweeping projects, the risks he had taken, and the losses he had incurred in this connection weakened the foundations of his political power. A growing reaction to his radicalism had developed in the ruling group. It brought together both conservatives and more cautious reformers. The coalition that downed him included both the elements Kozlov had sought to turn against him and a number of Khrushchev's former collaborators. Evidently Brezhnev, from his vantage point in the Secretariat, was well aware of the trend and assumed a key role in organizing the winning combination. The attack on Khrushchev this time, of course, was not the clear-cut orthodox challenge led by the Kozlov-Suslov faction in the Cuban aftermath, but its underlying motive was nonetheless conservative. It reflected the hostility of the heads of the bureaucratic fiefdoms of party and state to a leader bent on upsetting established relationships.

Khrushchev had alienated the political-ideological functionaries by his efforts to reshape the party institution; he had incensed the central planners and the economic czars of the state apparatus by his attempts to give the party the key role in economic management and by his successive projects to rechannel the direction of the economy; he had provoked opposition of important elements in the Soviet military establishment by repeated incursions into their sphere; he had aroused fears among the guardians of the party institution that his radical attacks on Stalin would get out of control and inflame discontents in society at large. He had offended too many powers within the regime too often.

THE KHRUSHCHEV LEGACY

The Khrushchev era was a transition in Soviet politics and Khrushchev may be seen as a transitional leader. Stalin's Draconian dictatorship—a mix of terror, storm and stress ideology, and forced draft industrialization—was an artificial but effective means for sustaining the forward thrust of the Soviet regime. It was scarcely a permanent answer, however, to the problem of rulership: how to make the party that was originally conceived as an instrument of revolution into an effective agency of governance. In fact, the party under Stalin was simply reduced to one of several major instruments of a personal dictatorship. Following Stalin's fall Khrushchev succeeded in restoring the political supremacy of the party within the Soviet system. As a result, however, the need to bridge the gap between the ideological-political mission of the party and the practical business of ruling and managing an advanced industrial society became the more pressing. Khrushchev's problem was not how to make or consolidate a revolution but how to perpetuate it.

He sought to square the circle between "revolutionary sweep" and "efficiency," ideology and reality, by turning the focus of the party from theory to practice, by making it less an ideological party and more of a managerial party. His emphasis on practice was a persisting theme, so much so that it was a point of political vulnerability. His successors have sharply attacked the Khrushchevian view of the role of the party, warning against divorcing practical problems from the ideological functions of the party and dismissing theoretical questions in the work of the party.

While a true believer in the Communist vision, Khrushchev saw the salvation of the party in its conversion into an indispensable functional agency in the operation of an advanced industrial society. His formula for adapting the party dictatorship to modern Russia was to transform it into an instrument of economic re-generation. His quest led him into an assault on orthodoxy in theory and practice at home and abroad and was epitomized by his radical reform of the basic structure of the party on the "production" principle in 1962. As might have been expected, his actions provoked both the ideologues and political functionaries, who saw the traditional ideological and political functions of the party being watered down, and also the administrators and economic managers of the state apparatus, who resented the intrusion of the party into their time-honored jurisdictions and who viewed the 1962 reform as irrational and inefficient. In short, Khrushchev tried to force the party institution into a mold which it violently resisted and into a role it was ill-equipped to perform.

Khrushchev's long-term outlook saw an expansion of the role of the party and a withering of the role of the state in national affairs as the U.S.S.R. entered the "higher stage" of Communist society. The notion that the party "withers" along with the state apparatus under communism was, in effect, relegated to the limbo of an indefinite future under Khrushchev's theoretical formulations. In practice his party of the future had all the appearances of a substitute state. The party reform sought to give primacy to the "party-of-the-whole-people" over the "state-of-the-whole-people" that seemed out of tune with the emphasis on the latter doctrine at the Twenty-second Congress. In fact, his successors have pictured the reform as a violation of the party constitution adopted at the congress.

Khrushchev's long-term aim, it appears, was to assure as far as possible that there would be no other institutions in the Soviet system that could effectually raise a threat to the political hegemony of the party. His industrial decentralization of 1957 and party reform of 1962 were practical measures in accord with this vision. With the establishment of the local Councils of the National Economy (*Sovnarkhozi*) in the 1957 reform Khrushchev attempted a major departure from the extreme centralization of the system of economic ministries in Moscow inherited from Stalin. Under the new arrangement the party rather than the state was to provide the operational guidance of the economy—an aim the 1962 reform of party structure was intended to effectuate.

Resistance to the more radical implications of Khrushchev's policy was evident, however, at the time of the Twenty-second Congress in the debate over the "withering of the state" and, later, in the sharp reaction the party reform caused within the regime. After Cuba the reaction was visible in the fact that the state economic apparatus began to regain some of the prerogatives it had lost to the party under Khrushchev. His successors placed new reliance on the managerial and administrative bureaucracy of the state for policy implementation and registered their opposition to reform schemes that might radically upset the institutional balance between party and state. Before the end of the year following Khrushchev's fall, his successors abolished the regional economic councils he had set up in 1957 and re-established the centralized system of economic ministries that had been formed under Stalin and retained under Malenkov. This action, combined with the earlier abolition of the 1962 party reform structure, completed the dismantling of the new managerial structure Khrushchev had sought to establish.

His concept of the long-range role of the party in modern Russia foundered with the revocation of the 1962 party reform. He offered a relatively consistent solution to the problem of justifying the role of an institution in danger of becoming an anachronism in a mature industrialized society. His successors rejected the solution but cannot now escape the problems he sought to solve.

Khrushchev's policy for the party also involved an attack on economic traditionalism within the regime. In order to put his

1962 party reform in perspective, it is necessary to see that it was intimately connected with his long-term effort to shift the focus of party policy to agriculture and the consumer, and away from steel and defense. He had met repeated frustration in this effort and it was against this background that he attempted to reshape the party into a more responsive instrument of his purposes and at the same time undercut and replace those who had raised obstacles. While the reform failed, however, Khrushchev's policy in the economic sphere was a mixture of success and failure. He succeeded in moving the regime away from the extreme economic imbalance produced by Stalinist economic doctrine and he provoked wide-ranging debates within the regime over economic policy and doctrine which continues in the successor regime. Doctrine inherited from the Stalin era became subject to critical challenge.

Under Khrushchev Soviet economists began to enjoy wide latitude in expressing their views on reforming the Soviet economic system. For example, with Khrushchev's blessing a powerful reform movement gained its head, pressing for widespread introduction of "profit" criteria in the operations of Soviet industrial enterprises. The movement that has acquired the name Libermanism after the unorthodox Soviet economic theorist who is among its chief inspirers has continued to prosper under the post-Khrushchev regime.

While he undercut the theoretical foundations of traditional economic policy and shifted the political ground in favor of change, his own program for reorienting policy toward agriculture and the consumer lost headway in his last years of rule. His repeated attacks on the sway of "steel" in the economy produced little result and after 1958 his claims to have cured the agricultural ills of the U.S.S.R. were nullified by lagging production and finally by the great harvest failure of 1963. When the agricultural situation began to worsen after 1958 Khrushchev berated the leading group for complacency and persistently argued for increased investments and incentives in this sphere. But it took the shock of the 1963 harvest disaster to convince them of the critical need for a change in policy. Ironically, Khrushchev's successors, while making the fallen leader a scapegoat for agricultural failures, have initiated a major agricultural program which they promise will do what Khrushchev in his last years insisted must be done.

In 1963 the traditionalists lost a powerful spokesman when Kozlov left, but their criticism of Khrushchev's initiatives in economic policy as overly radical and incautious nevertheless had a lasting corrosive effect on his leadership. His critics were able to marshal against him all those forces and interests upset by his efforts to engineer breakthroughs in policy. Following his ouster, charges were aimed at him for neglecting doctrinal criteria in economic policy, namely, that the "economic laws of socialism" had been ignored, and for disregarding "objective" conditions. Though the new regime promised to meet consumer needs, its statements in effect asserted that those needs could only be met as a result of general expansion and modernization of production and not by decree or "subjective" desires. He was accused of focusing excessively on material welfare to the neglect of the broader ideals of communism. One writer in *Pravda* ridiculed the Khrushchevian attitude as reducing communism to "filling the belly."[7] Shortly thereafter Suslov reiterated this theme, saying that communism could not be measured by material abundance alone; in an allusion to Khrushchev's leadership he complained that the party had become excessively absorbed in "current economic work" to the detriment of politics and ideology.

From the outset the new leadership indicated that consumption would remain subordinate to production in line with past practice. In fact the first speeches of the new First Secretary and Premier reasserted this traditional order of things in policy. Where Khrushchev, just before his fall, had called for a new plan directly aimed at satisfying consumer needs as the "main task" of the party, Brezhnev stressed that the main task in domestic policy was the "development of the productive forces of our society" and then "on this basis" popular welfare would be raised. Kosygin similarly asserted the primacy of productivity. He said that, while the party had no loftier aim than the "steady growth" of living standards, this was "inconceivable" without increasing productivity first.

---

[7] See the article by V. Stepanov, editor of *Kommunist*, in *Pravda*, May 17, 1965.

Probably reflecting criticism within the Presidium of Khrushchev's last consumer project as premature and unrealistic, he declared that abundance "will not drop from the skies" and could not come without "work" and "strain." While the new leadership could scarcely admit that it was less interested in consumer welfare than Khrushchev, these remarks sounded very much like a muted form of the same criticism Khrushchev had faced from his enemies in June, 1957, when they charged him with a consumer deviation in policy.

The corollary of Khrushchev's domestic policy was his emphasis on peaceful coexistence and economic competition abroad. This by no means meant he was averse to promoting Communist-led revolution in the underdeveloped world or to power plays as in Cuba and Berlin to undercut the position of the United States and the Western powers. Nonetheless, in his over-all policy he sought to cultivate an aura of limited détente in world affairs in contrast to the unremitting hostility in East-West relations that Communist China seeks to sustain. This strategy brought him into collision with Communist militants abroad, championed by Mao Tse-tung. The Chinese countered with a program stressing revolutionary militancy, which placed anti-imperialism and Communist revolution in Asia, Africa, and Latin America at the head of the list of priorities in Communist strategy.

Khrushchev was unable to deal decisively and effectively with the Chinese challenge because the Stalinist model of a monolithic Communist movement directed from Moscow had disintegrated. Paradoxically, Khrushchev himself took a leading hand in accelerating the breakdown, which in any case was scarcely preventable, with his attack on Stalin at the Twentieth Party Congress. His anti-Stalinism affected his ability to enforce discipline not only within the leadership but also in the Communist movement at large. Despite his efforts to develop a more flexible substitute concept in tune with the times, the Soviet loss of authority was irrevocable.

For reasons of general policy as well as personal prestige and power Khrushchev sought to put Mao Tse-tung and the Chinese militants outside the Communist pale; however, he encountered both internal and external resistance. The opposition from normally pro-Soviet parties abroad buttressed the reluctance within the Soviet leadership, which was sufficiently strong to prevent the official adoption of the proposition that dogmatism—the Chinese political line—rather than revisionism had become the main danger to Communist policy.

It is worth recalling in this connection that Khrushchev, after regaining his momentum in the summer of 1963, renewed his effort to force acceptance of this proposition. He succeeded in getting various foreign parties, notably the French, to press the line that dogmatism had become a mortal threat to the movement, yet he failed to get his own party to adopt it officially and un-equivocally. Although in August, 1963, the line appeared momentarily in a review of a Lenin work in *Pravda*,[8] it did not subsequently appear in official party statements or editorials. Even the Suslov report to the February, 1964, plenum calling for a world party conference stopped short of endorsing the proposition. Chinese "splitting" activity, not Chinese "dogmatism," was declared to be the main danger to Communist unity.[9]

There was a difference between the two and this difference was a measure of Khrushchev's failure to gain his point that the Chinese doctrinal and political positions as such were anathema and in themselves a justification for excommunicating the Chinese from the Communist movement.[10] Khrushchev's successors, consistent with their attempt to get off the collision course with the Chinese, initially resorted to the ambivalent line that the Soviet party wages a two-front battle against *both* dogmatism and revisionism,

[8] *Ibid.*, Aug. 23, 1963.

[9] *Ibid.*, April 3, 1964.

[10] Among the other notable telltales of the leadership's reluctance was its failure to respond in kind to *Red Flag*'s sustained personal vilification and abuse of Khrushchev in its series of polemical assaults on Soviet policy in late 1963 and early 1964. Probably alluding to criticisms of his personal vendetta against Mao Tse-tung, Khrushchev at a Moscow rally in mid-April, 1964, prophetically quipped that one day he might be criticized on this score for "subjectivism" at an international conference. The remark referred to a sharp personal attack on Mao he had just made. The criticism of Khrushchev for "subjectivism" came some six months later, not at an international conference but in a *Pravda* editorial a few days after his overthrow.

without committing themselves to the position that one or the other is the main danger.

During this period of challenge from the Chinese, Khrushchev also encountered internal resistance to the pre-eminence he gave the peaceful coexistence and economic competition themes in Communist strategy. When he was in retreat after Cuba he faced an effort within the leadership in February, 1963, to put anti-imperialism ahead of coexistence. The February letter of the CPSU to the Chinese party, it will be recalled, had upgraded the anti-imperialist and national liberation struggle to first place in offering an agenda for talks with the Chinese party. Only when Khrushchev was in a stronger position did a new letter restore coexistence and economic competition to first place.[11] It has been apparent that advocates of toning down the coexistence theme in favor of anti-imperialism have sought to press their advantage since Khrushchev's fall. Under the new group so far anti-imperialism and national liberation have initially been upgraded and peaceful coexistence put down a few notches. While the shift in emphasis has undoubtedly been designed to enable the Soviet leadership to compete more effectively with the militancy of the Chinese Communists, it entailed a movement closer to the orthodox view that the theme of world revolution must remain in the center of Communist strategy.[12]

Despite critics' charges that he depreciated theory, Khrushchev left behind an impressive body of theoretical revisions and innovations in Soviet doctrine. Taken together these doctrinal

[11] See pp. 175–76 of Chapter 9.

[12] One indication of the presence in the successor regime of those favoring a more forward strategy in support of revolution in the underdeveloped world was the re-emergence after Khrushchev's fall of the doctrine that the Communist bloc now functions as a "dictatorship of the proletariat" on a world scale, the doctrine which Suslov introduced in July, 1960 (cf. pp. 99–100 of Chapter 6). An article in *Kommunist* (K. Brutents, "The Contemporary Stage of the National Liberation Movement," *Kommunist*, No. 17, 1964, esp. pp. 31–32) advanced the concept and saw increased opportunity for revolution in the underdeveloped world. The article declared that the Communist bloc now acts as a "mighty proletarian vanguard" for the "peasant and semi-proletarian masses" of former colonies and semi-colonies. Here was a sophisticated rationale for promoting Communist revolution in regions where there are few proletarians in the Marxist sense and for justifying current Soviet efforts to subvert and convert new revolutionary nationalist regimes in Asia, Africa, and Latin America from within.

changes effected a significant departure from the Stalinist legacy
and revealed the underlying consistency of Khrushchev's outlook
on over-all questions of policy. The formulas he developed, which
he called "creative Marxism-Leninism" and his enemies condemned
as "revisionism," in fact, provide an interlinked, comprehensive
definition of that outlook in theoretical form. His pronouncements
on the non-inevitability of war, the possibility of peaceful transition
to socialism in the non-Communist world, and the end of the
"capitalist encirclement" provided the premises for the pursuit of
a highly flexible foreign strategy at once aimed at achieving limited
détente with the West and sapping Western strong points in world
politics. This strategy came under the headings of peaceful coexistence and peaceful economic competition. A set of related
propositions was concurrently developed in support of his domestic
policy of internal relaxation and consumer-oriented economic
development. Formulations on the waning of the class struggle
inside the U.S.S.R., the gradual withering away of the Soviet state,
the "final victory of socialism" in the U.S.S.R., the subordination
of politics to economics in party policy, the end of the dictatorship
of the proletariat, the formation of a party and state "of the whole
people," and the transition to the higher phase of communism in
the Soviet Union provided the doctrinal props for his internal
policies. The old Communist conservative Molotov, in his own
lights, had good reason for suggesting that this was a policy of
"communism-in-one-country."

The political importance of Khrushchev's theoretical legacy
should not be underestimated despite the proven capacity of Soviet
politicians to overturn past political lines. The Khrushchevian
formulas are embedded in basic party documents, including the
new party program, the second such programmatic document in
Soviet history replacing the outdated program of 1919. Those
who wish to continue the basic policy lines developed by
Khrushchev are provided a strong handle. Those who wish to
change policy, unless they win decisive victory in factional struggle,
are more or less compelled to work within the broad doctrinal
framework Khrushchev left behind. They must resort to a process
of selection, shifting emphases, and manipulation of existing

formulas in the effort to reorient policy according to their own views.

The denigration of Stalin was a virtual precondition for Khrushchev's overhaul of party doctrine and practice. Indeed, his first major revisions coincided with the attack on Stalin at the Twentieth Party Congress. The attack on Stalin, however, carried implications for Soviet politics that far exceeded the immediate value the action had for Khrushchev either as a means of removing obstacles to reform or as a weapon of factional politics. It led him to seek out sources of support beyond the immediate ruling circle and in the process he stirred latent but profound discontents and aroused dormant political forces in Soviet society.[13]

Khrushchev's strategy added to the uncertainties of the political environment within the leading group itself. He frequently sought to expand the sphere of conflict beyond the inner circle at critical junctures. Whether it was at a party congress, a plenum, a special party conference, or an expanded joint session of the Presidium and the Council of Ministers, he sought broader forums where he could bring outside forces to bear on the inner group to tip the balance in his favor. The classic example was his successful appeal to the Central Committee over the heads of the Presidium majority in June, 1957. Though Khrushchev probably believed he could stay master of the outside forces he exploited, any expansion of the arena of conflict creates a menace to the leadership group's control over latent political forces in the system at large. In October, 1964, however, the "insiders" denied Khrushchev an opportunity to resort to his tactic and succeeded in confining the confrontation to the inner circle. The status quo was thus preserved and the

---

[13] The Solzhenitsyn affair provides a recent illustration of this. Khrushchev used Solzhenitsyn's literary exposé of life in Stalin's forced labor camps as a political weapon gaining its publication over the protests of some of his associates. The book was political dynamite and later, according to Khrushchev himself, had resulted in a "flood" of anti-Stalin and protest literature into Soviet publishing houses. According to one account of the indictment of Khrushchev in the Presidium at his fall in the Communist-supported Italian periodical *Paese Sera* (Oct. 30, 1964), Khrushchev was hit for meddling in Soviet literary affairs through his sponsorship of Solzhenitsyn's *One Day in the Life of Ivan Denisovich*. The indictment asserted that the book otherwise would not have seen the light of day.

Presidium membership asserted its common interest in protecting its powers and privileges from outside interference.

Khrushchev, in any case, did little to place the channels of authority and decision-making on a firmer basis and was unable to arrange for an orderly transfer of power. His successors may consciously seek to institutionalize and regularize the proceedings within the leadership, but this will be difficult to achieve in conditions of an ideological, factional politics. Ambitious leaders and factions will always be tempted to take a leaf from Khrushchev's book in their efforts to gain the advantage in political struggle.

With the removal of the deadening weight of Stalin's terror politics, the Khrushchev era came to be characterized by a loss of the kind of firm discipline within the leading group that Stalin imposed. Contention between the various elements of the upper echelons pervaded the environment in which Khrushchev worked and may even more deeply affect post-Khrushchevian leadership politics.

Conflicts within and among broader groups in the Soviet system also began rising to the surface during the Khrushchev era. Soviet press organs and periodicals have more and more become sounding boards for such conflicts and it has become difficult for the regime to conceal or even effectively suppress them. While the conventions of a "monolithic" politics still affect the forms in which these conflicts are expressed, divisions and debates among writers, economists, legal theorists, and other professionals have become relatively more open and the arguments among regime politicians more easily discernible. Although this is still a far cry from the free debate of a democratic society, in time it may have important effects on the Soviet political process.

Against these trends must be balanced the natural and powerful inclination of the party officialdom to prevent any pluralistic tendencies from acquiring autonomous force within the system. The Stalinist legacy still lives in the political foundations of the regime and no mere exorcism could destroy it. Indeed, it would not be surprising if a countertrend were to develop against the extreme denigration of Stalin. The new leadership has already provided an opening wedge for such a trend. Within months after

Khrushchev's fall they advanced a more positive portrayal of Stalin's wartime leadership, countering Khrushchev's position that Stalin was responsible for all the failures and none of the successes of the U.S.S.R. in World War II. This move implied something more than a zeal for historical objectivity among party leaders.

Inevitably Khrushchev's iconoclasm placed the legitimacy of party rule in doubt. His critics often warned of the dangers of anti-Stalinist excesses and Khrushchev was not always free to disregard such warnings. The claim of the party to rule rests heavily on the proposition that it has been correctly led politically and ideologically throughout its history. In any case, as time goes on Khrushchev's successors may find less need and fewer pretexts for using the Stalin bugbear as a weapon of internal political struggle. It is possible that in time Stalin will be reappraised not too differently from the party line prior to the Twenty-second Congress —namely, that he made mistakes and was guilty of abuses but was a major leader of the party. Mao Tse-tung has shown his shrewd sense of history in rehabilitating Stalin and counterposing him to Khrushchev. In this regard one need only ask whether Stalin or Khrushchev is the more likely to loom the larger in Communist history after the memories of the purges and the terror recede in the party's political consciousness. The answer is by no means self-evident.

Those who have succeeded Khrushchev cannot escape the dilemmas with which he tried to cope. Whoever gains the prime place in the leadership must contend not only with conflicting elements in the party but with the demands of a changing Soviet society. Khrushchev's concept of the economics-oriented, managerial party has been discarded for the time being as the primary rationale for the contemporary party and any leader who would revive it must find new and more convincing variants on that theme. The broad alternative to this would be to revitalize the "ideological" party, a direction in which the successor regime has shown an initial tendency to move. Generally this alternative could involve reinforcing the emphasis on the world revolutionary mission of the party and reasserting the role of theory and doctrine in party practice. Theory might be subjected to a process of refinement and sophistication to adapt it more effectively to the complex realities of contemporary Soviet society. However, the leader who seeks to develop an over-all prescription for the party and its policy must develop it in terms of the actual spectrum of forces within the regime. The reformist forces Khrushchev sought to lead did not disappear with his fall any more than did the more conservative forces Kozlov once sought to marshal against him. Any new program must be forged in this context.

Just as leadership politics in the Khrushchev era revolved around Stalin's political and doctrinal legacy, so after Khrushchev it revolves around his revisions of that legacy. The long-term trend would seem to favor the general thrust of Khrushchev's policies. Great pressures in Soviet society virtually exclude a full-scale return to a regime of the primitive Stalinist type and even militate against more or less traditional solutions to the problem of leadership. The demand for reforms, popular pressures for greater welfare and material rewards, the desire for personal security and legality, and the stirrings for genuine freedom of expression among the intellectual groups will accumulate. The party regime nonetheless has its own logic and will to survive and will thus strive to retard and contain those pressures for change that threaten its political supremacy. Even Khrushchev's conception of reform, while radical in the context of inner party politics, was limited in terms of these broader pressures from society at large. It mainly sought the perpetuation of the regime through its transformation into an agency of economic regeneration. Khrushchev apparently assumed that the pressures on the party from without could be contained if the long-neglected material wants of Russian society could be satisfied. Such a formula for bridging the gap between party and society was inadequate on the face of it.

The tendencies and factors that shaped the Khrushchev period will influence but not predetermine the future course of Soviet politics. The unpredictable can play havoc with Soviet politics as much as any other politics. One of the critical variables remains a question mark at this stage—namely, the presence or absence of a capacity for creative leadership among Khrushchev's successors. Khrushchev possessed outstanding political abilities but suffered ultimate failure in sustaining his leadership. Will any of his successors surpass or even match him in this regard? The answer will critically affect the viability of party rule for Russia in the future.

In sum, Khrushchev succeeded in carrying the party through its perilous post-Stalin transition and left it intact as the dominant institution of Soviet society. But his effort to transform it failed. He sought to scourge the party of Stalinist practices yet could not fully free himself from them. He helped make unlikely a return to primitive Stalinism and shifted the center of gravity in the battle between reform and orthodoxy, but he did not overthrow the forces of orthodoxy and conservatism rooted in the regime. Similarly, in the external sphere his effort to reorient the world Communist movement in favor of his political lines only deepened the rift between orthodoxy and reform among and within the parties. Finally, he did not succeed in removing the underlying instability of Soviet leadership politics, which infected the political atmosphere during his own incumbency and infects that of his successors. Khrushchev left his successors an ambiguous legacy.

EPILOGUE: Away from KHRUSHCHEVISM—
The TWENTY-THIRD PARTY CONGRESS

Yevtushenko in his poem "Stalin's Heirs," written at the time of Khrushchev's renewed anti-Stalin campaign at the Twenty-second Party Congress, warned that there were still officials within the party who denounced Stalin from the rostrums but who secretly yearned for the old days. At the Twenty-third Party Congress in March, 1966, the first congress since Khrushchev's fall, a succession of party officials mounted the platform and sought to restore the respectability of the Stalin era, if not Stalin personally, in party history.

While the Congress delegates were assured that there was no danger of a return to Stalinism, it was apparent that powerful forces in the regime were bent on enforcing greater political and ideological conformity in Soviet society. Where the Twenty-second Congress had painted Stalin's rule as twenty years of tyranny over the party, speakers at the Twenty-third Congress intimated that the ten years of Khrushchev's rule had bordered on treason to the interests of the party. They implied that Khrushchev had permitted subversive ideas to gain a foothold in Soviet society and asserted that the time had come for imposing firmer ideological and political controls inside the country. The pressures for such a policy were apparent in a succession of developments on the eve of the Congress.

In February the trial of the Soviet writers Sinyavskiy and Daniel, charged with smuggling "anti-Soviet" manuscripts abroad under pseudonyms, ended with their being sentenced to seven- and five-year terms at hard labor. Shortly thereafter the Soviet press published articles of praise for A. Zhdanov, the figure who supervised Stalin's crackdown against alleged Western influences and heterodoxy among writers and artists after World War II. The ostensible occasion was the seventieth birth anniversary of Zhdanov, who had died in 1948 and had been given only meager attention in party histories in the Khrushchev period. At the same time the halls of the provincial party congresses preceding the Twenty-third Congress rang with complaints that hostile opinions and anti-Soviet propaganda were being spread by Soviet listeners of Western broadcasts. Aside from a brief mention in *Pravda*, the tenth anniversary of the Twentieth Party Congress and Khrushchev's de-Stalinization passed virtually unobserved.

In his keynote at the Congress the new party secretary, Brezhnev, skirted any mention of the abuses in the Stalin era. He thereby lent silent support, if not outright patronage, to the defenders of the Stalinist past in party history. Among the more outspoken was the head of the Moscow party, N. Yegorychev, who allowed that "some things might have been done better" in the past, but then proceeded to make it unmistakably clear that exposés of the Stalin era or the uncovering of "elements of so-called Stalinism in the country's political life" were now out of fashion.[1] It was such things, Yegorychev suggested, that had produced the troubles in the "ideological" education of the people, especially among the youth, and had given birth to "nihilism and skepticism" among "politically untempered people." He charged that neglect of ideology in party policy had allowed "plain ideological saboteurs" to penetrate the Soviet cultural community.

In terms similar to those Yegorychev had used, the Moldavian party chief, I. Bodyul, pinpointed the various sources of ideological infection, domestic and foreign. In this connection he denounced Solzhenitsyn's novel *One Day in the Life of Ivan Denisovitch*, which

[1] *Pravda*, March 31, 1966.

had been published under Khrushchev's personal sponsorship, as a gross distortion of the Soviet past and a preachment of pessimism and skepticism. As part of his call for greater vigilance in the ideological sector he demanded a closer scrutiny of cultural exchanges with the West. Such speeches lent substance to the general complaint at the Congress that the ideological functions of the party had been allowed to wither under Khrushchev.

The Twenty-third Congress also put its seal on the revocation of Khrushchev's major policy measures in the period after October, 1964, and gave short shrift to the new party program that was adopted at the Twenty-second Congress under Khrushchev. That the de-emphasis was intentional was confirmed in the May Day slogans issued the month after the Congress. For the first time the slogans contained no reference to the new program in any context. Also notably absent from them were the standard references to Khrushchev's doctrinal innovation at the Twenty-second Congress, namely that the U.S.S.R. had been transformed from a proletarian dictatorship to a "state of the whole people." That doctrine, which conveyed an image of the relaxation of the internal regime, was ignored, suggesting it had become controversial.

The Congress also confirmed the fact that the leadership had abandoned the ambitious goals Khrushchev had promoted, substituting a far more modest and gradualist economic program for the country. While the economic directives adopted at the Congress did not turn back the clock in economic policy, they were well designed not to upset any of the applecarts of the various major claimants to regime resources. While the Soviet citizen was promised a steady improvement in living conditions, the new leaders replaced Khrushchev's optimistic vision of a society on the verge of abundance with a far more sober outlook. The citizen was told that economic progress could proceed only within the limits of "objective conditions" and the "objective laws of socialism" and that no one's "subjective" wishes could alter this.

Alluding to Khrushchev's attempts to alter the basic allocations pattern of the economy, the plan directives denounced "subjectivism" in past policy and attempts to change the proportions of the economy arbitrarily. Brezhnev in his report revealed one major cause of the complaint—namely, Khrushchev's attempt to shift the center of gravity of the Soviet economy away from steel and metals through the preferential development of the chemicals industry. Adopting the position that Kozlov had once taken, he attacked the Khrushchevian argument that chemical synthetics could replace metals to a great extent. He attacked the "incorrect view" that the production of these synthetics would sharply reduce the demand for metals and said the view had exerted a "negative" effect on the development of metallurgy.[2] He said it was now necessary to make·"serious corrections" in the development of metallurgy.

In regard to the relative rates of growth of heavy industrial and consumer production, Brezhnev made it clear that the leadership was not contemplating any sudden shift of allocations in favor of the consumer sector. Under the next five-year plan, heavy industry's growth rate would continue to lead the rate of consumer output, but it was promised that these rates of growth would be brought closer together.

The Congress did show that Khrushchev's successors were still committed to a policy of significant reform in the sphere of economic management. The new leaders, principally Premier Kosygin, conveyed the idea that consumer and other needs of the economy could be met through improvements in efficiency, quality of production, rationalization of managerial methods, and the application of "profit" criteria in enterprise operations, rather than through basic allocations shifts. The virtue of this approach, politically, in contrast to Khrushchev's was that it did not impinge directly on the thorny issue of allocations.

In the sphere of external policy the Congress mirrored the movement away from Khrushchevian optimism regarding the prospects in world politics. While in practice pursuing a cautious course in foreign policy, his successors described the international situation in somber tones. Where Khrushchev had pictured his rule as a period when the danger of world war was receding, Brezhnev now viewed the Khrushchev era, and the present period as well, as a time of serious international tension. In this connection he stressed

[2] *Ibid.*, March 30, 1966.

the interdependence of internal and external policy. He offered the explanation to the Congress that improvement of living standards had been retarded by complications in the international situation. He asserted that the "aggressive actions of the U.S. imperialists forced us during the past few years to divert considerable additional sums to strengthening the defensive might of the country." He added in a swipe at Khrushchev that "due to a subjective approach in working out the seven-year plan [under Khrushchev] . . . an attempt to go ahead too fast was made." Kosygin's report to the Congress revealed that under the new plan increases in military spending in connection with the Vietnamese war had once again deprived the civilian economy of funds.

In view of such statements it was scarcely surprising that the Khrushchevian formulas that war was no longer fatalistically inevitable and that the time was near when world war would be removed from the life of society were absent from the Congress speeches. At the same time the coexistence line, while reiterated at the Congress, was associated with more militant themes, such as national liberation and anti-imperialism, in accordance with post-Khrushchev policy.

Brezhnev reasserted the ambivalent line that the Soviet party saw equal dangers from both extremes of revisionism and dogmatism in Communist policy. Brezhnev portrayed the party as adhering to a judicious middle road and offering the world Communist parties responsible leadership in implicit contrast to the extremism of their Chinese challengers.

Despite the steady outpouring of unbridled invective against the Soviet leaders from Peking, the Congress underscored the dogged adherence of the post-Khrushchev leadership to a policy of public self-restraint in the dispute. The cudgels were not taken up against the Chinese at the Congress and the leaders once again simply expressed regret that the "difficulties" in the movement had not been overcome. Where Khrushchev had sought to force matters to a head through the convocation of a world Communist meeting, Brezhnev indicated that the present leaders were in no hurry for a meeting and were prepared to wait indefinitely until "conditions" for a meeting were ripe. The policy suggested that Khrushchev's successors intended to wait out the storm in Peking and had not given up the hope for some kind of accommodation with Mao's successors. Evidently the Soviet leaders had not ruled out the idea that in time the Sino-Soviet axis might be salvaged as a basis of Communist power in world affairs. In any case, the policy has borne visible fruit for Moscow in terms of enhanced prestige among the parties and the increasing isolation of the Chinese in the Communist movement.

The Central Committee slogans issued for May Day after the Congress also contained a clear sign that Moscow regarded the Yugoslavs as further out on the fringes of the bloc of Communist states than either the Chinese or the Albanians. Ironically, it was a slap at the Albanian party in the slogans that conveyed the point. The greeting to the Albanians was taken from its customary position at the head of the alphabetical listing of the "socialist" countries and placed at the end of the list, but before the greeting to the Yugoslavs. Consequently it was clear that the appearance of the Yugoslav greeting at the end of the list was not due merely to its position in the alphabet. It would seem that the consensus in the CPSU Secretariat where the slogans are drawn up was that "revisionism" still held the edge as the chief danger to sound Communist policy.

The Twenty-third Congress thus indicated that the pendulum of Soviet politics in the period after Khrushchev's fall had swung to a more conservative position. Nonetheless the permanence of the shift could be doubted. Despite the retrenchment in policy, this was something of a "do-nothing" congress. In many spheres of domestic and foreign policy the new leaders seemed to be marking time. This in itself seemed to indicate that no party faction had yet won a decisive ascendancy in the post-Khrushchev regime. Notably both the restoration of the respectability of the Stalin era and the attack on Khrushchevism at the Congress were marked by caution and restraint. There was no direct criticism of the new party program that had been enacted at the Twenty-second Congress and the Khrushchevian themes embodied in that document; instead they were largely ignored. The departure from over-all Khrushchevian political strategy was marked not by outright rejection of all its premises but rather by omissions, shifts in emphases, and selection of themes. It seemed evident that the forces behind the shift in direction had to take care not to provoke dangerous opposition from the still powerful forces that had once been in Khrushchev's camp.

Khrushchev's overthrow had been the result of a marriage of convenience between party conservatives and the more cautious reformers disturbed by Khrushchevian radicalism. They did not join in coalition because they saw eye to eye on a positive political program. Thus in the interim between Khrushchev's fall and the Twenty-third Congress there continued to be many signs of conflict between the wings of the party. The point and counterpoint between the conservatives and the reform-minded reverberated in almost every sphere of policy.

The policy measures Khrushchev's successors have come up with so far are hybrids reflecting compromise arrangements. The regime's restructuring of industrial management after Khrushchev's fall is a case in point. A partial return to the Stalinist system of centralized planning and direction of the economy was combined with reforms giving greater autonomy to enterprise managers and introducing some self-regulatory mechanism in the planned economy.

The conflict over the relative weights to be given the consumer economy as against the traditional high investment in the heavy industry and military sector continues unabated. The new Premier Kosygin—although less radical than Khrushchev on the allocations issue—has evidently had to engage in a not overly successful effort to fend off powerful pressures for stepped-up military spending favored by party conservatives and the military. The latter have obviously exploited the Vietnam war to force an increase in military expenditures in the new economic plan.

Also, in somewhat altered form, the politics-versus-economics debate has continued into the successor regime. One major movement, strongly represented by the party *apparatchiki*, has stressed the primacy of Marxist-Leninist doctrine in all aspects of regime practice and the priority of ideological goals over mere problems of economics. Another current, strong among the economic managers, has focused on the application of scientific method, rational economics, and efficient management as the panacea for the country's domestic ills. The two trends have coexisted but their ultimate compatibility in Soviet politics could be questioned.

Despite the backtracking on the Stalin issue at the Congress and the harsher line toward writers, the conflict in these areas continues. Finally, there is visible the broad cleavage between those stressing the exigencies of the world conflict and Soviet responsibilities to the Communist movement as a whole and those stressing domestic problems and internal development, as well as the need to develop trade and economic relations with the West.

There are, of course, many shades of difference among the various leaders and groupings within the regime between these poles in policy. The evidences of conflicting pressures of continuity or change mark the far from resolved battle over the orientation of the post-Khrushchev regime.

However, one aftereffect of Khrushchev's rule has emerged with unmistakable clarity. The succession of changes that transformed the Soviet political and psychological atmosphere during his incumbency has produced a malaise inside the party. Much of the officialdom behaves as if it were under siege from the forces at work in the new world of post-Stalin society. They seem to fear that the grip of the party on the new Soviet generation is slipping. Signs of slippage have indeed been evident, especially among the intelligentsia and youth. The danger to the party, however, would seem to be less a danger of open disaffection but, what may be worse in the long run, of indifference and contempt for the official ideology and those who purvey it. Ironically, the ruling group has helped bring this result upon itself. The upshot of its internecine struggles has not only been the denigration of Stalin but of virtually all his heirs, including finally even Khrushchev himself. The official refrain that the party remained unsullied in spite of having been led by a succession of bad leaders is worse than no answer at all, and no amount of historical rewriting under the present leadership is likely to undo the damage.

At the same time, the body of critical literature that found its way into print in the less stringent atmosphere of the post-Stalin period has given voice to a broad undercurrent of social criticism among the educated class of Soviet society. Such criticism lands at the party's doorstep. This literature has also represented a breach in the party's monopoly over public communication.

Further, the breach itself was in part made possible by the rifts within the post-Stalin leadership and the consequences have been more far-reaching than even the most reform-minded of the leaders either anticipated or desired. The restoration at the Twenty-third Party Congress of the designations of "Politburo" and "General Secretary" for the highest policy council and the highest executive official of the party (i.e., the titles used under Lenin and Stalin) echoes the nostalgia in the ruling group for the time when the party leadership ostensibly faced society with a monolithic and unblemished public image.

As the fiftieth anniversary of the Bolshevik seizure of power approaches, the dominance of the party institution in Soviet society in terms of sheer bureaucratic and administrative power remains intact. However, there are signs of something of a crisis of self-confidence within party ranks as the leadership faces the problem of justifying its claim to rule. The challenge is not likely to be met by a leadership seeking refuge in ideological rearmament. Such a move will rather widen the gulf between the party dictatorship and society at large.

Khrushchev had sought to bridge the gap, and his promises of a society enjoying peace and abundance under Communist leadership lent impetus to a revolution of rising expectations in post-Stalin Soviet society. Despite the efforts of his successors to scale down these expectations they can ignore them only at their peril. Their initial attempt to combine a restoration of conformity in the ideological and political sphere with a gradualist program of modernization in the economic sphere (designed both to support the regime's political aims and satisfy popular needs) has yet to prove its adequacy. In any case, the initial post-Khrushchev mood in the party would seem to reduce the possibilities for the emergence of a dynamic leadership at a time when such leadership is needed if the vitality of the party institution is to be sustained over the long run.

APPENDIX: SKETCHES of SELECTED MEMBERS of the POST-1957 LEADERSHIP under KHRUSHCHEV

The following biographical sketches are not intended to be comprehensive, but simply a guide to identifying some of the political figures mentioned in the discussion of the post-1957 period.

ARISTOV, A. B.   (b. 1903)

Aristov, a party *apparatchik*, entered the Secretariat at the July, 1955, Central Committee plenum when Khrushchev defeated Molotov in debate over foreign policy. Along with a coterie of other Khrushchevites, he was rewarded with full Presidium membership at the June, 1957, plenum for his support in the defeat of the "group." He boldly indicated his personal loyalty to Khrushchev by praising his leadership in early 1957 in a public speech after the Hungarian revolt had struck a blow at Khrushchev's prestige and prior to the Molotov-Malenkov faction's challenge in June. He lost his post in the Secretariat at the time of the U-2 episode and began a decline which ended with his dispatch to Warsaw as an Ambassador. He finally lost his Presidium rank at the Twenty-second Congress.

BELYAEV, N. I.   (b. 1903)

An agricultural specialist, Central Committee Secretary (1955–59), and Presidium member (1957–60), Belyaev was sent to manage the virgin lands in December, 1957, as Kazakh First Secretary and was removed from that post in January, 1960, as the scapegoat for failure

231

in the virgin lands. His downfall paralleled that of his fellow secretary Kirichenko. He was transferred to a lesser regional party post and then, losing even that post in June, 1960, faded into obscurity.

BREZHNEV, L. I.   (b. 1906)

A Central Committee Secretary since 1956 with the exception of the period 1960-63 and a full Presidium member since June, 1957, he gained the First Secretaryship at Khrushchev's ouster probably because of the key role he played in engineering the overthrow. By all indications a loyal "Khrushchevite" up to the period shortly before Khrushchev's fall, he appears to have imitated with greater success the tactic of "Shepilov who joined them," one of his predecessors in the Secretariat and the Khrushchev protégé who turned against his patron in June, 1957. Brezhnev rose to high party posts from the Ukrainian apparatus under Khrushchev's direct auspices. He was a prime example of a presumed ally becoming a threat to the leader once gaining a position of power. In his public speeches he appeared among the most consistent supporters of Khrushchev's policies, but following the latter's ouster, at least initially, assumed the posture of a middle-of-the-road leader more cautious and conservative than his predecessor. The trust Khrushchev placed in him was early indicated by Brezhnev's direction of Khrushchev's virgin lands project at its crucial initial stages in 1954–55. At the time of the U-2 incident he lost out to Kozlov, his rival, in the Secretariat but regained his foothold in that body after Kozlov fell ill in 1963. A few months before Khrushchev's fall he gave up his post as titular chief of state to Mikoyan in order to work in the Secretariat full-time, a move that undoubtedly facilitated his participation in the plan to overthrow his chief.

BULGANIN, N. A.   (b. 1895)

A Politburo and Presidium figure with a background in defense affairs, Bulganin replaced Malenkov as Premier in February, 1955. Initially he played the role of Khrushchev's close partner in policy. However, as the leadership struggle intensified he made his availability as an alternate leader to Khrushchev increasingly evident by taking a neutral stance on key Khrushchev proposals. When the 1957 leadership crisis developed he threw his support on the side of Khrushchev's challengers. According to speakers at the Twenty-second Congress, he played an active role in the challenge by making his office available for meetings between members of the anti-Khrushchev faction and by placing guards around the Kremlin to keep out unwanted outsiders during the confrontation in the Presidium in June, 1957. Not without reason Khrushchev put the removal of Bulganin as Premier and exposure as a member of the group high on the order of business after the dust of the 1957 crisis had settled. Bulganin became the focus of Khrushchev's renewed drive against his defeated foes at the time of the Twenty-first Congress, but was more or less disregarded in the attack on the group at the Twenty-second Congress.

FURTSEVA, YE. A. (b. 1910)
One of the few women to enter the highest party posts, Furtseva was a loyal Khrushchevite who entered the Secretariat at the Twentieth Congress in 1956 from the post of First Secretary in the Moscow party organization. She gained full membership in the Presidium at the time of the purge of the "group" in 1957 when she reputedly played a key role in bringing Central Committee members into Moscow for the plenum that sealed the defeat of the anti-Khrushchev faction. She lost her post in the Secretariat in May, 1960, and was reduced to Minister of Culture. At the Twenty-second Congress she pressed a vigorous attack on the members of the "group". However, her decline was made complete at the end of the Congress with her removal from the Presidium.

IGNATOV, N. G. (b. 1901)
A Central Committee Secretary from 1957 to May, 1960, and a full Presidium member from 1957 to the Twenty-second Congress when he was demoted, Ignatov was deeply implicated in the factional struggles under Khrushchev and was among the most vigorous prosecutors of the attack on Khrushchev's fallen foes, the anti-party group. Khrushchev evidently brought Ignatov into the Secretariat in December, 1957, to strengthen his hand in that body. However, Ignatov lost his foothold in that body at the time of the U-2 affair and suffered a gyrating political decline afterward, suggesting that his fortunes were dependent on the course of factional politics between his patrons and his adversaries. While not a Khrushchev protégé, he appears to have been among the firmest supporters of Khrushchev's leadership ambitions.

ILICHEV, L. F.   (b. 1906)

Ilichev was the Central Committee propagandist and ideologue whom Khrushchev counterpoised to Suslov. Although he entered the Secretariat at the Twenty-second Congress and was made head of the special Central Committee ideological commission set up at the time of Khrushchev's party reform in November, 1962, he did not succeed in gaining the Presidium status that would have put him on a par with Suslov. He raised the Voznesenskiy case at the Twenty-second Congress, an issue that could be used against Suslov, and engaged in a veiled debate with Suslov after the Congress wherein he challenged Suslov's credentials as a theorist. Following Khrushchev's ouster, Ilichev was dropped from the Secretariat.

KAGANOVICH, L. M.   (b. 1893)

A member of the Politburo during most of Stalin's rule, Kaganovich was Molotov's prime ally in the leadership struggle after Stalin's death. Under Stalin he acquired the name of the "iron" commissar in connection with his careers as troubleshooter and purger, as well as a manager in the heavy industrial and transportation sectors of the economy. He is said to have proposed that the word "Stalinism" be added to "Marxism-Leninism" as the title of the official doctrine. After Stalin's death he called for a return to Bolshevik militancy in policy. He favored strict limitation of de-Stalinization and measures of internal relaxation. Kaganovich joined Molotov in opposition to Khrushchev's reforms including the virgin lands policy and the 1957 industrial decentralization. After their fall the two were also pictured as vigorous opponents of Khrushchev's MTS reform plan when it was being debated behind the scenes in early 1957. They also attacked Khrushchev for giving first place to catching up with the United States in meat, milk, and butter rather than to steel. At the Twenty-second Congress Kaganovich along with Molotov and Malenkov became a prime target in Khrushchev's campaign against the anti-party group.

KIRICHENKO, A. I.   (b. 1908)

A Presidium member (1955–60) and Central Committee Secretary until his sudden fall in 1960, Kirichenko was a manifest Khrushchev protégé whom the latter groomed in the Ukrainian party apparatus. He was second in command in the Secretariat until his fall and replacement by Kozlov. While the reasons for his fall remain obscure, it paralleled the fall of N. I. Belyaev, another Presidium member and Central Committee Secretary who was made scapegoat for failure in Khrushchev's virgin lands in 1959. His fall also occurred in a period when Khrushchev's Camp David strategy had begun to founder. An evident but abortive effort to save Kirichenko (and Belyaev as well) from total disgrace seemed entailed in their transfer to regional party posts. However, he lost this post and went into oblivion a month after the U-2 episode.

KIRILENKO, A. P.   (b. 1906)

A Ukrainian protégé of Khrushchev and linked with Brezhnev, Kirilenko was a strong backer of Khrushchev's effort to expel the members of the "group" from the party. Under Khrushchev he rose from head of the important Sverdlovsk party organization to become Khrushchev's chief deputy in the Central Committee Bureau for the RSFSR. He suddenly lost his status as a Presidium candidate at the Twenty-second Congress only to make a comeback six months later as a full Presidium member under Khrushchev's evident aegis. His re-entry into the Presidium coincided with Khrushchev's action against Kozlov's associate, Spiridonov, the Leningrad party chief after the Twenty-second Congress. Kirilenko's speech to the Twenty-second Congress was distinguished from Spiridonov's in one vital detail; while both denounced the "group" Kirilenko called for party expulsion of the group leaders and Spiridonov did not. After the Cuban crisis when Khrushchev was in retreat there were signs of factional moves against Kirilenko—his successor in Sverdlovsk delivered a sharp attack on the management of the Sverdlovsk party during the time Kirilenko was the incumbent and his name was placed below Kozlov's and Kosygin's in an otherwise customary alphabetical listing of the top leaders in *Pravda* in March, 1963.

KOSYGIN, A. N.   (b. 1904)

A full member of the Presidium since May, 1960, and Premier after Khrushchev's fall, Kosygin rose to high government and planning posts outside of Khrushchev's patronage. Having spent his whole career in the state apparatus and as a First Deputy Chairman of the Council of Ministers under Khrushchev, he is an example of the regime economic administrator par excellence. Under Khrushchev he repeatedly indicated his independence of mind in his evident distaste for the leader "cult" around Khrushchev and his opposition to further vendettas against members of the anti-party group. Khrushchev's ambitious chemicals program did not prosper when Kosygin headed the state planning agency and he was probably among the targets of Khrushchev's bitter complaints in 1964 against state planners for their failure to be sufficiently responsive to his policies. As a proponent of "scientific" and "rational" economics he has shown his dislike for Khrushchev's radical initiatives in economic policy and the latter's attempt to convert the party apparatus into an agency of economic management. In this connection he has been a defender of the traditional prerogatives of the state apparatus in the economic sphere. He represents himself as a leader who opposes extremes in policy, a middle-of-the-roader who opposed Khrushchev's "subjectivism" in economic policy and who stresses that consumer needs can only be met through modernization and rationalization of the productive apparatus of the whole economy on the basis of "objective" criteria rather than by decree "from above." With this approach he avoids giving the impression, as Khrushchev did, that he intends any radical shakeup of established interests in the regime and yet conveys a picture of himself as a forward-looking apostle of efficiency and "scientific" methods.

KOZLOV, F. R.   (1908–64)

A full Presidium member since June, 1957, and a Central Committee Secretary to the period shortly before his death in 1964, Kozlov rose rapidly to the status of second in command in the Secretariat and became Khrushchev's presumptive "heir." Kozlov was not simply a creature of Khrushchev's patronage like his predecessor Kirichenko. He rose to prominence in the powerful Leningrad party apparatus. That he was less than a favored protégé was indicated in early 1955 when he came under sharp attack from Khrushchev for his agricultural leadership in the Leningrad region. Of course, an important factor in Kozlov's elevation to full Presidium status was the support he gave in the June crisis against the "group." After his entrance into the Secretariat at the time of the U-2 episode, he at various times indicated his political independence revealing himself as a critic of Khrushchev's economic policy, intimacy with Yugoslav "revisionism," and tactics in the Sino-Soviet dispute. After the Cuban crisis he emerged as a key figure in the conservative turn in policy and as a challenger of Khrushchev's policy until he was suddenly incapacitated in April, 1963.

In this endeavor he appears to have often been in alliance with Suslov. In mid-1962 he signed a *Kommunist* article which propounded the traditional view of the party's role as a political-ideological institution that must eschew excessive involvement in economic management. Subsequently, he indicated his opposition to Khrushchev's 1962 party reform. The same *Kommunist* article also tacitly criticized Khrushchev's agricultural policy for having resulted in a detrimental loss of "operative" state control over agriculture. Kozlov was vulnerable to attack from Khrushchev for his linkage with the public build-up for the "Doctors' Plot" in early 1953 when he identified himself as a proponent of extreme vigilance against alleged "spies" and "enemies" within the U.S.S.R. Ironically, Kozlov, who died shortly after Khrushchev's fall, was buried with full honors and eulogies from party leaders, while Khrushchev, still in life, was in political disgrace.

KUUSINEN, O. V. (1881–64)
An elder Communist statesman, founder of the Finnish Communist party and a prominent figure in the Comintern of the 1920's, Kuusinen entered the Secretariat and the Presidium at the same time of the purge of the "group" in 1957. He thus lent his prestige as an "old Bolshevik" to the new Khrushchev administration which had just disposed of such elder figures as Molotov and Kaganovich. Kuusinen strongly supported Khrushchev's attack on Molotov at the Twenty-second Congress, particularly in the area of theory and generally assisted Khrushchev in his attack on the Chinese "dogmatists." He delivered the reply, for example, to the pamphlet entitled *Long Live Leninism!*, a Chinese attack on Khrushchev's policy in April, 1960. He was the editor-in-chief of the textbook on theory under Khrushchev, *The Fundamentals of Marxism-Leninism*.

MALENKOV, G. M. (b. 1902)
The one-time heir apparent in Stalin's last years and Premier from 1953 to 1955, Malenkov initially was Khrushchev's main competitor in the leadership struggle after Stalin's death, but not as an antagonist of reform as was Molotov, but as a rival reform leader. Until his defeat and removal as Premier, Malenkov pursued a policy of measured concessions to the population at home and a relatively cautious foreign policy. In many respects Malenkov resembles Khrushchev's successor in the Premiership, Kosygin, who presents himself as a judicious reformer and modernizer. Malenkov stressed rationality

and efficiency and reliance on the state apparatus as the prime directing agency in the economy. After his defeat he was charged with attempting to place the state above the party. He was associated with the short-lived effort after Stalin's death to place the economy under the centralized direction of a small number of super-ministries. The number of ministries was sharply reduced but in a relatively short time the plan was undone and ministerial bodies proliferated once again until the introduction of Khrushchev's 1957 reform. After his purge in 1957 Khrushchev tried to discredit the idea that Malenkov had favored reform and portrayed his old rival as an unscrupulous executor of some of the worst excesses of the latter part of Stalin's reign.

MAZUROV, K. T.   (b. 1914)

Under Khrushchev Mazurov was an example of an influential member of the territorial party apparatus who did not owe his position to Khrushchev and made his independence of mind evident. Mazurov held candidacy in the Presidium by virtue of his position as head of the Belorussian party apparatus where he spent his early career. Conflict between Khrushchev and Mazurov was evident at various points in the 1957–64 period. In December, 1960, Mazurov opposed Khrushchev's decentralization of the apparatus of the Ministry of Agriculture, complaining that the agencies of the Ministry were being "unjustly deprived of their age-old functions." At the Twenty-second Congress Khrushchev interrupted Mazurov's speech and sharply attacked him for reducing meat production in Belorussia. Mazurov has been clearly a defender of the traditional centralized ministerial system. After Khrushchev's fall he gained full Presidium status. Shortly before his elevation the Ministry of Agriculture regained its former functions, presaging the abolition of Khrushchev's decentralized system of economic administration as a whole and the restoration of the central ministries by Khrushchev's successors.

MIKOYAN, A. I.   (b. 1895)

A member of the Politburo and Presidium since 1926, Mikoyan was a senior and influential figure in the leadership. His most notable characteristic was his quite amazing survivability for close to four decades amid the perils of high-level factional politics of the Stalin and post-Stalin periods. He was Khrushchev's privileged ally who stood by Khrushchev against what initially appeared to be overwhelming odds in the June, 1957, leadership crisis but who also deserted him at the time of his ouster in 1964. He was perhaps Khrushchev's closest collaborator and adviser in policy matters and undertook important foreign missions in support of Khrushchev's foreign policy, including the trip to the United States in advance of the Khrushchev visit and the trip to Cuba in 1962 to conciliate Castro in the wake of the withdrawal of Soviet missiles. He clearly supported Khrushchev's general policy of pro-consumer economic reform and was a representative of the reform wing of the party. At the Twentieth Party Congress he made the strongest attack on Stalin prior to Khrushchev's "secret speech" sharply depreciating Stalin's rigidity in economic theory. Along with Khrushchev himself, he was among the least doctrinaire of the party leaders. While a backer of Khrushchev's general policy, he also was the boldest among the leaders in registering his opposition to any attempt by Khrushchev to gain absolute power or to press further purges against the anti-party group. It was perhaps his self-appointed role as a senior politician without ambitions for supreme power that partly explained his political success, despite many ups and downs in his fortunes. He became titular chief of state just prior to Khrushchev's fall, but has since resigned that post, allegedly for reasons of age and health. As a result he no longer sits in the party Presidium (now renamed Politburo) but retains his Central Committee membership.

MOLOTOV, V. M. (b. 1890)

Despite his defeat in the leadership crisis of June, 1957, Molotov remained a hovering presence behind the political stage in the years after. It was with good reason that Khrushchev made Molotov rather than Malenkov a major target at the Twenty-second Congress. As an old Bolshevik who had known Lenin personally and held top posts throughout the Stalin era, Molotov was the most prestigious political figure in the leading group after Stalin's death. Further, he had compromised himself the least of all the members of the anti-Khrushchev faction. In a bold rejection of convention, he refused to vote for the Central Committee resolution condemning the anti-party group; subsequently, he also refused to come forward in self-criticism. After 1957 Khrushchev faced the danger that an opposition might arise which would seek Molotov's services in a challenge to his leadership. Yevtushenko's poem, "Stalin's Heirs," broadly hinted that Molotov was hoping for just such an opportunity. Up to early 1962 Molotov had retained official posts first as Ambassador to Mongolia and then as Soviet representative to the International Atomic Energy

Commission in Vienna. Not until 1964, close to seven years after Molotov's purge, was it announced that Molotov had been expelled from the party. The announcement came not long after *Izvestia* had published "letters" from readers bitterly complaining that "certain people" were spreading anecdotes among the population obviously critical of Khrushchev and implying that the views of the anti-party group had proven right.

Molotov was something more than a straw man in Khrushchev's attacks on "dogmatism" in policy. The epitome of orthodoxy, Molotov's outlook on over-all policy was the antithesis of Khrushchev's. According to various speakers at the Twenty-second Congress, Molotov continued to voice criticisms of Khrushchev's policy after 1957. These accounts said that he, among other things, attacked the MTS reform while it was under consideration in 1958, submitted an article to *Kommunist* on Lenin in April, 1960, for the latter's birthday anniversary, and sent a criticism of Khrushchev's policies to the Central Committee on the eve of the Twenty-second Congress. At the Congress Kuusinen charged that Molotov was fishing in "muddy" waters in hope of gaining supporters either at home or abroad.

MUKHITDINOV, N. A.   (b. 1917)

An Uzbek party official who rose to head the Uzbek party organization in 1955 under Khrushchev's direct auspices, Mukhitdinov was one of the coterie of Khrushchevites who entered both the Presidium and the Secretariat in the wake of the June, 1957, purge of the "group." Mukhitdinov assiduously cultivated the leader cult around Khrushchev at the Twenty-first Party Congress and helped promote the attack on the anti-party group. He lost his posts in the Presidium and Secretariat at the Twenty-second Party Congress along with a number of other former Khrushchev supporters during the June, 1957, leadership crisis.

PERVUKHIN, M. G.   (b. 1904)

The remarkable thing about this top-level industrial administrator and planner was that he retained his foothold in the Presidium for over four years after he had taken part in the 1957 challenge to Khrushchev. He was reduced only one rank, from a full to a candidate member of the Presidium. He held his Presidium post despite the concerted attack upon him at the Twenty-first CPSU Congress in 1959 and his exile to the post of Ambassador to East Germany. In July, 1960, when Kozlov, Suslov, and Kosygin were taking unusually prominent roles in leadership activities, he returned home from Berlin and joined the Presidium "collective" in one of its public appearances.

He was finally dropped from the Presidium without fanfare at the Twenty-second Congress in October, 1961. Kosygin, an economic administrator and planner like Pervukhin, may well have been among the latter's protectors after 1957. It is noteworthy that after Khrushchev's fall Pervukhin was linked with Kosygin in a highly favorable context in an article in the Soviet military historical journal (*Voyenno-istoricheskii Zhurnal*, No. 5, 1965, p. 11) in connection with their work in evacuating Soviet industry to rear areas in World War II. In March, 1966, he reappeared as a member of Gosplan, the state planning agency. Both figures have one thing in common: both clashed with Khrushchev over issues of economic planning and industrial management.

PODGORNYY, N. V. (b. 1903)
A full Presidium member since May, 1960, and a Central Committee Secretary since June, 1963, Podgornyy rose to prominence in the Ukrainian party apparatus. While regarded as a Khrushchevite, he rose to head the Ukrainian party after Khrushchev's departure from the Ukraine and his career association with Khrushchev was thus less direct than in the case of Kirichenko. During the bad harvest year of 1960 Podgornyy was severely criticized by Khrushchev for agricultural mismanagement but survived the attack. However, Podgornyy appeared to be generally loyal to Khrushchev's policies and was one of the promoters of Khrushchev's 1962 party reform. Ironically, however, he also was the figure who gave the report to the Central Committee on the abolition of the reform after Khrushchev's fall. At the same time he had shown some independence of mind at the November, 1962, plenum which adopted the party reform when he complained of inadequate metal output in the Ukraine at the very time Khrushchev was saying that the regime was overproducing steel. His entry into the Secretariat along with his natural rival Brezhnev in June, 1963, after Kozlov's incapacitation placed him in the running as one of Khrushchev's potential successors. There was a possible hint that he was somewhat on the outskirts of the plan to overthrow Khrushchev since he evidently was the last Presidium member to link himself publicly with Khrushchev on the eve of the latter's downfall. On October 10, 1964, in Moldavia he told his audience that he had spoken with Khrushchev shortly before and was passing his personal greetings on to the Moldavians.

POLYANSKIY, D. S.   (b. 1917)

One of the younger party functionaries and economic specialists in the Presidium, Polyanskiy vigorously pursued the attack on the "group" in 1957 and after, yet his attachment to Khrushchev appears to have lessened with time. He gained candidacy in the Presidium in connection with his elevation to Chairman of the RSFSR Council of Ministers in 1958 and entered the Presidium as a full member in May, 1960. His downgrading to a Deputy Chairman of the Council of Ministers at the time of Khrushchev's party reform in 1962 should normally have eventuated in his removal from the Presidium. However, like his Presidium colleague Voronov, who was associated with him in the RSFSR apparatus and suffered a decline at the same juncture, he retained his Presidium post and reputedly delivered the indictment of Khrushchev's agricultural policies at the Presidium meeting ousting the Soviet leader in October, 1964.

PONOMAREV, B. N.   (b. 1905)

A Central Committee historian and specialist on relations within the international Communist movement, Ponomarev entered the Secretariat at the Twenty-second Congress in 1961. He was the chief editor of the new party history under Khrushchev and a member of the editorial board of *Kommunist*. While he participated in sharp attacks on the Chinese "dogmatists," he also indicated in a *Pravda* article shortly after the Cuban crisis his opposition to condoning Yugoslav "revisionism," and stressed that "revisionism" remained the "main danger" to the Communist movement. This line was out of tune with Khrushchev's effort to make "dogmatism" the greater danger. In this regard, his party history was criticized by the Yugoslavs for justifying the ideological grounds of the resolution expelling the Yugoslavs from the Cominform in 1948.

POSPELOV, P. N.   (b. 1898)

A long-time Central Committee historian and ideologue, Pospelov entered the Secretariat in 1953 and at the Twentieth Congress became a deputy to Khrushchev in the then newly formed Central Committee Bureau for the RSFSR. He lost his post in the Secretariat in the May, 1960, shake-up and subsequently his post in the RSFSR Bureau at the Twenty-second Congress and was given the lesser but still influential post of head of the Central Committee's Institute of Marzism-Leninism. Pospelov aimed a shaft at Suslov at the time of the

MTS reform criticizing those who failed to see the reform's theoretical significance. At the Twenty-first and Twenty-second Congresses Pospelov enthusiastically elucidated Khrushchev's doctrinal revisions and in early 1962 wrote a *Pravda* article which implied an analogy between Lenin's difficulties with "compromisers" in the party in struggles with his enemies and Khrushchev's own situation in his struggle against the Chinese and the Albanians.

SABUROV, M. Z.   (b. 1900)

From the standpoint of career and outlook Saburov was the twin of Pervukhin. A mechanical engineer by training, he rose to Presidium membership in his capacity as a planner and managerial executive in the economic-administrative structure of the state. His objections to Khrushchev's 1957 industrial reform were evidently similar to Pervukhin's. Both saw the reform as a threat to central control and planning in the economy. As a result of his part in the leadership crisis in June, 1957, Saburov was stripped of his posts as a Presidium member and First Deputy Chairman of the Council of Ministers. Unlike Pervukhin, he went rapidly into political limbo after June, 1957. In his statement to the Twenty-first Party Congress he conceded that he had displayed "political instability" in 1957 but stoutly insisted that he had not supported the challenge to Khrushchev's leadership as such. Notably, Saburov was virtually ignored in the renewed attack on the fallen anti-Khrushchev faction at the Twenty-second Congress.

SHELEPIN, A. N.   (b. 1918)

Another member of the younger generation in the leadership who rose to high posts as head of the Komsomol, Shelepin was made head of the secret police (KGB) in 1958 in a move designed to suggest that the police had come under strict party control. He vigorously pressed the attack on the "crimes" of the anti-party group at the Twenty-second Congress and gained entrance to the Secretariat at the Congress. Following Khrushchev's 1962 party reform he was made head of the newly formed party-state control commission, a potentially powerful agency designed to check upon and correct abuses by officials at all levels of the party and state apparatus. He evidently played an important role in arranging Khrushchev's overthrow, probably in part because of his connections in the secret police. Shortly after Khrushchev's fall he gained full Presidium membership and thus became one of the privileged figures in that body with a foothold in the Secretariat.

SHEPILOV, D. T.   (b. 1905)

A political-ideological functionary, Shepilov rose rapidly under Khrushchev's patronage in the 1954–57 period. He served with Khrushchev as a political commander on the Ukrainian front in World War II and evidently held Khrushchev's trust until he deserted him in the 1957 leadership crisis. In 1954–55 he was editor of *Pravda*. At the Twentieth Party Congress he gained candidacy in the Presidium and successively occupied posts as a CPSU secretary, Foreign Minister, and again as secretary before his purge in June, 1957. He was singled out in attacks on the fallen faction as "Shepilov who joined them" and portrayed as a "double-dealer." At the Twenty-first Party Congress he was ridiculed by one speaker for attributing his apostasy to the "instability" of Russian intellectuals of which he counted himself as one. At the Twenty-second Party Congress he was also accused of keeping a "dirty little black book" in which he gathered information for use against other political leaders.

SHVERNIK, N. M.   (b. 1888)

Like Kuusinen, another "old Bolshevik" brought into the Presidium at the time of the purge of the anti-Khrushchev faction in 1957, Shvernik headed the party control commission under Khrushchev and dutifully pressed sharp attacks on the members of the "group" at the Twenty-second Congress for their "crimes" under Stalin. His commission formally heard cases involving party expulsions and thus he was important to Khrushchev in the latter's effort to expel the "group" members from the party.

SPIRIDONOV, I. V.   (b. 1905)

A party official who built his career in the Leningrad party organization and who succeeded Kozlov as Leningrad First Secretary, Spiridonov led vigorous attacks on Malenkov's role in the "Leningrad Affair," the purge of the Leningrad party under Stalin in 1949, both at the Twenty-first and Twenty-second Congresses. His loyalty appears to have been divided between Khrushchev and Kozlov. At the Twenty-second Congress he made the proposal from the floor calling for Stalin's removal from Lenin's tomb, delivered a sharp attack on the "group," but conspicuously failed to demand party expulsions of the latter. He gained entry into the Secretariat at the Twenty-second Congress most likely under Kozlov's aegis only to lose that position and his post as Leningrad First Secretary at Khrushchev's hands six months later.

He thus became a casualty in the conflict between Khrushchev and Kozlov. However, his transfer to a ceremonial post in the Supreme Soviet indicated that he still had powerful protectors.

SUSLOV, M. A.   (b. 1902)

A Central Committee Secretary since 1947 and a full member of the Presidium since 1955, Suslov is an influential and senior member of the leadership who on various occasions indicated his political independence, his distaste for Khrushchev's pragmatism, depreciation of theory and penchant for radical innovations. As the regime's senior theorist and ideologist he has played key roles in relations with foreign parties, including major roles in the 1957 and 1960 world Communist meetings in Moscow, in the ideological supervision of the Soviet intelligentsia, as well as in over-all questions of policy. He indicated that he took exception to the theoretical aspects of Khrushchev's MTS reform, refused to treat Khrushchev's Twenty-first Congress report as a Central Committee document and pointed to the theoretical "difficulties" in working out the new party program for which Khrushchev sought to claim credit. He was vulnerable to attack from Khrushchev as a "dogmatist" and "Stalinist" because of his prominent public roles in Stalin's last years in the expulsion of the Yugoslav "revisionists" from the Cominform, in the ideological crackdown under Zhdanov, and in the attack on Voznesenskiy, the Politburo member executed at Stalin's orders. Khrushchev obviously regarded Suslov as a danger to his leadership and groomed the ideologist Ilichev as his rival. He resisted Khrushchev's effort to heap new punishments on his fallen enemies in the anti-party group and indicated his opposition to Khrushchev's anti-Stalinist excesses. He reportedly delivered the main indictment against Khrushchev at his ouster. According to the Italian Communist periodical *Paese Sera*, that indictment criticized Khrushchev, among other things, for "subjectivism" in the conduct of the polemic with the Chinese Communists, a desire to put "excessive" resources into the consumer economy to the detriment of heavy industry, and for sponsoring the publication of Solzhenitsyn's literary exposé of Stalin's labor camps.

VORONOV, G. I.   (b. 1910)

An official in the party apparatus specializing in agriculture, Voronov became a full member of the Presidium at the Twenty-second Congress. He had succeeded to Aristov's former position in the Central Committee's RSFSR Bureau in January, 1961, as a First Deputy

Chairman in that body. Voronov cannot be counted among Khrushchev's protégés since he had made most of his career outside Khrushchev's patronage. In this regard his speeches, including the one he gave at the Twenty-second Congress, virtually ignored the question of the anti-party group. One of the figures Voronov appointed to head the RSFSR agricultural ministry in 1962, N. I. Smirnov, actually had been subjected to severe criticism by Khrushchev just a few months before, an indication of Voronov's political independence and divergence from Khrushchev in agricultural matters. Kirilenko's entrance into the RSFSR Bureau at the time looked like a Khrushchev move to undercut Voronov's position in that body. Indeed at the time of the party reform Voronov was transferred to the post of Chairman of the RSFSR Council of Ministers, a somewhat lesser post. This action occurred at the very time Khrushchev was attempting to give the lead to the party apparatus in the economic sphere with his party reform. Nonetheless, despite this setback, Voronov retained his Presidium position.

VOROSHILOV, K. YE. (b. 1881)

An old Bolshevik and, like Molotov, a long-time intimate of Stalin, Voroshilov lent his considerable prestige as an elder party figure to the cause of the anti-Khrushchev faction in June, 1957. As a consequence, he became a special target in Khrushchev's drive to heap further humiliations and punishments on his defeated enemies. At the same time, however, Voroshilov had protectors in the leadership after 1957, most visibly Mikoyan. Voroshilov did not lose his ceremonial position as Chairman of the Supreme Soviet until July, 1960. And despite his belated exposure as a member of the anti-party group at the Twenty-second Congress in October, 1961, he did not suffer complete disgrace at Khrushchev's hands. Voroshilov's fear that Khrushchev would press his vendetta against him even to the point of a political trial was indicated in a curious account Khrushchev gave of a private conversation with the elder figure in late 1959. Khrushchev said Voroshilov had pleaded with him to stress that "we do not now have any cases of political crime to prosecute" (see Khrushchev's speech to Soviet journalists, *Pravda*, Nov. 18, 1959). Voroshilov was not without grounds for such a fear. At the Twenty-second Congress Khrushchev charged Voroshilov with grave political crimes under Stalin. After Khrushchev's fall, however, he returned to full political respectability, regaining Central Committee membership.

ANNOTATED BIBLIOGRAPHY

PRIMARY SOURCES

Pravda is a basic source for major political documents, decrees, leaders' speeches, etc.; however, it is important to approach Soviet newspapers and journals on a comparative basis and to watch for instances of divergent treatment of issues or developments that often provide clues to the regime's inner politics. For those who do not read Russian, the *Current Digest of the Soviet Press*, New York, N.Y., edited by Leo Gruliow, provides an extensive selection of key political materials from the Soviet press and publications.

DOCUMENTS

THE RUSSIAN INSTITUTE, COLUMBIA UNIVERSITY (ed.). *The Anti-Stalin Campaign and International Communism*. New York: Columbia University Press, 1956.

    A useful collection of documents in English including Khrushchev's "secret speech" to the Twentieth Party Congress.

GRULIOW, LEO (ed.). *Current Soviet Policies*. Vols. I, II, and III. New York: Praeger, 1953–60.

    The documentary records of the Nineteenth, Twentieth, and Twenty-first CPSU Congresses in English translation.

KHRUSHCHEV, NIKITA S. *Stroitel'stvo Kommunizma v SSSR i Razvitiye Sel'skogo Khozyaystva* [*The Construction of Communism in the USSR and the Development of Agriculture*]. 8 vols. Moscow: Gospolitizdat, 1962–64.

A goldmine of Khrushchev's speeches, statements, interviews, and memoranda on agricultural policy. Some of the material was not previously published in the Soviet press. Materials from September, 1953, to March, 1964, are included.

KUUSINEN, O. (ed.). *Fundamentals of Marxism-Leninism.* Moscow: Foreign Languages Publishing House, 1961.

————. *Fundamentals of Marxism-Leninism.* 2nd ed. rev. Moscow: Foreign Languages Publishing House, 1963.

The official doctrinal and theoretical textbook. The changes in the 2nd edition reflected the sharpening of the Sino-Soviet dispute and readjustments in the political line after the Twenty-second Congress.

Plenum Tsentral'nogo Komiteta Kommunisticheskoy Partii Sovetskogo Soyuza, Stenograficheskiy Otchet [Plenum of the Central Committee of the Communist Party of the Soviet Union, Stenographic Record]. Moscow: Gospolitizdat.

Stenographic records appearing under the above title have been published by Gospolitizdat (State Publishing House for Political Literature) for the plenums which took place on the following dates (place and date of publication noted): Dec. 15–19, 1958, Moscow, 1958; June 24–29, 1959, Moscow, 1959; Dec. 22–25, 1959, Moscow, 1960; July 13–16, 1960, Moscow, 1960; Jan. 10–18, 1961, Moscow, 1961; March 5–9, 1962, Moscow, 1962; Nov. 19–23, 1962, Moscow, 1963; June 18–21, 1963, Moscow, 1963; Dec. 9–13, 1963, Moscow, 1964; Feb. 10–15, 1964; Moscow, 1964.

PONOMAREV, B. N., *et al. Istoriya Kommunisticheskoy Partii Sovetskogo Soyuza [The History of the Communist Party of the Soviet Union].* Moscow: Gospolitizdat, 1959. Also 2nd ed. enl. Moscow: Gospolitizdat, 1962.

A history reflecting the current political line. Editions can be usefully compared for changes in line in the intervening period.

STALIN, J. V. *Economic Problems of Socialism in the USSR,* in Leo Gruliow (ed.), *Current Soviet Policies.* Vol. 1. New York: Praeger, 1953.

————. *Sochineniya [Works].* 14 vols. Moscow: Gospolitizdat, 1946–55.

XXII S'yezd Kommunisticheskoy Partii Sovetskogo Soyuza, 17–31 Oktyabrya 1961 Goda, Stenograficheskiy Otchet [22nd Congress of the Communist Party of the Soviet Union, October 17–31, 1961, Stenographic Record]. 3 vols. Moscow: Gospolitizdat, 1961–62.

Vneocherednoy XXI S'yezd Kommunisticheskoy Partii Sovetskogo Soyuza, 27 Yanvarya – 5 Fevralya 1959 Goda, Stenograficheskiy Otchet [Extraordinary 21st Congress of the Communist Party of the Soviet Union, January 27 – February 5, 1959, Stenographic Record]. 2 vols. Moscow: Gospolitizdat, 1959.

REFERENCE MATERIALS

Bol'shaya Sovetskaya Entsiklopediya [*The Large Soviet Encyclopedia*]. 2nd ed. 50 vols. Moscow: Large Soviet Encyclopedia, 1949–58.
Useful source of biographical and political information.

Knizhnaya Letopis', Letopis' Zhurnal'nykh Statei, Letopis' Gazetnykh Statei [*Book Chronicle, Chronicle of Journal Articles, Chronicle of Newspaper Articles*]. Moscow: Izdatel'stvo Vsesoyuznoi Knizhnoi Palaty [Publishing House of the All-Union Book Chamber].
Comprehensive but not exhaustive indices to current Soviet books, journals, and newspapers published weekly. Also includes author index.

Politicheskii Slovar' [*Political Dictionary*]. Moscow: Gospolitizdat, 1956, 1958.
Provides brief statements of the current political line on a variety of subjects including political leaders.

Spravochnik Partiynogo Rabotnika [*Handbook of the Party Worker*]. Moscow: Gospolitizdat, 1959–63.
Contains useful collections of party documents, resolutions, etc. on variety of topics.

Vedomosti Verkhovnogo Soveta [*Proceedings of the USSR Supreme Soviet*]. Publishes decrees of the Supreme Soviet.

NEWSPAPERS AND JOURNALS

Soviet Central Press:

Ekonomicheskaya Gazeta [*Economic Gazette*]
Weekly organ of the Party Central Committee on economic affairs, Moscow.

Izvestia [*News*]
Organ of the central government, Moscow.

Krasnaya Zveszda [*Red Star*]
Organ of the Ministry of Defense of the U.S.S.R., Moscow.

Literaturnaya Gazeta [*Literary Gazette*]
Organ of the Soviet Writers' Union, Moscow.

Pravda [*Truth*]
Organ of the Party Central Committee, Moscow.

Sovetskaya Rossiya [*Soviet Russia*]
Organ of the party and government of the Russian Federation (RSFSR), Moscow.

Trud [*Labor*]
Organ of the Soviet trade unions, Moscow.

Soviet Provincial Newspapers:

Bakinskii Rabochii [*Baku Worker*], Baku.
Kazakhstanskaya Pravda [*Pravda of Kazakhstan*], Alma Ata.
Kommunist [*Communist*], Yerevan.
Kommunist Tadzhikistana [*Communist of Tadzhikistan*], Dushanbe.
Leningradskaya Pravda [*Leningrad Pravda*], Leningrad
Pravda Ukrainy [*Pravda of the Ukraine*], Kiev.
Pravda Vostoka [*Pravda of the East*], Tashkent.
Sovetskaya Belorussiya [*Soviet Belorussia*], Minsk.
Sovetskaya Kirgiziya [*Soviet Kirgizia*], Frunze.
Sovetskaya Latviya [*Soviet Latvia*], Riga.
Sovetskaya Litva [*Soviet Lithuania*], Vil'nyus.
Sovetskaya Moldaviya [*Soviet Moldavia*], Kishinev.
Turkmenskaya Iskra [*Spark of Turkmenia*], Ashkhabad.
Zarya Vostoka [*Dawn of the East*], Tbilisi.

Soviet Journals:

Kommunist [*Communist*]
    Theoretical organ of the Party Central Committee.
Novy Mir [*New World*]
    A literary journal of the U.S.S.R. Writers' Union known in recent
    years as a mouthpiece of the liberal wing of Soviet writers.
Oktyabr [*October*]
    A literary organ of the RSFSR (Russian Federation) Writers'
    Union known in recent years as the journal often presenting the
    views of the conservative wing of Soviet writers.
Partiinaya Zhizn' [*Party Life*]
    House organ of the Party Central Committee focusing on
    organizational questions and internal party affairs.
Voprosy Ekonomiki [*Problems of Economics*]
    Organ of the Institute of Economics of the U.S.S.R. Academy of
    Sciences.
Voprosy Istorii [*Problems of History*]
    Organ of the historical department of the U.S.S.R. Academy of
    Sciences.
Voprosy Istorii KPSS [*Problems of CPSU History*]
    Organ of the Institute of Marxism-Leninism under the Party
    Central Committee.
World Marxist Review
    The Soviet bloc journal published in Prague as a successor to

the defunct Cominform journal. Pro-Soviet in orientation in the bloc dispute, it is intended as an organ for the Communist movement as a whole. It appears in numerous languages and also appears in Russian under the name *Problems of Peace and Socialism*.

Foreign Party Press:

Borba [*Struggle*]
> Organ of the League of Communists of Yugoslavia.

Hung ch'i [*Red Flag*]
> The theoretical journal of the Chinese Communist party.

Jen-min jih-pao [*People's Daily*]
> Organ of the Chinese Communist party.

L'Unita
> Organ of the Italian Communist party.

Neues Deutschland
> Organ of the East German Communist party (SED-Socialist Unity Party of Germany).

Zolnierz Wolnosci [*Soldier of Freedom*]
> Organ of the Polish Ministry of Defense, Warsaw.

Western Press:

The New York Times
The Washington Post

SECONDARY SOURCES

Books

ARMSTRONG, JOHN A. *The Politics of Totalitarianism, The Communist Party of the Soviet Union from 1934 to the Present*. New York: Random House, 1961.
> A detailed political history of the Soviet Communist party using 1934 as the starting date when the regime begins to display the traits of full-blown totalitarianism. Complements Leonard Schapiro's history by providing a fuller account of more recent party history.

CONQUEST, ROBERT. *Power and Policy in the USSR*. New York: St. Martin's Press, 1961.
> A pioneering work in the study of Soviet leadership politics. Combines a thorough discussion of the problems of evidence and methodology in the study of Kremlin politics with a detailed history of leadership struggles from Stalin's last years to the Twenty-first Party Congress in 1959. Contains extensive appendices providing some key sources and useful basic information on the political leadership.

————. *Russia After Khrushchev*. New York: Praeger, 1965.

A wide-ranging examination of the character and pattern of contemporary leadership politics. Stresses the pervasiveness of the power and factional struggle in the party and the instability of the leadership arrangement.

CRANKSHAW, EDWARD. *The New Cold War: Moscow v. Pekin*. Baltimore: Penguin, 1963.

A popular but useful account of the development of the Sino-Soviet conflict. Especially valuable for its accounts of the two crucial Soviet-Chinese confrontations behind closed doors at the world party meetings in Bucharest and Moscow in 1960.

DJILAS, MILOVAN. *Conversations with Stalin*. New York: Harcourt, Brace, and World, 1962.

A valuable source of first-hand observations not only on Stalin but on the figures around him such as Molotov, Malenkov, Khrushchev, etc.

FAINSOD, MERLE. *How Russia Is Ruled*. Rev. ed. Cambridge, Mass.: Harvard University Press, 1963.

The classic and standard work in the study of Soviet government revised and updated.

LEONHARD, WOLFGANG. *The Kremlin Since Stalin*. London: Oxford, 1962.

A detailed and comprehensive history of Soviet politics from the time of Stalin's death to 1960.

PETHYBRIDGE, ROGER. *A Key to Soviet Politics: The Crisis of the Anti-Party Group*. New York: Praeger, 1962.

A thorough and detailed study of the available evidence on the challenge to Khrushchev in June, 1957, by the Molotov-Malenkov faction and an interpretation of the event's significance to an understanding of contemporary Soviet leadership politics.

PISTRAK, LAZAR. *The Grand Tactician: Khrushchev's Rise to Power*. New York: Praeger, 1961.

A political biography of Khrushchev which is especially useful for its extended account of the Soviet leader's early rise to high posts before Stalin's death.

PLOSS, SIDNEY. *Conflict and Decision-Making in Soviet Russia, A Case Study of Agricultural Policy, 1953–1963*. Princeton, N.J.: Princeton University Press, 1965.

Not only a detailed and perceptive examination of conflict and decision-making in the crucial area of Soviet agricultural policy but an important contribution to the study of contemporary Soviet leadership politics.

RUSH, MYRON. *The Rise of Khrushchev*. Washington, D.C.: Public Affairs Press, 1958.

A Kremlinological history of the leadership struggles after Stalin's death that led to Khrushchev's victory over his challengers in 1957. An important contribution to the development of contemporary methodology in the study of Soviet leadership politics. Contains an essay on "esoteric communication" in Soviet politics in the appendices.

———. *Political Succession in the U.S.S.R.* New York: Columbia University Press, 1965.

An historical and conceptual analysis and interpretation of the problem of political succession in the Soviet regime. Focuses on the political and institutional milieu that has made succession a critical and unpredictable process in the U.S.S.R.

SCHAPIRO, LEONARD. *The Communist Party of the Soviet Union*. New York: Random House, 1960.

A comprehensive history of the Russian Communist party from its origins to the contemporary period. Contains detailed and illuminating treatments of the controversies in which Lenin engaged as leader of the Bolshevik faction before 1917 and of the political struggles in the post-revolutionary ruling party leading to Stalin's seizure of dictatorial power.

TUCKER, ROBERT C. *The Soviet Political Mind*. New York: Praeger, 1963.

A perceptive collection of essays on Soviet politics containing many valuable insights into the Soviet political milieu in both the Stalin and post-Stalin eras.

ULAM, ADAM B. *The New Face of Soviet Totalitarianism*. Cambridge, Mass.: Harvard University Press, 1963.

A collection of essays ranging over the historical role of Marxism, ideology in Soviet foreign policy and Soviet politics under Khrushchev.

———. *The Unfinished Revolution*. New York: Random House, 1960.

An original analysis and interpretation of the historical role of Marxist ideology in the modern world. The author seeks to show why Marxism has an appeal in societies going through the throes of modernization and industrialization.

WOLFE, THOMAS. *Soviet Strategy at the Crossroads*. Cambridge, Mass.: Harvard University Press, 1964.

A thorough analysis of developments and debates within the military establishment concerning strategic doctrine which, at the same time, sheds light on Khrushchev's often thorny relations with the generals.

ZAGORIA, DONALD S. *The Sino-Soviet Conflict, 1956–1961.* Princeton, N.J.: Princeton University Press, 1962.

A comprehensive study of the development of the Sino-Soviet conflict from the time of the Twentieth Party Congress in 1956 to the Twenty-second Party Congress in 1961. Contains a useful discussion of methodology in the study of Communist sources and in analyzing political developments in the Communist world.

ARTICLES

BELL, DANIEL. "Ten Theories in Search of Reality: The Prediction of Soviet Behavior in the Social Sciences," *World Politics,* X (April, 1958), 327–65.

An excellent survey and critique of the various approaches that have been employed in the scholarly community in the study of the Soviet world.

CONQUEST, ROBERT. "The Struggle Goes On," *Problems of Communism,* IX (July–Aug., 1960), 7–11.

———. "After Khrushchev: A Conservative Restoration?," *Problems of Communism,* XII (Sept.–Oct., 1963), 41–46.

A contribution to the discussion on Khrushchev's leadership in the above issue of *Problems of Communism* but dealing with the question of the succession after Khrushchev.

"The Future of Russian Studies," *Survey, A Journal of Soviet and East European Studies,* Vol. 50 (Jan., 1964). See especially section entitled "Kremlinology," pp. 154–94.

A valuable collection of essays on Soviet studies by various recognized authorities. Contains an especially useful discussion of Kremlinology by Arthur Adams, Robert Conquest, Alec Nove, and T. H. Rigby.

GALLAGHER, MATTHEW. "Military Manpower: A Case Study," *Problems of Communism,* XIII (May–June, 1964), 53–62.

An excellent example of a careful analysis of conflict within the regime over a specific issue of military policy based on a close reading of statements of party and military leaders and articles in the Soviet press and journals.

GORDEY, MICHEL. "Vanka-Vstanka," *Problems of Communism,* XII (Nov.–Dec., 1963), 64–65.

Another commentary in the above journal's discussion of Khrushchev's power.

JOHNSON, PRISCILLA. "Russia: Poetry, Politics and the Unpredictable," *The Reporter*, Vol. 29 (Nov. 21, 1963), pp. 44–48.

———. "The Regime and the Intellectuals: A Window on Party Politics," *Problems of Communism, Supplement* (July–Aug., 1963).

Perceptive articles on the inter-relationship between literary conflicts among the writers and inner-regime politics.

LEONHARD, WOLFGANG. "An Anti-Khrushchev Opposition?," *Problems of Communism*, XII (Nov.–Dec., 1963), 61–64.

A commentary on my article in the preceding issue and T. H. Rigby's critique.

LINDEN, CARL. "Khrushchev and the Party Battle," *Problems of Communism*, XII (Sept.–Oct., 1963), 27–35.

Some of the principal elements of the views contained in this study are developed in this article, which was part of a discussion of the nature and extent of Khrushchev's political power in the above journal.

———. "Facts in Search of a Theory, A Reply," *Problems of Communism*, XII (Nov.–Dec., 1963), 56–58.

A reply to T. H. Rigby's critique of my article in the previous issue of the journal.

LOWENTHAL, RICHARD. "The Nature of Khrushchev's Power," *Problems of Communism*, IX (July–Aug., 1960), 1–7.

PLOSS, SIDNEY. "Political Conflict and the Soviet Press." Paper delivered to a panel on Methodology in Soviet Studies at the Annual Meeting of the American Political Science Association, Chicago, Sept. 10, 1964.

An excellent discussion of how policy conflicts in the Soviet regime are echoed in its press and publications.

RIGBY, THOMAS H. "How Strong Is the Leader?," *Problems of Communism*, XI (Sept.–Oct., 1962), 1–8.

An institutional analysis of Khrushchev's political power.

———. "The Extent and Limits of Authority (A Rejoinder to Mr. Linden)," *Problems of Communism*, XII (Sept.–Oct., 1963), 36–41.

A critique of my views on Khrushchev's power and fortunes in the above journal's discussion on the subject.

TUCKER, ROBERT C. "The 'Conflict Model,'" *Problems of Communism*, XII (Nov.–Dec., 1963), 59–61.

A commentary on my article in the preceding issue and T. H. Rigby's critique.

WOLFE, THOMAS W. "Political Primacy vs. Professional Elan," *Problems of Communism*, XIII (May–June, 1964), 44–52.

An examination of party-military politics under Khrushchev.

INDEX

Adventurism: Chinese criticism of Khrushchev, 154, 155

Adzhubei, Alexei: on error in Yugoslav slogan, 178n; defends Khrushchev under Stalin, 179; slated for Secretariat, 205

Agricultural policy: Khrushchev-Malenkov rivalry (1953–54), 27–29, 31; at 1961 plenum, 106–7; Khrushchev opposes diversion of funds from agriculture, 140; experts on fertilizer goals, 188; 1963 harvest failure, 189, 206, 211; after Khrushchev, 211–12; opposition to decentralization, 229. *See also* Economic Policy; Khrushchev

Agrogorod, 25, 84

Akhundov, V. Yu., 94

Albanian leaders: attacked at Twenty-second Congress, 131–33

Allocations, resource. *See* Resource allocations policy

Andreyev, A. A., 80

Andropov, 102

Anti-imperialist struggle, 175, 215

Anti-party group: opposition to Khrushchev's view of party, 33; in post-1957 politics, 40–41; tactics in 1957, 41–43, 52; *Pravda* complaint on attention to, 47; divisions on group issue, 75–76, 125–28; Khrushchev's power, 78; and Stalin issue at Twenty-second Congress, 118–28; Twenty-second Congress resolution on, 126; hit Khrushchev's economics line, 149; "guilt" in Stalin's crimes, 179; expulsion of Molotov *et al.*, 182, 184, 186; *Izvestia* complaint on anecdotes, 231; mentioned, 133, 174

Anti-Stalinism. *See* Stalin issue in Soviet politics

Aristov, A. P.: at Kapitonov's demotion, 77; fall from Secretariat, 95. *See also* biog., 231

Artists, Soviet: 1962 letter on revisionism, 158

Arts, policy on. *See* Literary-artistic policy

Arzumanyan, A. (economic theorist): attack on economic orthodoxy, 196–97, 197n

Barghoorn case, 190

Belgrade nonaligned conference (1961), 115

Bell, Daniel, 8

Belyaev, N. I.: scapegoat for virgin lands failure, 95. *See also* biog., 231–32

Beria, L. P.: execution, 12, 160; support of internal relaxation, 35; hid crimes from party, 137; blamed for Stalin's repressions, 160

82–83; at Pitsunda, 99; report to Twenty-second Congress, 119–20; concluding speech at Twenty-second Congress, 122; seventieth birthday, 187; intentions for Twenty-third Congress, 200; legacy, 208–21 (and mentioned *passim*)
—revisionism-dogmatism issue: emphasis on dogmatism danger, 54–55, 162, 214; attacks on dogmatists and conservatives, 73, 107, 109
—Sino-Soviet conflict: vs. Mao on revisionism-dogmatism issue, 54–57; on dogmatism danger, 55; pro-Yugoslav moves, 55, 56, 146, 180; witholds support of Mao on Taiwan, 82; veiled criticism of Chinese communes, 86; tactics at Bucharest meeting, 100–1, 102–4; speech at Bucharest, 104; confrontation with Chinese at Twenty-second Congress, 131–33; attacks exaggerators of Yugoslav danger, 161–62; project for world party meeting, 174, 200, 203; jibe at Chinese on Macao and Hong Kong, 175; charges Chinese with attempting his overthrow, 180, 181
—the Stalin issue: on Stalin's neglect of agriculture, 27; on opposition to exposure of Stalin, 34; secret speech, 35; use of anti-Stalinism, 35–36, 213; group issue as weapon, 38; post-1957 purge view of Stalin, 47–48, 59; on Stalin after Hungarian revolt, 47; on Stalin's merits, 60, 159–60; Stalin and "Doctors' Plot," 81; the anti-Stalin campaign at Twenty-second Congress, 118–28; on Kirov affair, 122; on execution of Tukhachevskiy, 122; on Ordzhonikidze's suicide, 122; sponsors Yevtushenko's *Stalin's Heirs*, 147–48; post-Cuba retreat on Stalin issue, 157–61; his role under Stalin, 179, 185; anti-Stalin speech at July, 1963, rally, 180; 1935 attack on

Yenukidze, 185; sponsors Solzhenitsyn novel, 224
—theory and practice: criticized for neglect of ideology, 24–25, 209; on practice, 24, 25, 209; as theoretician at Twenty-first Congress, 83; declares socialism-in-one-country obsolete, 85; on final socialist victory, 85; on end of encirclement, 85; on end of proletarian dictatorship, 85; on state of the whole people, 85, 109–10; on simultaneous transition to communism, 86; formulations on withering of state, 109–13; revisions of theory, 215–17
—writers and artists: 1957 speeches on literature and art, 59; July, 1960, speech on literature, 98; sponsors anti-Stalin literature, 147–48, 180; at art exhibition, 159; on party line toward arts, 159; backtracks on literary policy, 159–60; dampens conservative drive against writers, 179; mid-1963 reconciliation with writers, 180, 190
Kirichenko, A. I.: enters Secretariat, 61; at Kapitonov's removal, 77; Khrushchev protégé, 95; stood by Khrushchev in 1957, 95; his fall, 95–96. *See also* biog., 234–35
Kirilenko, A. P.: removed from Presidium, 141; re-enters Presidium, 141. *See also* biog., 235
Kirov, S. M.: attempt to curb Stalin's power, 14, 184–85; murdered, 122, 127
Kochetov, V.: controversy over his novel, 143–44
Kommunist: editing of Suslov lecture, 137–38, 138–139n; intervenes in dispute over Kochetov novel, 143
Kosygin, A. N.: on heavy industry, 50; as Gosplan chief, 70; and chemicals lag, 70; moderate on group, 78–79, 125; Twenty-first Congress speech, 78–79; gains full Presidium rank, 96; July, 1960, report on technology, 98; on Cuban crisis, 156; target of Khrushchev

Malinovskiy, R. Ya., Marshal: attacks Zhukov, 43; on combined arms, 92–93; on troop cuts, 92, 93n, 191; on military policy, 157; on military's policy-making role, 192

Mao Tse-tung: challenges Khrushchev, 54, 56, 82–83; anti-revisionism line, 56; defense of Stalin, 219; mentioned, 176, 200, 213

Material incentives, policy on, 140, 165, 166

Matskevich, V. V.: on Molotov's effort to sabotage MTS reform, 63; attacks on Bulganin, 76

Meetings, Central Committee. *See* Central Committee

Metal-eaters, 106–7

Metallurgical Committee, State: Khrushchev's criticism of, 195

Methodology, 8–9

Mikoyan, A. I.: defends Khrushchev's consumer line, 67–68; opposes further purge of group, 67–68, 75, 125; attacks dogmatism, 68; defends Voroshilov, 80; on indispensable men, 80–81; U.S. visit, 86–87; temporary decline in April, 1960, 94; on Molotov's opposition to coexistence, 121; on Molotov's opposition to new stage concept, 131; at 1934 congress, 185; mentioned, 136. *See also* biog., 238–39

Military leadership, Soviet: stress on heavy industry, 52; resistance to troop cuts, 91, 92, 191–92; and Cuban crisis, 155–57; and Khrushchev's fall, 205. *See also* Khrushchev—the military

Military policy: combined arms, 92–93, 115, 191–92; shifts in summer of 1961, 114; debate over, 190–94; and chemicals program, 194. *See also* Khrushchev—the military

Military Strategy, 156n

Militia, territorial concept: opposition to, 68–69

Militias, volunteer, 84

Ministries, central economic: restored after Khrushchev's fall, 210

Molotov, V. M.: admission of error, 22, 32; orthodox conservative, 23, 35; opposes Khrushchev's 1954 housing plan, 31; February, 1955, hard-line speech, 31; clash with Khrushchev on foreign policy, 32; opposed to party's de-politicization, 33; abstains at 1957 plenum, 46; heads group at Twenty-second Congress, 54; accused of dogmatism, conservatism in 1957, 54–55; vs. rapprochement with Tito, 55; opposes MTS reform, 63; pictured as Beria accomplice, 74; sends article to *Kommunist* (1960), 94; criticizes party program, 113, 117, 131; linked with Chinese positions, 118, 131; return to Vienna canceled, 134; expulsion from party, 174, 203; mentioned, 118, 126, 189. *See also* biog., 239–40

Moscow, Spirit of, 174, 190

Motylev, A., 170, 172

MTS (Machine Tractor Stations), reform of: Stalin attacks plan, 17–18; criticism of, 61, 62, 63–67; Khrushchev overturns Stalin doctrine, 61–62; controversy over, 61–69; local experiments, 62; group opposes plan, 63; mentioned, 58, 60

Mukhitdinov, N. A.: enters Secretariat, gains full Presidium rank, 60–61; promotes Khrushchev cult, 96; stresses consumer welfare, 106; removed from Presidium, Secretariat, 142. *See also* biog., 240

National Liberation Struggle, 175, 215, 215n

Nazi invasion, Twentieth anniversary of, 115

New Party Program. *See* Party program

Nicolaevsky, Boris, 5

Nihilism: attacked at Twenty-third Congress, 223

designer: Cecilie Gaziano
typesetter: Baltimore Type and Composition Corporation
typefaces: Baskerville (text) and News Gothic (display)
printer: The Murray Printing Company
paper: Lindenmeyr Schlosser—Book Smooth (cloth edition); Allied Offset (paperback edition)
binder: William Marley Company (cloth edition); The Murray Printing Company (paperback edition)
cover material: Columbia Riverside Linen (cloth edition)

DATE DUE

FEB 4 1981			

GAYLORD   PRINTED IN U.S.A